Searching for the Ideal School around the World

T0394281

Arts, Creativities, and Learning Environments in Global Perspectives

Series Editors

Tatiana Chemi (*Aalborg University*)
Anu M. Mitra (*Union Institute & University*)
Chunfang Zhou (*Aalborg University*)

VOLUME 6

The titles published in this series are listed at *brill.com/acle*

Searching for the Ideal School around the World

School Tourism and Performative Autoethnographic-We

By

Alys Mendus

BRILL

LEIDEN | BOSTON

Cover illustration: Image by Alys Mendus

All chapters in this book have undergone peer review.

The Library of Congress Cataloging-in-Publication Data is available online at https://catalog.loc.gov

Typeface for the Latin, Greek, and Cyrillic scripts: "Brill". See and download: brill.com/brill-typeface.

ISSN 2589-9813
ISBN 978-90-04-50602-2 (paperback)
ISBN 978-90-04-50601-5 (hardback)
ISBN 978-90-04-50603-9 (e-book)

In loving memory of my amazing Grandmother

Valerie Rickerby O.B.E
1924–2020

For my partner and our daughter
Bozz Connelly and Ginny Connelly-Mendus

For without their love and support the writing of this book could never have happened

∵

My family linocut

Contents

Foreword

In March 2017 I had the pleasure of taking two weeks of my sabbatical leave from Southwestern University to travel to the United Kingdom and Ireland, visiting schools and meeting or reconnecting with professional colleagues sharing an interest in play and play research. In Plymouth, England, my friend and colleague Rod Parker-Rees had arranged meetings and a school visit. His department at Plymouth University happened to be hosting a conference, *Beyond words: Privileging the Unspoken in Arts & Communities in a Posthuman World* and he arranged for me to attend. One session in the program immediately caught my attention: *In search of the 'ideal school': a rhizomatic journey.* My long-standing pedagogical interest in visiting innovative schools with pre-service teachers, along with my own use of Deleuze and Guattari's metaphor of learning as a rhizome – an underground plant stem system that sprouts roots from its nodes – made this session my first priority.

I was delighted to find a kindred spirit in Alys Mendus. She called herself a "school tourist," and presented her emerging dissertation research as performances and stories from multiple voices and perspectives. We chatted after her session, and both of us recognized enthusiastically the "rhizomatic node" of the moment. I mentioned that I would soon be bringing several students to New York City to visit innovative schools and invited her to join us if she was interested in adding more schools to her quest to find the ideal school. The logistics fell into place, and she joined the four of us "touring" schools. Alys' experiences as a school tourist, a qualified teacher, a Waldorf teacher, a Forest School teacher, and her brilliant insights enhanced the experience for all of us. Together we all wrote and performed a play and published a book chapter about the shared experience.

Alys has now visited over 180 schools in 23 countries and shares her journey as a school tourist, a theoretician, a teacher, a poet, a feminist, and a parent with the world. This book brilliantly combines art, academic writing, poetry, a travel journal to ask important questions about schools, education, and learning. She creatively presents her PhD work in this book as if it were a rhizome, inviting readers to mingle with the text in their own way, as nodes between rhizomes emerge for the reader. From parents trying to understand school options for their child, to graduate students embracing theory, to professors preparing teachers, to researchers interested in performative autoethnography, to teachers looking for alternatives, this book is ideal.

Dr. Mendus takes us on a journey with her as a school tourist. Energized by her dissatisfaction with both traditional state schools and their alternatives, she begins her quest to find the ideal school. She questions the culture of schools, the hierarchy, the rules, the assumptions, and even the notion that school is the answer. She brilliantly explores schools deeply and critically while highlighting pedagogical kindness and inspiration – the "gems" she describes. This book will raise the bar for understanding what school could be, should be, but perhaps can't be.

Michael Kamen
Professor, Education Department
Southwestern University
Georgetown, Texas
23 January 2021

Preface

Alys the Guide

Yuggera Country, Brisbane, Queensland, Australia, Thursday 9th April 2020

Our daughter is 11 months old today. She woke up alert, bright and happy around 6am and nuzzled me until she found my breast and began sucking energetically. Sated, she rolled over and looked me in the eye and said, grinning, 'Hi Mem!' My heart melting, I can't help but lift up my heavy eyelids and smile right back at her.

I realise it is even more important now than ever to be reminded of the joys from simple things in life, like love and connection. As we, like a third of the population of the world in this moment, are living under lockdown. 2020, the year I write this book turning my PhD thesis into an accessible text, is the year of the Coronavirus, of COVID-19. The year the world stood still. People are dying from a respiratory virus all over the world. It is egalitarian in who it affects, but not necessarily egalitarian in how those affected people access health care. It just depends on where you are living. Boris Johnson, the UK Prime Minister, is in intensive care, suffering with this illness and so many, many more are sick or dying. Others are recovering and, thankfully, children and young people seem to have more resilience, but they could be carriers.

In relation to this book, I write this preface as so many children are being educated at home. Schools are shut in many countries except to those whose parents are essential workers, from medical practitioners to people who work in shops and distribution centres. Home-learning in this moment of time is normality. When I wrote my thesis in 2017 (Mendus, 2017c) and drew conclusions that home education could be one way forward that would help bring about a paradigm shift in education, this current situation was far beyond my wildest imaginings.

However, what is happening now in terms of home education and learning at home is very different than before-COVID-19 home education. I would always argue that home educators are barely at home! So many of the freedoms of home education are in the ability to set a time-table for your own family that involves going out into the community, nature, culture, sports with other children and people of all ages. Under lockdown, home education is closer to schooling by the fact that people are 'at-home.' An hour's exercise is allowed per day in the UK near your home and currently here in Queensland how long you exercise is not fixed, but most people are staying closeby. Some schools are using zoom to teach whole classes and to check in with students, other schools have sent homework and guidance. Distance and correspondence learning is not so unusual in Australia, with a history of educating children living out on cattle stations, but it is definitely not the norm (Reiach, Averbeck, & Cassidy, 2012).

The ramifications for this dramatic shift in what is education and the learning environment is massive and currently, living in this moment, it is still impossible to know. Only a few weeks ago, children went to school in a physical room and were taught set lessons by an individual teacher. Now, children are being grouped differently, using the internet for chats but also to access resources and apps and different skills for music, languages and the very popular Joe Wick's workouts. The kudos should go to schools who managed virtually overnight to transform their thinking and approaches to learning and move almost everything online. As Chemi (2020) points out, for teachers and university lecturers now working online creativity "was not an option anymore, but the necessary response to crises" (p. 1).

As a lover of technology for myself but having concerns about the overuse of it in education, particularly in the early years, I am fascinated by how this transformation is going to affect some of the schools that are educating differently to traditional mainstream settings, particularly Steiner Waldorf, where avoiding technology is part of the pedagogy. One school I have had contact with has had a morning check in online with the whole class for one hour and then gives creative guidelines for the rest of the day. This way, screen time is limited but the rich content of stories and singing together can be kept.

The onus of all this change to education moves to the children and their parents. It is down to the motivation of both to engage with the work that has been set and to balance their days. My social media feed is full of parents sharing stories of realising how much more their children are learning at home and others are questioning the role of traditional schooling. However, many parents are also working from home and there are multiple siblings and not necessarily space to play or access to technology to join into these online classes. These families, and many others, are missing the cultural experience of 'school.' Shutting schools comes with a caveat of privilege; those who have outdoor space, technology and food, and others in crowded dwellings who rely on free school dinners. Bradbury-Jones and Isham (2020) argue that there has been an increase in cases of domestic violence during Lockdown in 2020. Living together in close proximity has the potentiality for many shifts to occur in relationships, this is before adding the anxiety of sickness. The messages to physically distance ourselves from others (and thereby we socially distance ourselves) can lead to a higher chance to feel isolated. But, of course, the number of cases are increasing each day and to actually become sick with a potentially life-threatening disease is a very real and present possibility. This is our current time and the post-COVID-19 consciousness will never be able to unlearn this vibrational shift on our bodies.

However, I completed my PhD thesis in 2017, a different time. A time when high-stakes testing, hierarchy, league tables (where schools in the UK are put in lists of most successful in terms of exam results and outcomes from inspections), government inspections and order were much more of the norm. In the UK, in 2020, all exams and inspections have been cancelled for this school year. An overnight shift. As an educator I have riled against the system as I did not fit satisfactorily into the niche of 'teacher.' This book is a sharing of stories from my journey exploring, visiting and working in a wide variety of places of learning around the world. It is written in a series of voices of myself to give different perspectives and understandings of the experiences. I write now as Alys-the-Guide, as I lead you through one possible pathway through the stories. However, I feel education, learning, schooling and, hopefully, a paradigm shift is beyond my own guiding and this book can be read as a Choose your own adventure story following key themes, pedagogies and possibilities that interest you as a teacher, parent or young person.

Acknowledgements

I acknowledge and pay respect to Aboriginal and Torres Strait Islander peoples past, present and emerging. I recognise that the sovereignty of the land that I am on was never ceded and that it remains Aboriginal land. I am writing this from Gubbi Gubbi Country, Moreton Bay, Australia.

I would like to thank Bozz Connelly for all the support and time he has given me throughout 2020 to write, talk about, and discuss my book, and then for all the copy-editing and feedback. And to Ginny for keeping us both smiling!

I would like to thank the following people for helping me get this book published!

Davina Kirkpatrick for her friendship and expertise in getting the images ready for publication.

John Bennett and Henriët Graafland for their support at Brill. Tatiana Chemi and the rest of the editors in the *Arts, Creativities, and Learning Environments in Global Perspectives* book series for seeing the potential of this book. I received invaluable feedback on draft chapters and sections from Lisa Siegel, Sandra Wooltorton, Johnny Lupinacci, Michael Kamen and from Michael's students at Southwestern University, Texas. Thank you to Annie Audsley, Dan Arkle, Emma Hughes, Tessa Wyatt, Michael Kamen, Margo Bruins, Barbara Whitesides and Ginny Connelly-Mendus for their images that help to bring this text alive. To the Bodies Collective who help me trouble and enjoy(!) the fringes of the academy: Davina Kirkpatrick, Jess Erb, Mark Huhnen, Sarah Helps, Claudia Canella, Ryan Bittinger and Ines Barcenas Taland. To the members of Sustainability Environment Arts Education (SEAE) cluster at Southern Cross University who have allowed me in 2020 to widen my experiences and knowledges within Australia.

I want to acknowledge and thank those involved in the original research – the people and places of learning/schools/homes that have welcomed me into their settings and given their time to share their experience with me. Thank you for being part of this story.

The main research of this book is the accumulation of my PhD journey (2014-2017) and I want to thank my main supervisor, Max Hope, for letting me follow my own journey and Joseph Ploner, my second supervisor. I also want to thank Peter Kraftl and Gill Hughes for examining my thesis and for their feedback. I also want to thank the members of the Freedom to Learn project as the conversations we had at many different events helped me develop and position my work: Catherine Montgomery, Michael Fielding, Diane Reay, Helen Lees, Dan Ford, David Gribble. Through becoming part of the International Congress of Qualitative Inquiry community, I want to recognise the help and support from many academics whose work has inspired me: Tami Spry, Carolyn Ellis, Jane

Speedy, Jonathan Wyatt, Ken Gale, Elizabeth St. Pierre, Stacy Holman Jones, Dan Harris, Carolyn Ellis, Kitrina Douglas and Phiona Stanley. I also want to thank people from the University of Plymouth, UK where I found a lot of support for my interest in methodologies and alternative education: Cath Gristy, Joanna Haynes, Paul Warwick, Mel Parker and Ciaran O'Sullivan. I would also like to thank Paul Magnuson at Leysin American School, Switzerland for inviting me to be a visiting scholar. To the many people from the Steiner World including Neil Boland (University of Auckland) for inspiring me with Waldorf 2.0, Susan Perrow (for the stories), Janni Nichol, Michael Rose and Linda Fryer for the guidance and belief in helping me think differently. For support with my Come Dance my PhD project: Karen Doyle, Carran Waterfield, Gale Simon, D. Soyini Madison and all the dancers in my workshops.

To Vanny McVanface, the red van that was our home as we lived as nomads travelling around the UK visiting schools, visiting friends and family and writing a PhD. Thank you to my parents and sister, all our friends, colleagues and other family members who hosted us and joined in discussions about the future of education and to your kitchen tables, tasty dinners, glasses of wine, soft beds and hot showers that kept us going when we needed some respite.

Figures

All photographs and artwork taken and made by Alys Mendus unless otherwise specified.

About the Author

Alys Mendus

is an independent scholar based in Australia. She has a PhD in Education from the University of Hull, UK which she completed on a scholarship as part of a wider 'Freedom to Learn' project in 2017. Once finding autoethnography and arts-based approaches to research, her networks expanded and she is now an active member of the Bodies Collective, an international group of Early Career researchers exploring ways of giving voice to the body and unsettling hierarchies. She is also a member of CANI-net in the UK and SEAE, based at Southern Cross University, Australia. Alys works as a Casual academic and in 2020 worked online for University of Melbourne Graduate School of Education and Southern Cross University. Alys continues to write and to research and is looking for an exciting post-doc.

Alys and her partner, Bozz, and their toddler, Ginny, currently live on Gubbi Gubbi Country, just north of Brisbane, Australia. They hope to continue their nomadology in their new van, Valerie.

Alys continues to be a free spirit...

Introduction

1 Alys the Guide

I begin with the Guided Meditation I used at my Come Dance my PhD workshops in Cumbria, UK in April 2018 (Mendus, 2018a, 2018b, 2019). I invite you to sit comfortably, maybe have a decent hot cup of coffee by your side as you read this section and I encourage you to view my film, 'A cup of instant coffee: A van-dwellers' assemblage' (Mendus, 2018a) and listen to the words being read aloud, surrounded by the images of my journey researching this book.

> Imagine a cup of instant coffee, its bitter taste wrapped around your mouth, add now the taste of cheap milk and the slightly curdled flavour of your coffee gone cold and you are beginning to enter into the materiality of my life, my quest, my journeys.
>
> For I had been a teacher in the local mainstream state funded school, rushed off my feet with expectations, pressure, assessments, marking, curriculum and a life similar to prison, run by bells, hierarchy and strict rules and endless cold, instant coffee to wash it down.

FIGURE 1 A kitchen table arrangement (Artist: Annie Audsley, Uphall, Scotland, 2018)

© KONINKLIJKE BRILL NV, LEIDEN, 2022 | DOI: 10.1163/9789004506039_001

Ever since I trained to be a teacher in 2004, I was unhappy [Fed up] with the system. I struggled with the curriculum, the rules, the uniforms, hierarchies, homework and assessment. I managed to teach for two years before I had a retirement party in 2007. I then began my search for something else. I first found Steiner Waldorf and Forest Schools and continued to work in outdoor education, now focussing more on international expeditions and special needs groups. However, I was unsatisfied. So, I retrained in Early Years and completed an MA in education exploring alternatives to behaviourism. I was still unsatisfied, but I had hope. I was sure out there, somewhere, would be the new pedagogy for the 21st century, so I began visiting schools and places of learning that educated differently. This journey took me around the world to over 180 schools in 23 countries. I was a School Tourist. I visited Montessori, Steiner, Democratic, Reggio Emilia, Krishnamurti, Forest Schools, Progressive, home education, Project-Based learning and many many more, but I was never fully happy.

One day I was in Bali on a teacher's course at the Green School and one of my colleagues said to me, "Alys, why are you so negative? Nothing is good enough for you" and it was an epiphany. I realised that this was true as the Ideal School was an oxymoron and so I refocused and began to see the 'gems' in each place. I called these gems, that exist within the neoliberal system, the "edge-ucation" and one of the ways I saw myself was as an 'edge-dweller.'

This journey was very complex and using Deleuzian theory I saw my life (as an itinerant vagabond/nomad living in a van) and my journeys performing School Tourism as a rhizome. I was ever moving between the centre and the periphery, sometimes flowering into a nodal point that would then die and compost into the rhizome to nourish another journey. I also realised that although I was using autoethnography that it was not about the 'I,' so I wrote the thesis in different voices of the Alys-we. Towards the end I realised that it is a much bigger picture, that of the Earth-we that needs to be explored. It is a consciousness shift, not some new pedagogy or approach. (Mendus, Guided meditation for my Come Dance my PhD workshops [Edinburgh, April 2018])

This book is for those of you who are interested in thinking differently about education who want to follow the journey of someone who was 'Fed up with the System' and was keen to use their time, resources and ingenuity to visit as many places that educate differently as possible.

Those voices ending that short film ('A cup of instant coffee: A van-dwellers' assemblage'), northern voices, position my life and identity as being part of a want for change; supporting the concept that my PhD, and now book, are fundamentally about a life subverting the current paradigm. Following the words of my PhD examiner, Peter Kraftl:

> [Traditional] Schools are dehumanising and anti-democratic... they obstruct creativity in favour of learning knowledge by rote... they simply institutionalise children to become good, neoliberal workers and consumers. (Kraftl, 2013, p. 10)

When I began my journey 'Searching for the Ideal School,' my challenges were with the educational 'system,' particularly the current, what I saw as, traditional approaches to mainstream education in the UK. I was frustrated by the early age of formal schooling, the use of high-stakes testing and grading, as well as the strict hierarchies, homework, uniforms, single age classrooms, school 'day' formats, choice of subjects, and even the environment of the school buildings and classrooms. I argue that traditional, mainstream education has not moved on from the England and Wales 1870 Education Act, when society and the economy needed a literate and compliant workforce. Even now in the 21st century this need has continued, with standardised achievement of teachers, schools and children seen as the main currency of education.

I also felt uncomfortable with my feeling that there had to be a new way of learning, but I was unsure if it could be found in the state funded school system and I was aware of the issues of privilege and social justice to who would have access to these different approaches. I initially qualified as an English state-school teacher and immediately began to find out about other teaching pedagogies and found Steiner Waldorf. I then trained as a Steiner Waldorf teacher. My school teaching career is diverse, eclectic and short-term, although it spanned from 2002-2018. I have taught mainstream secondary Science, taught special needs schools, taught casually in Primary schools in England and Scotland, run an Early Years setting, lead Forest Schools, undertaken short-term teaching in multiple Steiner Waldorf schools in the UK, run home-education groups for under 8's, lead Parent and Child sessions, worked at an International Boarding School in Switzerland and worked as an outdoor instructor in the UK and on international expeditions.

My teaching experiences mirror my frustration with the system. After two years in my first school I had a 'retirement party' as I was keen to experience other teaching environments, particularly outdoors. I began to realise the more experiences I had, the greater my depth of understanding about education grew and I also felt I could turn up fresh and excited about teaching and not be distracted or annoyed by school politics and teacher bureaucracy. This did mean I could often be quite lonely, flitting in and out of different settings and not really ever being part of any. However, I decided to see this as a strength as I did not have to completely abide by school policies if I was only in a setting for a day. I was free to not return to that school. With hindsight, I realise that I was in the early stages of my nomadology. This idea of nomadology is explored further in Chapter 2.

Through the chapters of this book I offer my readers a snapshot of stories of places of learning/schools that I visited around the world. I hope that by engaging with my poems, stories and playscripts you will be able to have the confidence to make changes in how you teach in your classrooms or how you choose where to study, or what place of learning/school is best for your child by becoming aware of current approaches within education. The book was written in multiple voices of Alys to emphasise the different relational aspects within myself and within each reader. You may or may not resonate with all, some, or none of the voices, but I hope it will allow you to think about the way in which you look at education, learning and schooling. Alys-the-guide will lead you through the stories as I share my journey: how I lived, how I travelled, where and who with, how I lived in a van, how I fell in love, how I chose places to visit and my emotional connection to the all-encompassing experience. This voice aims to help pull the experience into a story of becoming, a story where I moved beyond searching for the Ideal School into an understanding that a paradigm shift is needed in how we view education. However, it does not aim to scare the reader, but to mobilise change within the current system to move towards a new future. This can be in small (or large or anywhere in between) alterations in teaching pedagogy, outlook, behaviour and environment within state funded schooling. It could be new alternative schools, confidence to home educate or to be the voice to speak out about the unfairness of the current system. It also could be an awareness that there is the possibility of doing things differently to the current educational trope.

I used the term 'educating differently' to describe places that are teaching differently to the traditional, mainstream approaches of set curriculum, high-stakes testing, grading, behaviourism and hierarchy. Places that are educating differently may still have some of the more traditional elements in place, and the change may only be undertaken by a small fraction of the school or it could be totally radical and be unlike our usual comprehension of 'school.' I decided not to use the term alternative education as in many countries around the world this term is used for education for children who are at-risk or who have been excluded from mainstream schooling. From my collaborations with Michael Kamen (see Foreword), I am coming to use the term 'innovative' as it brings with it a momentum of creative change without the labelling of a binary of one type of schooling or another. A place of learning/school can be innovative, but so can an activity in a lesson or a teacher or the children or... it continues.

One of the main methodologies of this book is performative autoethno-graphic-we. My understanding of autoethnography follows Ellis' that "autoeth-nography involves a back-and-forth movement between experiencing and examining a vulnerable self and observing and revealing the broader context of that experience" (2007, p. 14) with Spry's definition of Autoethnography, as "a self-narrative that critiques the situations of self with others in social contexts" (2001, p. 710). So, for my research, my autoethnography is a cultural critique of my experiences searching for the Ideal School around the world. However, I realized that my autoethnography was more complex than a single voice and it includes many aspects of performance including the dialogic engagement (Spry, 2016) and sharing the stories from visiting places of learning/schools. Therefore, I see my work as performative autoethnography where "Perfor-mance is not an added scholarly bonus... performance does not "illuminate" the text, rather it assists in the creation of the text; it is in itself performative" (Spry, 2011, p. 28). This book was written to reflect this understanding, it shares the performance and storytelling of my performative-autoethnography in a variety of writing styles: vignettes, ethnodramas, poems, images, journalling, reflective stories and case studies from places of learning/schools.

This arts-based approach is written in different voices from the multiplicity of Alys-we, supporting my understanding that my experiences and stories are beyond the singular Alys. This recognises that there are many embodiments of 'Alys,' as well as my collective dialogues with others and the more-than-human world, seen as a decentring of human exceptionalism, becoming an entangle-ment of human, non human, nature, culture and others in between (Springgay & Truman, 2018). I explore the multiplicity of Alys-we further in Chapter 1. I recognise, as defined by Spry, that "autoethnography is not about 'self' but the wilful embodiment of 'we'" (2016, p. 15) and realise that these multiplicities of 'Alys' and 'other' are co-present and need a voice if I am to critically reflect on the sociocultural privilege that the autoethnography carries (Spry, 2016). This is the performative-autoethnographic-we.

One way that this will be shown on the page is through using quotes from my journalling during the research process. I have been constantly travelling (as a van-dweller performing School Tourism), so the place and time in which the journal entry or reflection was written will be added. For example: Mendus, Type of Journal entry, [Place written, Date written]. By adding this temporality to the text, it is hoped that the reader will be able to connect to the text-body in a different way (Bennett, 2015). Journal entries, my voice within a story and poems are written in italics throughout the book to highlight their difference from the main text.

2   Part 1 Covers…

Part 1 covers the background to the research and my positionality. For some, moving straight to the stories from the places of learning/schools that I visited in Part 2 may be of more interest and I suggest you hop straight there. The book is written to be dipped into and for the reader to be in charge of their experience, choosing to move between stories and theory where needed. Of course, you can also read the book cover to cover if you prefer!

Chapter 1 explores performative autoethnography and the multiplicities of the Alys-we in more detail and shares stories and understanding of why I am 'Fed up with the system' in relation to the mainstream education system and the dominance of neoliberalism.

Chapter 2 explores my van-dwelling and the nomadology of my research.

Chapter 3 focuses on a realisation that came during my research that the Ideal School was an oxymoron and that creating a new dogma from a mix of different approaches was not only impossible but also unethical as the ideal is so different to each person, family, or culture. Also, fundamentally for this book, defining an 'ideal' school would be creating a new schooling system and in Chapter 3 I argue that actual school/schooling as we know it is not the answer and that we need to move beyond what we can currently comprehend and 'think the unthought' (St. Pierre, 2011).

> One of the multiplicities of the Alys-we is the School Tourist (someone who visits schools). School Tourist is something that I have been labelling myself for a while to describe my life visiting schools around the world. Throughout my life, when I come to a new place I would always look over the wall into the playground of the village school and wonder… what would it be like to live here? To go to school here? That sense of longing or curiosity seems to be part of my identity. This role of Alys-the-School-Tourist has been a major methodology of living my life (and this interest in schools and places) through visiting a school and thinking, "What if?" (Mendus, Autoethnography drafts [Dartmoor, September 2016])

My research has developed performing School Tourism as an embodied approach, a feeling journey, that connects the 'School Tourist' with the more-than-human world of ways of 'educating differently.' Through the performance of the travelling-to, inhabiting the space of the visit and then travelling-from creates new understandings of what is possible and implants new stories and potentially non-normative views of education and learning. The School Tourist then has a political choice to share these stories with others, to act on their own learning from the experience they had with their own family or in places of learning/schools in which they work, or to keep quiet. The multiplicities of Alys-we that wrote this thesis are also present in all School Tourists – not the same multiplicities, but their own multiplicities that too are part of their own rhizome that intra-acts (see Barad, 2007) with other School Tourists and people and the natural world. For we are all part of a larger network. School Tourism could work with other places/things other than 'schools'... (Mendus, Journalling on the contribution to knowledge [Suffolk, August 2017])

3   Part 2 Covers...

Part 2 'Educating Differently' shares my autoethnographic journey exploring places and pedagogies educating differently around the world. As part of my journeying visiting places of learning/schools, I was inspired by Kraftl's (2013) ideas that 'alternatives' to mainstream education "provoke reflection about alternative visions and versions of life-itself" (p. 229) away from the dominance of neoliberalism. As I have been lucky enough to visit over 180 places of learning/schools in 23 countries, I have not been able to include stories from each visit in this book. However, each visit is part of my own embodied experience and understanding of innovative pedagogies in action and has a role in framing the lens through which I see new places of learning/schools. In Chapters 4 and 5 this is initially moving alongside my role as a mainstream teacher with my explorations into Steiner Waldorf education. This part dances around, sharing key descriptions of the approach with stories and poems about the different stages of the pedagogy – Kindergarten, Primary School and High School. Throughout this section, Alys the Guide will lead you through the process of their developing relationship with Steiner Waldorf education, their frustrations with particular aspects and how they realised that some of the ideals could be used and be more accessible in mainstream education. Being Fed up with this particular (Steiner Waldorf) system kept me exploring further and led me to visit other places educating differently, focussing on progressive, democratic and Montessori schools in my continued search for the Ideal School. This journey is shared in Chapters 6-9. I have tried to not label places of learning/schools myself, but to be authentic to each place's own choice to label or not label their approach. This is incredibly complex as there are many entanglements between the terms, philosophies and pedagogies that I notice through visiting so many places. I am aware that the places of learning/schools may not be familiar with the other terms or ideas and I aim to not become too judgmental. Chapter 6 shares stories and thinking from the start of my School Tourism. Chapter 7 raises issues of social justice and the political challenge of Democratic Education, which sees itself as education for the future, although I trouble this as I argue that the future is not our current understanding of democracy. Chapters 8 and 9 continue to share my journey. Throughout these autoethnographic chapters, I try to offer the richness of current examples by sharing stories from the 'gems' of my School Tourism of places that have attempted to begin this shift, to explore this edge-ucation. These stories aim to give hope that the reader could visit, attend, or include these approaches into their lives.

By sharing these autoethnographic chapters I hope that the insights and felt experiences can be embodied by the reader opening up the possibility to feel they too have been in that classroom or also visited that school. I also hope to help the reader ponder the question; what is education?

4 Part 3 Covers...

Part 3 reflexively 'intra-acts' with the autoethnography. Using the term 'intra-action,' defined by Barad as "the mutual constitution of entangled agencies" (2007, p. 33), is helpful as it allows distinct aspects to emerge within the key themes that are arising from my autoethnographic journey performing School Tourism. As the reader you may find different gems from my stories than the ones that I highlight and this is why I encourage you to become a School Tourist yourself (see Chapters 10 and 11) and share stories of your own. I realise that from learning about places educating differently and/or even becoming a School Tourist yourself that change could begin to happen around the world as "in some places, at some moments, they [places educating differently] offer distinct challenges to dominant assumptions we hold about bodily habits and dispositions, about mess, about interpersonal love, and about life-itself" (Kraftl, 2013, p. 229).

Chapter 10 theoretically explores performing School Tourism and Chapter 11 explores the question of what is a School Tourist and invites the reader to become one themselves. Chapter 12 proposes a new way of thinking about education, thinking no longer with the multiplicities of the Alys-we but now with the Earth-we towards a consciousness shift for change.

This book sits happily within the book series on *Arts, Creativities, and Learning Environments in Global Perspectives* with the storying (Phillips & Bunda, 2018) of Alys-we's experiences performing School Tourism around the world. The encounters that happen in these visits to places of learning/schools are made accessible for the reader through creative writing approaches, poetry, ethnodrama, journalling and prose. Alys-we, in their searching for the Ideal School, came across a very diverse range of possibilities for learning, varied cultures and environments with young people from birth to adulthood. Alys-we acknowledges and troubles their position of privilege and subjectivity as they visit and share stories from places in a different culture to their own. However, it is through the arts-based approaches and performative autoethnography that I hope with this book to move from the researcher's own stories to inspire the reader to become a School Tourist themselves, to add their perspectives and understandings to the stories that are shared about education, thereby creating a larger collective consciousness of possibilities to help with a paradigm shift and a broader reframing of arts for learning, for society and for the future.

This book moves between chapters of stories, contemplation and theoretical chapters trying to make sense of these experiences on a meta-level. Manning (2015) puts this perfectly, "the relational movement through which the present begins to coexist with its futurity, with the quality or manner of the not-yet that lurks at the edges of actual experience" (pp. 45–46). The hope is that the reader can dip in and out of the sections that make sense for their own journey.

This book is to be read as a snapshot of an assemblage,
an amalgamation of a rhizome,
an entangled mess of ideas, schools, pedagogies,
Alys-we, Earth-we, the reader, lives, objects, old vans,
dappled sunlight, thoughts, dreams,
love;
all moving,
constantly moving,
changing, becoming, changing the system.
Images of schools, van-life, the nomadology,
appear between chapters and embedded in the text as
photos, lino-cuts and sketches
adding colour
and a sense of place
to this multi-sense-making experience of learning about performing School
Tourism
And calling to you to become a School Tourist yourself!

5   Alys the Guide

And now, where next is up to you! Choose your own adventure through the book.

If you want to explore the thinking behind the multiplicity of the Alys-we then head to Chapter 1, if you want details on my nomadology go to Chapter 2 and if you want to read my conclusions that School is Not the Answer then head to Chapter 3.

However, if you want stories about my school visits then head directly to Part 2.

Chapters 4 and 5 are about Steiner Waldorf, Chapter 6 Progressive Education, Chapter 7 Democratic Education, Chapter 8 Montessori and Chapter 9 'Gems' within state-funded education.

If you want to go straight to the theory behind performing School Tourism and find out how to become a School Tourist yourself, go to Part 3, Chapters 10 and 11. For more information about my asking for a change in our collective consciousness, head to Chapter 12 on Composting the Rhizome: The Earth-we.

Enjoy!

PART 1

Fed up with the System

∵

FIGURE 2   Kookaburra – What do I see outside as I write this book? (Linocut)

CHAPTER 1

'Fed up with the System'

1 Alys the Guide: Introduction

Defining Alys is tricky. Defining self is a challenge. Who am I when I walk into those classrooms? Who are you reading this book? Thinking about education; what privileges and assumptions do we all hold in some capacity? What agency do we have to make a difference, to change what the question is for the future of learning on our planet? What can we do with our agency to be part of the paradigm shift?

When I wrote that I am fed up with the system it may have started as a tongue-in-cheek phrase, but it really is an activist agenda, a place to begin to shake up the system and begin to not just think into change but start living the new story. This book is written in the multiplicities of Alys, giving voice to many (but not all) of the different voices of Alys as they go about their journey Searching for the Ideal School around the world. The voice of Alys the Guide is new, added in when writing this book to give more accessibility to the reader to ponder with the multiple Alys' about the whole journey, but also to remind Alys to 'tend to self' (Lupinacci, 2020). This Alys the Guide learns from Johnny Lupinacci's (2019) call for scholar-activists to move beyond neoliberal relationships of self and to rescript our understandings to do things differently. Lupinacci (2020) reminds Alys-we of their normativity, their relationship to a hyper-consumerist world, their role in white supremacy and the patriarchy and calls out to them to join the dance. Alys-we is also very aware that they are now writing this book in Australia as a settler-colonial (Country et al., 2019) migrant, which adds another element of complexity to their position, acknowledging the critical and complicated responsibility of a settler-academic "attending to life lived on stolen Indigenous land" (Rowe & Tuck, 2016, p. 6). Returning again to Lupinacci helps Alys-we to commit each day and in each place of learning/school visit to address this privilege whilst at the same time tending to themselves with love, healthy food and time in nature.

This chapter aims to position the book to realise why I was 'Fed up with the system.' The first two sections through story hope the reader will gain a glimpse of my challenges with my early experiences as a school teacher in the UK and the role of neoliberalism as a dominant approach influencing education. Then the following sections are more theoretical helping the reader to explore performative autoethnography and the styles in which this book has been written and then to explore the multiplicities of Alys-we and their voices throughout the book.

2   Fed up with the English Education System

2.1   *Alys the Educator: Retiring from Full-Time Traditional Teaching in 2007*

I never wanted to be a teacher, I always saw it as a failure and wanted to do something else. I was well aware of the words of George Bernard Shaw "those who can, do, those who can't, teach" (1903/2009, Maxim 36) and didn't want to fall into the 'trap,' but it had always been 'known' I would be a teacher from childhood.

> I have a younger sister, who followed me through primary school, two years below. She was young for her year and initially struggled with her reading. Family story has it that after once belittling her ability to read I then set about teaching her. We would often play schools and it was thought by my family that I would be a teacher. (Mendus, Journalling – Childhood memories [Sheffield, November 2015])

Then years later, while living and working in New Zealand, (2001–2003) I was earning some money working in preschools and nurseries and the 'calling' returned:

> "When you go home you need to go and train to be a teacher," the Preschool Manager ordered me one day, "you are a natural." (Mendus, Journalling – Gap year memories, 2001–2003 [Sydney, February 2016])

Even the following year when I returned to the UK I still didn't want to be a teacher, I wanted to be an Archaeologist (the job I had been doing predominantly in New Zealand) and in a way it was only money that stopped me as I had a place on an MSc in 'Archaeology and Geographical Information Systems' to start the same September as I had a place for a Post Graduate Certificate of Education (PGCE). It was only because I got paid to do teacher training and would have to pay them to do the Masters that I chose teaching. So I did the PGCE, with many tears. My lack of caring made it a fun year, I could teach quite easily, was organised and got my work done and played a lot of rugby for Bath Ladies Rugby Football Club, so I kept fit and I could cave on the Mendip Hills. Life flowed quite nicely until I had to get a job:

> Alys, get a job! Why have you not got a job already? You will get your student loan paid back and get a golden hello (government bonus for teaching a shortage subject) if you teach Science. What is stopping you?
>
> The voice of my father rang out when by the end of June in my PGCE year I had not 'got a job.' It wasn't because I couldn't teach. I kept getting flying colours on my teaching observations. It was because something was stopping me. Something deep down was preventing me from entering a profession that I felt was fundamentally flawed, I just couldn't put my finger on how or what... (Mendus, Autoethnography of my life journalling [Cumbria, May 2016])

So maybe the truth is that I had always known that it wasn't 'right,' but I did end up getting a job at a school in the town where I had studied for my undergraduate degree in Archaeology and I knew that it was in a 'nice' part of town and that the students didn't have to wear uniform. I had always hated uniform:

> "It's Friday choosing day! What would you like to wear to school today Alys!?," my Mum asked me. There wasn't even a uniform at my tiny Primary school in the rural Lake District but my Mum liked uniform, so she made us wear it every day except for Fridays when she let us choose what we wore... My secondary school had uniform all the way to 18, including new colours and ties (and girls could wear trousers) in the sixth form. I hated it but I didn't change schools to the neighbouring town which my sister, after me, did. (Mendus, Autoethnography of my childhood journalling [Sheffield, November 2015])

The day before I got the comprehensive job I had had an interview in a Steiner Waldorf school in Scotland. I'd first come across Steiner Waldorf in January 2002 when living in Christchurch, New Zealand and one of my housemates had gone to the Steiner school so they took me for a visit. I'm not sure that I was very impressed. It was just a school and I was in a phase of my life where I saw myself as an 'archaeologist' and not a teacher, but the concept of a 'different' type of school stayed with me and when I was doing my PGCE I remembered that Steiner school in New Zealand and found one in a nearby town to visit.

It was a wet, January morning and I hurried into the old Georgian building. The entrance hall was bare and much needed some attention. Nes-
tled at the bottom of the stairs was a table filled with knitted animals
and other handmade crafts for sale. I thought back to my village and to
the Methodist chapel bring-and-buy sales and laughing at the twee hand-
crafts... I was taken upstairs to a Y6 room, except it was called Class 5, and
stepped inside. A narrow room with a long blackboard across the back
wall, children (in their own clothes) standing behind old wooden school
desks. I felt like I had stepped back in time. I perched in the corner and
watched as the class sang songs, recited long poems, did a complicated
jumping game connected to the times tables, played recorders and said a
verse that mentioned God and ended up with their arms crossed against
their chests. Weird, but strangely fascinating. I spoke to their teacher
at break-time, excited at my new 'find' about how to become a Steiner
Teacher. The teacher told me they had trained at a school in Glouces-
tershire and the thought of more training appalled me. I felt I had done
enough learning. (Mendus, PGCE notebooks [Bath, January 2005])

So why hadn't I gone for that job in Scotland? The truth is, I wanted to earn
more money. At 25 I had never earned money before and the mainstream job
would pay me £5000 more and give me a £4000 golden hello after two years if
I taught Science. My PGCE was in Middle Years Science, so I had the choice of
Primary or Secondary for a job and I hadn't enjoyed the end of Primary teaching anyway, too much marking and time spent learning Maths and English
facts for the SATs exams that I wasn't inspired to fill my brain with, and then
the staff:

"I'm not going to work in a Primary school," I told one of my school friend's
mothers, "as it is full of old women talking about babies, grandchildren
and diets." Her mother was a Reception teacher and Deputy Head of an
Infant school. It has to be said that that quote has not been forgotten.
(Mendus, Memory of a conversation, April 2005 [Sheffield, November
2015])

And who I was, and maybe who I am now, is well suited to banter and play
and the creativity in how you teach and manage behaviour with teenagers. As
I have begun to learn more about Steiner Waldorf education (Rawson, Ritcher,
& Avison, 2014; and see Chapters 4 and 5, this volume), it suggests that this is
because those children at end of Primary school need an authoritarian figure
to have knowledge, hold clear boundaries and be fair, and I aim to manage

classes by friendly relationships rather than power and control (behaviourism is also discussed further in Chapter 5).

Going to work in a comprehensive, a UK state funded 11–18 school, was full of delights. In the first couple of terms especially, I would join the other young staff, teachers and support staff, in the local pub. We called it 'period 6' and would see each other in the corridor and ask if they were going to period 6 later. We thought we were hilarious! And we would have a laugh and I would usually be drunk and asleep by 9 pm on a Friday. When thinking back with hindsight I wonder, is getting drunk on Friday the only way to cope with a stressful job? I know it is done the country over, but is that the point of working? Really? I went less to the pub in my second year of teaching as my life had begun to change focus and I ended the week on the Upper School site with a lower ability group of 15/16 year olds for Science:

> "Thank you for turning up. Please settle down," I would say as a 15 year old boy wandered into my classroom, cap on back to front, haze of smoke, trousers hanging from his buttocks, pants pulled up to the waist, hoody up. And I would try to teach a group of young people written off by the school. Some were in there as they had real additional learning needs and others because they messed around so much in the higher ability set that they were destroying learning (and the chance for the school to get the much needed number of pupils to a set GCSE grade). I began to realise that it is an art to be able to teach such a chaotic mix and I had to rely on my resilience and quick thinking to get through that hour. It wasn't, as deemed by my department, an easy class relying on those with lower level Scientific knowledge (aka me with an Archaeology degree), but a baptism of fire. I planned about 10 minutes actual work or a short practical and then winged it. I didn't need to give homework which I disliked anyway on three counts; one I had to mark it, two they had to do it in their free time which I think should truly be free time and three they never did it anyway so I had to chase it up and give them detentions (which also seemed pointless to me). I was beginning to see myself as different. The number of things I was unhappy with was increasing by the moment.
>
> And then there was that one lesson with the maggots. A hideous GCSE coursework experiment on respiration of maggots. I saw this group once a week. Friday, last lesson, and I was a brand new teacher. No teaching assistant and down in a dark out-of-the-way lab. Of course, the class were bored and a few boys decided to chuck maggots at the girls. One girl began screaming and hyperventilating. As I sent for some assistance a few boys grabbed the cup of maggots and ran riot around the school,

chucking maggots into each classroom they could find. Someone from
Senior Management appeared and the girl was looked after, but all other
staff were too busy to help with the ensuing maggot disaster.

I turned my attention back to the rest of the class and in the corner
one boy was happily munching on a maggot having been bet a pound he
wouldn't...

I asked, "Why?"

"It's well worth it for a pound," he answered... I drank a lot that night.
(Mendus, Memories of being a secondary school Science teacher 2005–
2007 Journalling [Sheffield, December 2015])

Even with the youthful energy of my mid-twenties, the constant battles with
behaviour and impossible targets and student disinterest in curriculum began
to wear on me:

Although I knew that I enjoyed working in education, I was really appre-
hensive about completing a PGCE as I had a gut feeling that I would find
the regimental structure of working under the National Curriculum and
National Strategies a challenge. Two years into teaching I still find this. I
teach mostly lower ability Science and I find behaviour to be poor, but
attitude to learning and lack of engagement with wanting to learn much
more upsetting. So I began to look around at different approaches to
teaching. (Mendus, 2006, Excerpt from MA Module 'Learning from the
NQT year' [Sheffield, July 2006)

Speaking to a teaching assistant from the time, they reminded me of how angry
I had been, which was something I had 'forgotten' when I was brainstorming
about this period of my life. Of course, a lot of this was my inner issues and
challenges coming to the forefront in this job, but it was through writing about
setting up the school garden for an action research module for my MA Education that I was able to express and explore my feelings for something different
in education:

This feeling of isolation was new to me as I am always driven and put
everything into something I feel passionately about... I really cared about
creating a pleasant space within the school grounds, about the children
who were able to learn new practical and creative skills and about the
team of adults that I worked with creating the garden. Also, it became very
important to me to bring inclusive outdoor learning as an opportunity for

some pupils… The fact that I really cared drove the project forward but also opened my eyes to realise I would be happier working more in the outdoors with troubled youngsters. I was also very aware that this need of mine did not make my project a high priority to others. (Mendus, MA Learning and Teaching assignment [Sheffield, May 2008])

I did take that love of learning and teaching in the outdoors with me and explored different ways of working in the outdoors once I 'retired.' So, like many new teachers, I left after only two years, following Weale (2016) who writes in the Guardian newspaper "Of the 21,400 who began teaching in English state schools in 2010, 30% had quit by 2015." I had lots of ideas but no real plan except going on a caving expedition to India the following February and to explore outdoor learning and supply teaching.

I gave a speech when I left, as was customary at the school, but wrote mine as a 'retirement' speech and I received 'retirement' cards from friends. My difference had been recognised by the school Head and he did agree to have a meeting with me about my career:

The trouble with you, Alys, is that you are a free-spirit. And as I recall this memory the word 'trouble' seems so forceful and I am not sure it would have been a word he would have used, yet even if my memory is incorrect, it was that sentiment that I carried with me. And now maybe I wear it as a badge of honour. (Mendus, Memory of a conversation, April 2007 [Sheffield, November 2015])

When I 'retired' I was 27, almost 28, on the cusp of what astrologists would call my 'Saturn Returns.' This is a belief that every 27–29 years a person faces a key identity crisis and creation period. For me it was a time of empowerment as I was now relatively solvent, owned a vehicle, and had a professional qualification that I could begin to do what made sense for me and if I truly was that 'free spirit' that my Head had described, I could begin to explore what that meant. I did not believe in the system and I was prepared to go into the unknown rather than stay in a space that made me unhappy. But all the time at the back of my mind a little voice kept reminding me, what about the children? Reay (2016) puts this so well:

While teachers are leaving the profession in increasing numbers (Weston, 2013) in despair at this sterile, joyless practice of teaching to the test, children do not have a choice to leave. (Reay, 2016, p. 326)

3   Fed up with Neoliberalism in Education

The influences of neoliberalism are seen throughout this book, arising in the background philosophies of many different types of schools and places of education. Following Au (2016), I see neoliberalism as a paradigm that "operates on the assumption that human progress and development is best served through economic systems based on free trade, deregulation of markets, and individual, entrepreneurial freedom" (Au, 2016, p. 316). It is important to be aware that it has been argued that the central message of neoliberalism is that there is no alternative (Mason, 2015). However, my research and this book argues that there are alternatives, just that some are still yet to be imagined.

In terms of education, Au (2016) argues that neoliberalism is seen through the privatisation of education and the continued use of high-stakes tests as a way to evaluate the market success of these schools through profit making companies such as academies, charter schools, exam boards, textbooks and curriculum. The influence of neoliberalism in education leads to different responses in the classroom. For example, Wrigley (2016) argues that for some the top-down pressure for teachers is always to do what they are told by staying:

> safely within the narrow confines of a lesson plan... to transmit pre-processed knowledge from the front... do this because it might be in the exam, hand it in after an hour, and you'll get a grade or mark. (p. 336)

This approach of 'teaching to the test' as Wrigley (2016) described has become a continual critique of the traditional, mainstream educational system, see the poster in Figure 3 as an example from a school in the US protesting against high-stakes testing. This argument is added to by Biesta (2010) who argues that education has changed for the worse and turned what is seen as 'legitimate knowledge' into anything that can be examined on high-stakes tests. The controversial outcome here is that in some cases neoliberalism can become normalised, as Joldersma (2016) argues that when this happens neoliberal approaches can no longer be seen as politically charged. However, the argument continues that education is politically charged (Joldersma, 2016; Spry, 2016) and the outcome of this, as Joldersma (2016) argues, is that alternative education (and, in this book, places educating differently) can be seen as a political challenge to the status quo.

Therefore, this book and work by others exploring educational alternatives (Kraftl, 2013; Lees & Noddings, 2016) are entering a deeply political debate as every school (including those that see themselves as alternative to more

FIGURE 3
One test does not fit all

traditional approaches) operates within its own socio and political environment and most of these are neoliberal. As such, I am aware that through the evocative nature of sharing stories of places 'educating differently' that they may challenge, and in turn it may make changes to, how people think about education, learning and schooling away from the current dominant discourse of neoliberalism. This follows Fielding and Moss's (2010) argument that within this present system there is "no alternative but to explore alternatives" (2010, p. 38). However, it is also a very fine line to walk as some aspects of neoliberalism, I realise, have influenced the growth in state-funded educational alternatives, such as the concept of 'choice,' which has allowed the UK Free School and academy programme to open different types of schools (including Steiner Waldorf, Reggio Emilia, Project-Based Learning). The privatisation of the state-funded education system in the US through Charter Schools and the UK through Free Schools and Academies has supported the neoliberal ideal of choice.

The focus of social justice is seen throughout this book as it was a framing of my research from my scholarship in Freedom to Learn from the University of Hull, UK which was part of a wider ESRC project called 'Freedom to Learn.' A paper that my supervisors, Max Hope and Catherine Montgomery, wrote argues that the "one of the main aims [of the Freedom to Learn project] has been to consider how a freer, more Democratic Education might contribute to a socially just society" (Montgomery & Hope, 2016, p. 307).

4   Alys the Guide

The need for the stories of this book to interrupt the dominant paradigms positions itself with Reay's (2012) argument that what we desperately need in contemporary neoliberal times are totally different ways of envisioning education; ways that accord respect and value to all children and their teachers. Reay brings to the forefront the importance of social justice by explaining that:

> While the three Rs are important, teaching children to be caring, respectful, cooperative, knowledgeable about their own and others' histories, and well informed about contemporary global issues is equally, if not more, important. (2016, p. 328)

This book aims to share stories from places educating differently to traditional approaches, places that are attempting to envision education in new ways.

Choose your own adventure: The next two sections position the theoretical and methodological approaches of performative autoethnography and the multiplicities of the Alys-we. If you want to jump to the next part of the storying narrative jump to Chapter 2: My nomadology or even straight into Part 2: Educating Differently for the stories of the places educating differently that I visited.

5   Performative Autoethnography

To understand autoethnography in greater depth I attended the International Congress of Qualitative Inquiry in Champaign-Urbana, Illinois in May 2015, which gave me the necessary insights and confidence to refine my approaches. It was from speaking to Tami Spry and watching her papers using performative autoethnography that made me realise that the performance is not an afterthought and is essential. Positioning my work alongside Spry, who reminds the reader that "we offer our performing body as raw data of a critical cultural story" (Spry, 2005, p. 501), gives permission for innovative approaches for sharing stories and opens a gap for those stories to fill. This can be extended further following Spry's argument that "Performative Autoethnography can interrupt master narratives that become "stuck in time" through its continual re/creation of knowledge by critically reflecting back on who we are, and where, and when" (Spry, 2005, p. 501). Therefore, performing School Tourism (explored in detail in Chapters 10 and 11), the approach I used to visit and share stories from places of learning/schools around the world, uses performative autoethnography.

Performative autoethnography has influenced the research methodology and the way in which this book has been written. Denzin (2006) draws to my attention that "through our writing and our talk, we enact the worlds we study… instruct our readers about this world and how we see it" (2006, p. 422). Therefore, I realised that it is not just about the 'performance' or a piece that I 'act' or a story that I stand up and 'tell,' it is also about the style in which I write the book. As Hamera explains, performance ethnography "lifts up the 'graph,' the always taken-for-grantedness of writing" (2011, p. 320). As I learnt more about autoethnography I was excited by Denzin's (2011, p. 673) description that:

> Autoethnography is feminist… queer in its attempts to fill necessary gaps in social and academic discourse, disrupt harmful assumptions of normalcy, foreground identity politics, and take an activist-orientated, critical sensibility to understanding experience.

Knowing this allowed me to feel empowered that my identity could be a position of activism and that a traditional academic style was not the only way to write. I took heed of advice that my writing could include "poetry, art, and music; and dialogue… collaboration" (Denzin, 2011, p. 673) as well as following Ellis's argument that 'flexibility is the mantra'" (2004, p. 74). With autoethnography, I really felt like I had come home with the methodological approach and within the ICQI conference community (I attended and presented again in 2017 and 2018).

A major focus of my research is storytelling. I see this in my research, orally sharing experiences from visiting places of learning/schools. Following Poulos, who reminds us that humans are fundamentally "storytelling creatures… we arise in – and out of – our stories. We are, as co-narrators, ever in the act of creating new realities, narratively" (2008, p. 127).

> I see 'story' as the personal retelling of an event that has happened, such as the thoughts and feelings connected to a place of learning/school visit, the chronology of events such as who I met and what I observed, my observations and influences from my senses. It could be in simple language, very matter of fact, or in more eloquent prose AND, most importantly, it changes depending on the audience to which I am sharing the story of the experience. It is a political event – I aim to not insult but to share observations and thoughts, not direct criticisms, as often people are deeply connected to their school or educational philosophy and I want to be invited back to visit more schools. Stories are situated within the time and place that they are told but they are also part of the rhizome,

so interconnected with stories and experiences from my past and future. (Mendus, Journalling [Brighton, August 2016])

Although Ellis argues that there is "nothing more theoretical or analytical than a good story" (2004, p. 194), Ellis, Adams and Bochner (2010) argue that just telling stories is not autoethnography, it is the grappling with theory and positioning the story within culture that is the challenge and scope of the work. Therefore, no separate analysis is needed as the words on the page or the body on the stage (Spry, 2011) do the work. Harris and Holman Jones clarify this further, reminding us that by "Writing for performance, the performer, the character, and the audience member exists in (and is affected by) this temporal and physical distance" (Harris & Holman Jones, 2016, p. 12). Therefore, critical theory can be used to provide a framework for writing and thinking in understanding the dynamic relationships between theory and story (Bunda, 2017; Denzin, 2003, 2006; Hamera, 2011; Holman Jones, 2016; Madison, 2008). Holman Jones explains that, "theory tells a story – in non-ordinary language (which Judith Butler, 1997, says jolt us out of our complacency and into attention) of how things are and helps us discover the possibilities in how things might be" (2016, p. 228). Therefore, within my writing I need to be continually aware, as Holman Jones explains, of using "language that unsettles the ordinary while spinning a good story" (2016, p. 229) whilst being aware of Pollock's advice that theorising in critical autoethnography is an "ongoing, movement driven process" where the author is continually, "doing theory and thinking story" (2006, p. 8).

In practice, within this book performativity has been embodied creatively within the text through journalling, storytelling, vignettes, dialogues, ethnodramas and poems. However, when I began writing my autoethnography I took guidance from Adams, Holman Jones and Ellis (2015) to situate myself in my own story from my own research and from stories that others have told. From this I continued to follow their guidance and examined my "personal and cultural texts, including photographs, personal diaries, popular press books, blogs, films, and podcasts" (Adams, Holman Jones, & Ellis, 2015, p. 49)

I spent a week at my parents' house digging through old papers, files, diaries, searching for more information about key times in my educational journey. I realised that the only evocative/emotional insights that I had recorded were from essays and journals when I trained to be a Steiner teacher and from essays for my MA, particularly one on how setting up a school garden led to me leaving that school and begin looking for educational alternatives. I recognised that I must rely more heavily on my memory of the time and not my written records from the past. This inspired me to begin journalling so I had a personal record of my research journey. (Mendus, Reflections on using Autoethnography Journalling [Totnes, December 2015])

Gale's (2014) work helped guide the use of vignettes in this book to allow "new utterances to emerge and new meanings to unfold" (Gale, 2014, p. 6). These vignettes are essential for developing the argument for the power of sharing stories as they:

> Offer a little window, an in/out/sight, a glimpsing of an image that is lit-erally smaller than the original and yet provides subtleties and flavours, nuances, and qualities that might otherwise not be seen, felt, or heard: a sharpening of focus, a heightening of awareness a touching upon inten-sity. (Gale, 2014, p. 3)

Gale (2017), in a paper at Beyond Words conference at the University of Plym-outh, explained he had found out the origin of the use of the word 'vignette.' It was a message written on a vine leaf that could be shared and then would wither and die and go back to composting the earth. This reminded me of a nodal point of a rhizome that also flowers (like a lily) and then dies and puts energy back into the network. So, for me the use of vignettes in my book does just that, it highlights an idea before retreating back into the rhizome.

I use dialogues to represent conversations that happened or aspects of conversations that might have happened with me, one or many of the mul-tiplicities of Alys-we, or via the internet to illustrate the intra-active (Barad, 2007) nature of the conversations and storytelling between different places of learning/schools and about different pedagogies. These dialogues are similar to ethnodrama, a way to "present and represent a study of people and their cul-ture-ethnography" (Saldana, 2005, p. 2) written from "journal entries, personal memories, historical documents, and other data [which] are dramatised into a theoretical script" (Chilton & Leavy, 2014, p. 411).

I use poems to give voice to the multiplicity of the Alys-we, inspired by Leavy who explains, "in my work toward integrating my a/r/t identities, and thus producing holistic and fulfilling work, I have turned largely to poetic forms of inquiry" (2010, p. 240). Pelias eloquently adds there is a need for "writings that mark a different space. They collect in the body: an ache, a fist, a soup" (2004, p. 11). I feel that poetry can feed into that 'ache' to share the thoughts and feelings of the different voices of the Alys-we and perform a different purpose of con-necting to the readers emotions. As Leavy argues, "poems use words, rhythm, and space to create sensory scenes where meaning emerges from the careful construction of both language and silences" (Leavy, 2015, p. 78). Therefore, by using poetry within this book I aim to add another layer to the patchwork text, the rhizomatic weave of my experiences searching for the Ideal School.

My research and writing approaches are post-qualitative (see MacLure, 2013a; St. Pierre, 2011, 2016). I am aware of the juxtaposition between autoethnography and post-qualitative work. However, through my rhizomatic autoethnographic-we I hope to follow St. Pierre (2016) who called for academics to "refuse methodology" (2016, p. 11) and I know from personal communication that St. Pierre sees the rhizome as 'anti method' as it is not slotting thinking into pre-existing categories. The post-qualitative argument suggests moving away from the artificial separation of set sections of research and coded analysis as this does not include space for the transgressive 'data' – the emotional, dreams, sensual and memory (St. Pierre, 2011) and in methods such as autoethnography where writing is analysis (Richardson & St. Pierre, 2005), it cannot be disentangled. Coding sees words as data in a positivist manner as it treats words as un-interpreted data rather than already interpreted data and St. Pierre would argue that words are, "already products of theory," as well as leaving space for using "thinking in analysis" (2011, p. 621).

Therefore, in my research I have moved away from calling my observations, journalling, memories and old photos 'data,' as that would suggest, as St. Pierre argues, they are, "words... waiting to be analysed" (2011, p. 621). I agree with St. Pierre (2011) that I continually theorise and analyse my subject so there was no separate data/data collection or data analysis as this would create an artificial separation of the research from matter that cannot be disentangled. I also agree with MacLure that, "coding recodes that which is already coded by language, culture, ideology and the symbolic order" (2013a, p. 170), but by writing a performative autoethnographic rhizome I can allow an embodied aspect to the work and give space for a data 'glow' (MacLure, 2010, 2013b). The data glow has been described as:

> Some detail – a fieldnote fragment or video image – starts to glimmer, gathering our attention. Things both slow down and speed up at this point. On the one hand, the detail arrests the listless traverse of our attention across the surface of the screen or page that holds the data, intensifying our gaze and making us pause to burrow inside it, mining it for meaning. On the other hand, connections start to fire up: the conversation gets faster and more animated as we begin to recall other details in the project classrooms, our own childhood experiences, films or artwork that we have seen, articles that we have read. (MacLure, 2010, p. 661)

I apply this concept of data glow to my research throughout this book when I talk about the 'gems' that sparkle when I visit places of learning/schools around the world.

6   The Multiplicities of the Alys-We

Inspired by the work on multiple identities (Clandinin et al., 2006; Etherington, 2002, 2004; Speedy, 2000; Zemblyas, 2003), many sections of this book are written in different voices of the author, the multiplicity of the Alys-we. By viewing my life as a complexity of selves following Etherington's argument that, "we are many selves which are constructed and change over time in response to the social contexts of our lives and experiences" (2002, pp. 222–223), the book aims to give different viewpoints to the experiences of searching for the Ideal School. By embodying the many different voices of Alys, following Cisneros's (2002) and Clandinin et al.'s (2006) idea of how lives intertwine, I aim to create a 'patchwork text' (Winter, Buck and Sobiechowska, 1999) where the reader can follow the plotlines of the Alys-we as these voices, as Cisneros describes "convolute and spiral' as "coincidences collide, seemingly random happenings are laced with knots, figure eights, and double loops" (2002, p. 429).

Drawing upon Cisneros's (2002) argument that acknowledges that no one can make up our own lived experiences, Alys-we recognises that often when writing in one voice an author does not get a chance to share the many aspects of self that intra-act (Barad, 2007) with their thoughts, feelings and, in this book, the journey as a School Tourist. Clandinin et al. (2006) extends this further, describing the voices as "storylines, these multiple identity threads, do not exist in isolation from one another or from the broader social and cultural milieu in which... [one] lives" (p. 26). It is essential to recognise this positioning of multiple voices in relation to society and culture as this supports the autoethnographic-we (Spry, 2016) methodology. The voices of Alys-we are moving away from the 'autoethnographic-I' which focuses on the one voice of 'self' (see Ellis, 2004). For, as Butler says, "The "I" has no story of its own that is not the story of relation," (2005, p. 8).

This book recognises that the relationship between the voices of the multiplicity of Alys-we are more complex than the singular 'Alys' as rhizomatically they are always intertwined. Wenger (2010) argues that, "identity is a nexus of multimembership" (Wenger, 2010, p. 6) and this book sees multimembership as referring to the different aspects of Alys-we. This could be seen as the nomadic-space, as Tedlock (2011) argues is a space "beyond unified identities" (p. 333). These multiple and non-unified identities of the Alys-we also include my collective dialogues with others and the post-human world. Therefore, the objects and things (Bennett, 2004; Harris & Holman Jones, 2019) connected to my journey and to performing School Tourism in terms of the visit themselves are all entangled within this nomadic space. This can be extended further by following Speedy (2000) who argues, "through the telling and retelling of many stories that contributed to [the multiple] identities" also make it possible to develop "a sense of agency" (Speedy, 2000, p. 364), it is possible to add a level of rhizomatic entanglement to the thoughts and feelings in this nomadic space that are shared within the stories in this book. It is this agency that helps subvert views that identity is fixed, towards a view that identity is something that is becoming, it is "constantly being reconstructed and constituted through interpersonal processes and 'performed' through the stories that we tell" (Etherington, 2004, p. 76).

Alys-we, as a concept, can be developed further through recognizing the connection between my life as it "moves beyond unified identities" (Tedlock, 2011, p. 333) and Zemblyas's work that the identities of Alys are continually 'becoming' (Deleuze & Guattari, 1980/1987). Therefore, when writing in one voice of Alys there needs to be an understanding of the dynamic character of identity that is being continuously re-defined (Zemblyas, 2003).

Wenger (2010) extends this further to explain that identity is multi-scale, so in terms of the rhizome of Alys-we, some of the voices/identities may be louder or more visible than others. It is important to be aware here of the political aspects of these voices. Alexander (2013) explains that "the 'I' is never singular but embodies multiple selves competing for the authority to interpret a story for their own benefit" (p. 551). Following Wenger (2010), these voices may "merely coexist or... [they may] complement, enhance, or conflict with each other" (p. 6). Therefore, an awareness is needed that the voices of the Alys-we are all facets of my identity, politically influenced by my life experiences and subjectivity which includes the aspects that I may hope to disidentify with. For example, when I attempt to 'deschool' my background as a mainstream teacher, or times when I have been less aware of my own privileges. I acknowledge that writing and sharing an autoethnography puts the writer in a vulnerable position. However, I argue this is essential to engage the reader with my arguments through story as, following Pelias (2013), "I wish to be accepted or rejected on the basis of who I understand myself to be. I do not want to live a hidden life" (p. 388).

In my research alongside Alys the Guide these voices included: Alys the Educator, Alys Educating Differently, Alys and Steiner, Alys the future parent, Alys the PhD Student, Alys the Theorist, Alys the School Tourist, Alys the Performer, Alys the Van-dweller, Alys the Nomad, Alys the Edge-dweller and the Queering

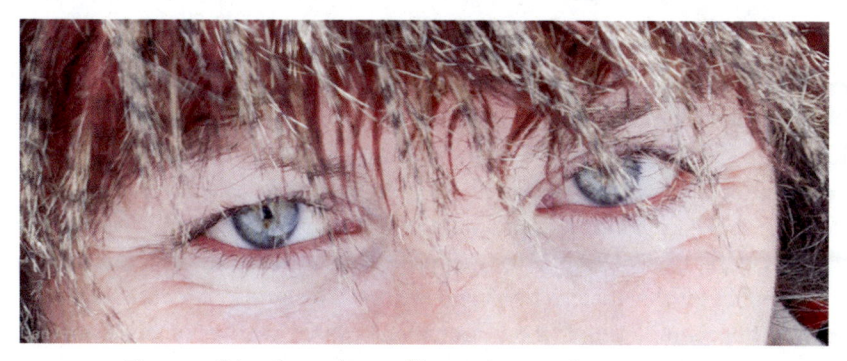

FIGURE 4   The eyes of the Alys-we (Dan Arkle, Cumbria, April 2018)

of 'Bad-Alys.' Wyatt and Gale's (2013) concept of assemblage autoethnography can also be used with the multiplicity of Alys-we as it allows for the depth and complexity that develops when the shift "from the individualisation of the 'auto' towards the felted dynamism of Deleuze and Guattari's (2009) notion of assemblage with its flow and effect, time, space and place" (Wyatt & Gale, 2013, p. 301) happens. By seeing the multiplicity of Alys-we as an assemblage it adds a dynamic level, allowing for a continual iterative flow and change in the voices and opinions as well as a space for more identities to emerge.

As I wrote about my visits to different places of learning/schools that I visited, read further about educational pedagogy and learnt more about theory and methodology, I began to see different voices appear in my writing. Schultz and Ravitch would argue that developing these additional 'professional identities' is not surprising as, "these identities are not intrinsic or separate from social contexts and interactions; rather they are embodied and enacted in practice" (2013, p. 37). Therefore, some voices have emerged towards the end of my studies; that of Ecological-Alys and Alys the guide and others are only appearing now such as 'Dr. Alys' and 'Alys the new parent.' I see myself, like Greene, that "my identity has to be perceived as multiple" because "neither my 'self' nor my narrative can have… a single strand. I stand at the crossing point of too many social and cultural forces; and, in any case, I am forever on my way" (Greene, 1995, p. 1). The mobility of being 'forever on my way,' I argue, develops the 'felted-dynamism' (Wyatt & Gale, 2013) of my assemblage-autoethnography further as the nomadology of the voices of the Alys-we continually change. In Part 3 there is a further shift away from the voices of the Alys-we still connected to the author, to a meta-level looking at giving voice to the Earth-we. The Earth-we is a voice for the collective consciousness of the planet, including all people and non-human elements. For now, these voices, the multiplicity of Alys-we, will be woven into the performative autoethnographic rhizome that is Part 2.

Nevertheless, I recognise that there are infinite possibilities of different voices of Alys that could have been included in this book, taking guidance from Etherington (2002), who suggested that narrative inquiry could include different viewpoints of the same incident and Mason (2009), whose PhD thesis was written as a dialogue of three different identities. I decided to use the voices that spoke the loudest in my journalling, in my thinking and theorising about this work, the voices of Alys-we connected to performing School Tourism, the search for the 'Ideal School' and my life as a van-dweller and Student/Theorist whilst completing this research. I am aware that this means that this whole book could be re-written in alternative voices of Alys-we, giving priority to alternative voices which may have created a very different performative autoethnographic-we.

Therefore, I argue that the multiplicity of the Alys-we speaks into/with the assemblage autoethnography/performative autoethnographic-we and helps weave the complexity of my identity in the form of a patchwork text of multiple voices and stories. This patchwork text starts from a story of performing School Tourism and 'Searching for the Ideal School.' It is through the different voices of the Alys-we that speak in the different pieces of writing/poetry that allows the assemblage to "'open up' endings, continue themes, explore contrast, and consider experiential and intellectual origins and alternatives," (Winter, Buck & Sobiechowska, 1999, p. 65). Therefore, all the voices are seen as integral within/to the rhizome. I realise that sometimes, some voices are louder than others, and I recognise that although a hierarchy could be seen to be created, as they are all inter-connected voices of the Alys-we it just suggests a more dominant multiplicity at that time and place. I invite you in Part 2 to play with my voices and multiple identities as they explore with each other, with you and within School Tourism, my stories from my autoethnographic-we Searching for the Ideal School around the world.

7   Summary

- Follow Lupinacci's call for scholar-activists to do things differently and be aware of their own privileges in the work.
- Performative Autoethnography influences how this book has been written and researched. The book includes storytelling through poems, journalling, ethnodramas, vignettes and images.
- The book is written in the multiplicities of the Alys-we, inspired by work on multiple identities and Spry's work on autoethnographic-we, remembering that *"autoethnography is not about 'self' but the wilful embodiment of 'we'"* (2016, p. 15).

- The essay Fed up with English Mainstream education shares my autoethnographic story of my schooling and early career as a teacher and helps position why I was so unhappy and why I began Searching for the Ideal School around the world.
- Fed up with Neoliberalism in education explains my issues with high-stakes testing, league tables, grading and why I was looking for educational reform.

My Nomadology

1 Alys the Guide

This chapter introduces the reader to the nomadology of my research: I share where in the world my travels took me searching for the Ideal School, then explore my itinerant van-dwelling in the UK and the mobility of writing and thinking and visiting places of learning/schools whilst on the move and of no fixed abode. I also position my nomadology within the theory of nomadic inquiry.

2 Alys the School Tourist: Where Did I Travel?

This section is a description of my journeying, searching for the Ideal School around the world to give an understanding of where and when I travelled to

FIGURE 5   Our van in Scotland, April 2017

© KONINKLIJKE BRILL NV, LEIDEN, 2022 | DOI: 10.1163/9789004506039_003

these different countries and schools. I visited over 180 schools in 23 countries and the stories from some of these journeys are shared in Part 2 (see Figure 14 for a shaded-in Peter's map of the world showing where I travelled).

In January 2013 I found myself on the East Coast of USA with a couple of months left on my visa:

> "What shall I do?"
> One of my new friends who heard that I was interested in alternative education asked me why wasn't I visiting schools?
> So I began to wonder?
> Why am I not visiting schools?
> I wasn't really sure what type of schools I wanted to visit... I didn't even know which key words to search for so started with 'progressive.' (Mendus, Journalling, Newton, MA, USA, April 2013)

From January to March 2013, I visited 14 different schools/home education groups/places 'educating differently' in the USA, which I wrote up in an article for the journal 'Other Education' (Mendus, 2013a). Once I returned to the UK I continued my School Tourism, visiting large independent progressive schools and others inspired by alternate philosophies such as Krishnamurti, Democratic Education and to a conference on radical education at Tamera Ecovillage in Portugal.

These experiences in 'educating differently' influenced my work choices and I spent a half-term teaching in the Upper School of a state funded Steiner Waldorf school in the UK before a term teaching at a progressive American semester school for 12–14 year olds in Switzerland.

Once starting the PhD from September 2014, performing School Tourism has been characterised by occasional visits followed by more in-depth school visits in certain areas or countries. There are examples of solo-visits, working on a project within a school, group visits, and consulting.

In January 2015, I visited two schools in Switzerland spending several days in each, then in June 2015 I visited many different places 'educating differently' in the South West of England, spending a half-day in each. After working for Die Freunde, (a German Steiner Waldorf charity), as a storyteller with refugees on Lesbos, Greece in October 2015 (see Mendus, 2016a), my school visits changed focus back to Steiner Waldorf schools where I was also giving a talk to the teenagers on my experiences.

I designed a research trip to Australia and Bali for February/March 2016. I attended a week-long educators course in Bali, spent a week observing a friend who had trained to be a Steiner Waldorf teacher with me in the UK and is now working in Australia and then spent another two weeks visiting places for a half day or full day that were 'educating differently' (including autonomous, democratic, Reggio Emilia, holistic and Steiner Waldorf).

In October 2016 I spent ten days at the Tamera community in Portugal exploring community based and Montessori Education, as well as a half-day visit to Florescer home-education project in Lisbon. After Portugal, recognising that I did not understand Montessori Education, I planned a couple of visits to a Children's Garden (3–6s) and a home school project for 6–12s in Scotland.

In March 2017, I spent 10 days working at Leysin American School (one that I had visited in 2015), this time working with the Middle School Students on their own projects into their 'Ideal School.' I came in as the 'expert,' giving ideas and suggestions and observing the use of the eduScrum approach for Project-Based Learning in action. The Middle School students made posters of their work and presented them at a conference where I gave a talk on 'Searching for the Ideal School.' The project was written up and published (Magnuson & Mendus, 2017).

In May 2017 my journey exploring performing School Tourism took a new direction when I joined Professor Michael Kamen (who had seen me give a paper at a conference in Plymouth in March 2017) and three pre-service teachers from Southwestern University, Texas on a week visiting schools in New York, USA. We visited charter schools, independent and state-funded schools covering many ways of 'educating differently' as well as continuing to explore what it meant to visit schools, particularly for the identity of pre-service teachers. This experience was turned into an ethnodrama performed at the Performing the World conference in NY in September 2018 and the whole script was positioned within affect theory and published as a chapter in a book on Performance and Affect theory (Mendus et al., 2020).

In June 2017 I was asked for the first time to use my experiences of visiting so many schools to visit a British school in Germany as a consultant. I then

FIGURE 6   Map showing the countries where I performed School Tourism

continued this visit to the Netherlands to visit Willy Wijnands, the founder of eduScrum, and watch the project-based learning approach in his school and also to visit De Ruimte democratic school using the sociocratic method. This was my last planned School Tourism trip during my research.

Since September 2018, living on the East coast of Australia I have visited 9 places educating differently, as well as taking my 18 month old daughter to the local Steiner playgroup.

3 Fed up with Fixed Home Dwelling: Introducing My Embodied Nomadology

> *I used to live within the old stone walls of a house*
> *Sheltering from the storms*
> *Securely tethered onto the earth*
> *In that exact spot.*
> *I could leave but I would come back*
> *There.*
>
> *Now I do not live anywhere*
> *I cause a daily headache to the system*
> *Partly an activist choice to not get*
> *Stuck*
> *Glued to a space on the earth.*
> *And partly a finger up at the establishment*
> *The UK does not like travellers*
> *I know as I live as one*
> *We move almost daily in our*
> *Metal shell*
> *An old builders van to the untrained eye*
> *And stop, explore, connect with nature and the people*
> *Then move on,*
> *Always moving on.*
> *The signs say quite blatantly that we*
> *Are not welcome here*
> *"No overnight parking"*
> *An anxiety sits with me all the time*
> *This becoming, being a pariah*
> *For not living normatively*
> *But I could be more 'normal'*
> *Be human, be local, just live in a van*

If parking, or being of no fixed abode
Was not such a challenge to society.
(Mendus, Journalling, North Devon, November 2017)

This section shares my methodology as a van-dwelling nomad through poems, theory, images and story. The aim is for the reader to be aware of the role of nomadology in the research so that when reading Part 2, where Alys-we shares stories from travelling around the world visiting places that educate differently, the reader will have a deeper understanding of the complexity of the process. It introduces the reader to the nomadology of my research: the mobility of writing and thinking and visiting places of learning/schools whilst living a life on the move and of no fixed abode. This book, although not written from a vehicle, has been written in multiple houses in two different states of Australia. It is a response to the call out by Braidotti (2012) to write into the nomadic subjectivity to fill the gaps that are unspoken in society.

> The central concern for my nomadic subject is that there is a noticeable gap between how we live – in emancipated or postfeminist, multiethnic, globalized societies, with advanced technologies and high-speed tele-communication, allegedly free borders, and increased border controls and security measures – and how we represent to ourselves this lived existence in theoretical terms and discourses. (Braidotti, 2012, p. 4)

The nomadology of writing is therefore integral to the style in which this book is written: A mobile writing approach.

FIGURE 7
Alys the van-dweller (Cornwall, July 2016)

4   Alys the Van-Dweller Describes Their Life in 2017

I have owned a van since 2007, as a reaction to waking up in a tent full of water and knowing it was time to have somewhere dry to keep stuff, to change in and sleep. My passion for the outdoors comes from my childhood growing up in the rural Lake District, UK with the lakes, mountains and crags on my doorstep. One of my main identities until around 2008 was a rock-climber. I went to university in Sheffield in 1998 so I was close to the Peak District for rock-climbing and returned to teach in 2005, again to be close to the rocks. The risks I choose to take may have changed but as I type these words I am parked up by the ocean, waiting impatiently to take my first naked dip of the day. The wilding of my identity and its influences on living close to nature are visible in my nomadic lifestyle.

I bought my second van in Autumn 2011 and since then I have not had my own home, instead being based from the van, sleeping in it sometimes and other times in friends or families homes or at short-term house-sits when in the UK. As I was spending more time being based from the van the conversion style had changed from needing lots of storage to more home comforts, including book-shelves and a more comfy bed. Every winter since 2013 I have been away for several months, escaping the damp of the UK weather. Since May 2016, a new chapter of my life began, with a new van and a new partner. Together, we stayed predominantly in the van when in the UK for over 18 months. It was during this time that I was writing the bulk of my thesis. This new van continued to have bookshelves but now had lighting, places to charge a laptop, a fridge and, most importantly for a student, the PhD desk. This was a tiny piece of reclaimed oak which was big enough to squeeze a tiny Macbook air and an enamel cup of espresso on as I perched on the end of the bed to write, see Figure 8 for a glimpse of working in such a small space.

Living an itinerant lifestyle is an essential thread of my research as being part of an ever moving rhizome is physically embodied in the life of the researcher. I write in different places. I look out on an ever-changing landscape and interact with numerous people. Our life is not planned, I have a thesis to complete

FIGURE 8   Alys the PhD student working in the van

but our day-to-day is inspired by 'following our highest excitement,' an idea from my friend Chloe, so we look at the weather and see what and where draws us next. I am incredibly lucky as the 'Freedom to Learn' PhD scholarship from the University Hull comes with a bursary which has given me relative solvency and freedom to live this life. I read 'Walden on Wheels' (Ilgunas, 2013) about a Graduate student living on the university campus in his van in the USA to save money but that van stayed put and from descriptions in the book had not been converted into a tiny-house-on-wheels like our van.

It is sometimes difficult for those looking in at my van-dwelling and varied itinerant life to understand how it works. One friend, working hard in the city in London, described my life as that of 'a trust fund child' as I seem to do whatever I want and travel extensively like I have an endless pot of money. The voice of Alys-the-van-dweller is reminded to share not just the highs but also the challenges, complications and anxieties as well, following Ingold:

> The wayfarer has to sustain himself, both perceptually and materially, through an active engagement with the country that opens up along [their] path. (Ingold, 2007, p. 76)

For example, for the van-dweller these questions arise; Where is it safe to park? Where can we wash and go to the toilet? Do we have enough power or WIFI? This section from a poem written in September 2016 illuminates these challenges further.

FIGURE 9   Alys the nomad. Parked up in a carpark by the sea (Newquay, Cornwall, August 2016)

5   **An Ode to the Car Park – 13th September 2016**

Sitting in yet another carpark
The life of a gas-station-hippy
Oh! there are pretty views of the breaking waves or the dew dappled grass
But there is also reality
Do we have enough water and gas and power?
Like the rest of Babylon just
A little more in our face and omnipresent
And where to poo?
That was the first question a 6 year old friend of mine asked me on a tour of the van
"So where's your toilet?"
I wonder how much of an idyll is our life?
We are not really cut off from society as we cannot grow our own food – except
for a few sprouts by our cooker
We don't even have solar panels – next year we say
And the truth is we spend more time in shops, around people in the society we try
to extradite ourselves from than those house-dwellers we look down on
Yet this morning waking, snuggled into a warm embrace, hearing the loud patter
of heavy rain on the roof I sprang out of bed
Pulling on my bikini (for common decency) I led the way dodging raindrops
across the carpark to the dark, treacle-like majesty of the Dart
And, gingerly at first, then proudly stepping off and into its current floating
down at speed until caught by an eddy and in to rest
The cleansing and anointing of the fresh water sending tingles to my toes and
washing my hair as I swam.
A run back to the van and happy smiles, fresh coffee, a few strums of a new tune
on my ukulele and back to it.
Sitting there like any PhD student up-and-down-the-land, head down, laptop
open, feet planted (on the floor of the van), working... working-in-an-unusual-
space but still working.
Not really edge-dwelling but edge-dancing in and out of the rhizome of Babylon.
And for one-who-does-not-like-to-compromise what is happening here? At times
van-dwelling is freedom but it is still living in this neoliberal, capitalist world.
Is it time to stop and be actually a bit different, actually living on the land?
Changing by doing rather than staring and looking in from the outside?
This Summer there were two of us in the van
And maybe soon there will be three.
I wonder where we will be?
(Mendus, Writing in the van outside Morrisons [Totnes, Devon,
September 2016])

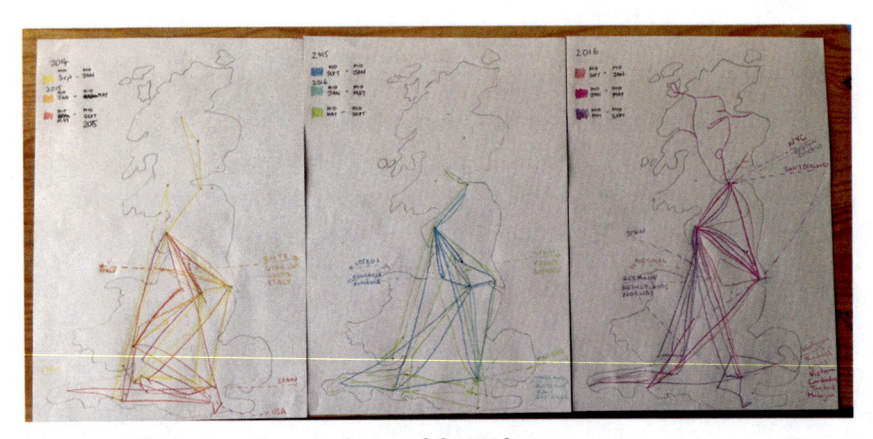

FIGURE 10   Three maps of my travels around the UK from 2014–2017

After completing my PhD I spent some time "mapping and threading those journeys" (Mendus, 2019, p. 58) looking for patterns around places, seasons and reasons for travelling (see Mendus, 2018b, 2019). Figure 10 visually shares my travels around the UK, highlighting places I regularly went and those I did not.

When I share these stories of my nomadology, it is not only the van, the multiplicities of the Alys-we that are travelling around the UK and the world visiting places of learning/schools, so is the laptop and the scraps of paper on which the thesis is written. It could be argued that even the writing of the thesis has been a performance as the thesis was written itinerantly. Van-dwelling can be viewed as a 'live method' (Back & Puwar, 2012), it is mobile process, where the writing happens on the PhD desk in the back of the van parked up in numerous locations with many writing possibilities – sometimes with stunning vistas of the sea or mountains and other times with the door firmly shut to the keep out the chill breeze and the smell of petrol fumes from the city smog outside. I also write in other locations, nowhere near the van: at a table in a coffee shop, on my parents' dining room table where I sit with memories of sitting at the same chair and desk struggling through schoolwork and an old painting of my long deceased grandfather watching me from the wall, to friend's kitchen tables, seats on planes, trains and buses around the world. Figure 11 shows me working in a cafe in Chiang Mai, Thailand in December 2016.

I would sometimes write outside when the British weather allowed on park benches or sitting on the grass leant up against the van. There was no office in which the PhD was written, but there were rhythms that set me in a writing routine – best early in the morning, with fresh coffee and discipline: dropping into 90min sessions knowing soon I could chat to my friend or hop out of the van for a walk or swim.

FIGURE 11 Two photos showing Alys-we working on the PhD in Chiang Mai, Thailand, December 2016

There are some days in the PhD life when it just makes sense

I'm in the back of our van perched on the bed, snuggled up against some sheepskins, my bare knees squeezed under a beautiful piece of reclaimed oak that is my desk. My laptop open and a pile of books beside me.

The cars are rushing by on the road outside, but I am stopped here.

Bozz is gently breathing... snoring slightly? As he sleeps behind me. My coffee sits in its little enamel cup waiting to be cool enough to drink and I lick the last remnants of croissant and home-made strawberry jam from my lips and smile. (Mendus, 2017a, from a paper presented at the ICQI conference)

Positioning my life through the lens of a van-dweller (someone who lives in a van as their main place of accommodation in continually changing locations), I find resolve in Sheller and Urry's (2006) understanding of "dwelling-in-motion" and from bel hooks assertion that for richer households in the west "home is no longer one place. It is locations" (1991, p. 148) or, like Urry (2000) argues, being "on the move" (p. 50) has become a way of life for many.

I am interested by ethnomethodological studies of driving and 'passengering' (Laurier et al., 2008) as they show contrasting ideas of what it is like to drive/be a passenger in an automobile similar to that of a van-dwelling School Tourist, but not covering the living-in-a-vehicle aspects. Sheller (2011) builds on this further in their discussion on travelling in a vehicle, drawing out the importance of the affects and feelings that are produced that are "neither located solely within the person nor produced solely by the car" (p. 5), or van. It could therefore be argued that 'van-dwelling' is a more-than-human experience because it combines 'motion and emotion' (Sheller, 2004, p. 227) and the van-dweller becomes 'kinaesthetically intertwined... through a conjunction of bodies, technologies, and cultural practices' (Sheller, 2004, p. 227).

FIGURE 12   Alys the van-dweller, photo of our cooker

6   Alys the Nomad

I am aware that writing this book in Australia adds a different dimension and criticality compared to if I had continued to live in the UK and written the book there. This is because as well as living in a different hemisphere and place, I now live on stolen land as a settler-academic (Country et al., 2019; Rowe & Tuck, 2016), where terms that I have used, such as 'nomad,' have different connotations and understandings. Following Country et al. (2019), I acknowledge that there are many tensions when a settler-academic attempts to be morally accountable, for example, not "intervening without imposing in unjust situations, representing learnings and knowledges without silencing or romancing, engaging with theory while remaining grounded…" (2019, p. 691). Therefore, I have included the vignette below to show my attempts at response-ability, described by Country et al. as "an ability to pay close and careful attention as part of more-than-human worlds, and an imperative to respond as part of these worlds" (2019, p. 682), as a settler-academic through my critical reflection with Alys-the-theorist and Alys-the-nomad to show why I have decided to continue to explore and use the term 'nomadology.'

7   Vignette 1: Alys the Theorist with Alys the Nomad – A Dialogue Troubling the Term 'Nomad'

A created conversation from an email conversation between Dr Sandra Wooltorton, University of Notre Dame Australia, and myself after they watched a recording of a presentation I gave to Southern Cross University about my research (Mendus, 2020).

Alys:	Thank you so much for watching my presentation on my research. Can you give me some clarification of the challenges of using the term 'nomad'?
Sandra Wooltorton:	'Nomad' has some unfortunate historical connotations in Australia. The incorrect view is that Aboriginal people are/were wandering opportunists with no attachment to any places (or the like). However, almost every part of this sentiment is untrue and ridiculous. So, the word nomad can bring up racist sentiments which reflect the ignorance of the first settlers, and those attitudes can still be heard today.
Alys:	Thanks! I am still worried that my use of the term 'nomad' may now be inappropriate as I now live and work as a settler-academic in Australia.
Sandra Wooltorton:	I think most people – particularly in the Kimberley where I live – know that the real transients (or nomads) have always been settlers and settler descendants. These people travel across Australia or the length and breadth of their state, in search of work, or travelling to explore the country!!! Like yourself. :) We have this term: 'grey nomads' to refer to retirees who travel around the state or the nation in camper vans or towing caravans.
Alys:	So, as long as I frame 'nomad' to be a settler identity and settler lifestyle choice I can distance myself from the incorrect labelling of Aboriginal people?
Sandra Wooltorton:	Yes! For example, many school teachers and public servants are still transient (or nomadic), staying a year or three in schools and then moving on in search of some holy grail – usually a lovely place to live and this often includes a 'better school' to teach at. So, you've just shortened that process with school tourism! A healthy proportion of rural/remote school teachers move around, and over their lives manage to teach in ten or more schools.

Wooltorton's final comment is an interesting cultural observation of the itinerant teacher in Australia and it reminds Alys-we that their assumptions of what it is to be a teacher are very much framed by their initial experiences in the UK where I have many friends who, 15 years on, still work at the first school that they got a teaching job with. It does, however, suggest that this book could be very helpful for those Australian teachers who often move jobs to know more about what to look out for in each school they visit or work at. In terms of usage of the term 'nomad,' it could be argued that it needs to be claimed by these teachers and that the response-ability of the settler-academic needs to be to educate people that Indigenous people in Australia are not 'nomadic' (Pascoe, 2014). As Country et al. (2019) reminds me to keep challenging, to "derail damaging and dangerous discourses" (p. 694) such as unconscious use of terms such as 'nomad.'

Therefore, I argue that having a greater awareness of terms that I choose to use to identify myself is essential to be a continuing reflexive practitioner. Therefore, I find it helpful to follow Bauman (2011), who uses several metaphors for modern life (such as tourist, vagabond, nomad). Although they were written to be separate entities, I see a van-dwelling School Tourist fitting into more than one category. For example, by living in a van, as my home also is constantly moving, my life is that of a 'vagabond' which Bauman describes as, "the vagabonds... know that they won't stay in one place for long" (2011, p. 22). 'Vagabond' casts images of the 'down-and-out' in the stratified, consumer society (Bauman, 2011). As Bauman explains:

> Those "high up" and "low down" are plotted in a society of consumers along the lines of mobility – the freedom to choose where to be. Those "high up" travel through life to their hearts' content and pick and choose their destinations by the joys they offer. (2011, p. 17)

Reading Bauman's words make me smile as it reminds me directly of one of my life's mottos: to be able to spend at least a day, if not my whole life, following my highest excitement. Realistically, is following my highest excitement fundamentally about privilege? For it is true, who can be a School Tourist is deeply connected to the ability to be mobile and, therefore, to privilege. As Skeggs argues, "mobility and control over mobility both reflect and reinforce power. Mobility is a resource to which not everyone has an equal relationship" (Skeggs, 2004, p. 49). How many people really have that choice as I 'pick and choose' as a vagabond School Tourist? I may be on a low-income (comparatively in the UK in 2017, under the Living Wage), but I am not destitute or homeless. I just choose (at present) to live an itinerant life as I know it means I have more disposable income and freedom than renting a physically fixed room in a house – more possibilities to follow my highest excitement than be stuck dreaming of the time to do things.

FIGURE 13   Bozz's profile. Looking out to sea from the van (Cornwall, September 2016)

I am well aware that being a van-dweller and a School Tourist are not self-reliant on each other. My being a van-dweller at the time of developing this approach gave me the funds and flexibility to embody the approach, but they are not mutually exclusive. It is possible to carry out School Tourism from a base-location, it would just be more expensive (in terms of running a home that you may not always be physically present in) and thereby give less opportunities to visit so many international schools. The itinerancy gave this particular study extra depth as I was able to stretch my money further. It is also worth mentioning that a well-funded School Tourist would not necessarily need to live an itinerant life. For example, during my research I met and visited schools with Professor Michael Kamen, Southwestern University, Texas, who has also visited innovative schools all around the world, but returns each time to a home base, job and responsibilities.

The influence of an embodied itinerant life will be apparent throughout, giving opinions from the journey(wo)man School Tourist. And the reader should not feel sorry for the van-dweller as it is also an activist choice, a place of privilege to resist the normatively of fixed-home-dwelling, "because "staying at home" in a world made to the measure of the tourist is a humiliation and a drudgery" (Bauman, 2011, p. 22). However 'Fed up with the System' I may be, it is important to mention that Heller's (1995) suggestion of loneliness or uprootedness could also be applied to a van-dwelling School Tourist, always constantly moving, looking in at 'others' but not having a 'community' (a school?) of their own. Boland (2017) recognised that following a non-normative line of enquiry, such as his work questioning dominant discourses in Steiner Waldorf

FIGURE 14   Alys and the van waving at fellow nomads (SW England, June 2016)

education, meant that at times it was 'lonely work' and isolating. However, there is a correlation here to joys of connection with like-minded others for the School Tourist as Boland recounts, "discovering fellow nomads on their own journeys is a moment of mutual celebration" (2017, p. 55).

Other theorists have seen the 'vagabond' or 'tourist' (Bauman, 2011) as the 'nomad.' For example, Braidotti (2012) sees the nomad as "a dynamic and changing entity" (p. 5). This dynamism or mobility of the nomad has been argued to be the nomadology (Deleuze & Guattari, 1980/87) or nomadic subject (Braidotti, 2012). Another way to understand this complexity is through rhizomatic theory and nomadology (Deleuze & Guattari, 1980/1987). For example, the journey of a School Tourist (with aspects from the vagabond/tourist/nomad) can be viewed as a rhizome, for it is not linear, it twists and turns, sometimes returning to a 'home' location and other times not. This is similar to Ingold's (2007) idea for a wayfarer or seafarer, the van-dwelling School Tourist has "no final destination, for wherever... [they are] , and so long as life goes on, there is somewhere further... [they] can go" (Ingold, 2007, p. 77). Following Braidotti (2012), the journey could also be viewed as an unsettled dialogue between an ever-changing-peripheral and its centre. This unsettling can be argued to represent the nomadology of the Alys-we as they travel in multiple ever-moving ways, visiting places of learning/schools, questioning normative views about education and life.

It is important to be aware that School Tourism and Van-dwelling/Vagabond living differ here from the nomadism argued by Bauman (2011) and Braidotti (2012). Braidotti (2012) explains that:

> The nomadism in question here refers to the kind of critical consciousness that resists settling into socially coded modes of thought and behavior.

> Not all nomads are world travelers; some of the greatest trips can take place without physically moving from one's habitat. Consciousness-raising and the subversion of set conventions define the nomadic state, *not the literal act of traveling.* (p. 24; emphasis added)

I argue that it is "the literal act of travelling" that is essential for School Tourism as it is an embodied spatial practice following Urry (2002) that virtual travel does not substitute corporeal travel. I recognise that it is possible to use the internet to visit place of learning/school websites, watch documentaries on particular schools or read articles to be 'visiting' the schools abstractly, however this is not School Tourism as it misses the emotional aspect of the practice (Zembylas, 2003) and, as Braidotti also argues, that embodied accounts, "illuminate and transform our knowledge of ourselves and of the world" (2012, p. 16).

It is the 'visit' itself which could be seen as a 'nodal point,' as Gale explains that from each nodal point flows the "possibilities of each new rhizomatic encounter" (2014, p. 2). Following Urry's (2007) argument that, "people... desire to know a place through encountering it directly. To be there for oneself is critical" (2007, p. 261), then School Tourism is about those corporeal spatial visits as "a further sense of co-presence, physically walking or seeing or touching or hearing or smelling a place" (Urry, 2007, p. 261). This co-presence is also about "'facing-the-moment' as 'what is experienced is a 'live' event programmed to happen at a very specific moment'" (Urry, 2007, p. 262). The word 'embodied' itself is contested as some say that it too can be virtual (Kilteni, Groten, & Slater, 2012). However, for School Tourism I am arguing 'embodied' to mean a physical visit, following Harris and Holman Jones, "embodiment for performing bodies exists and is enacted in place and time, including both virtual and 'live' spaces" (2016, p. 13). Therefore, it is through the nomadology of my research, my life and my writing that these experiences of places educating differently to traditional education can be shared.

8   Summary

– I lived as a nomad, as an itinerant van-dweller throughout my PhD studies, travelling around the UK.
– The nomadology of my research is visible in the mobility of writing and thinking and visiting schools whilst living a life on the move and of no fixed abode. Following Country et al. (2019), I acknowledge that there are many tensions when a settler-academic attempts to be morally accountable and I am aware of the incorrect usage of the term 'nomad' for Indigenous people

in Australia.The nomadism of performing School Tourism is different to that argued by Bauman (2011) and Braidotti (2012) in that it is "the literal act of travelling" that is essential for School Tourism.

– My nomadology gave me an extensive wealth of experience as I visited over 180 schools in 23 countries.

FIGURE 15   The van at night (Hay Tor, Dartmoor, Devon, September 2017)

CHAPTER 3

School Is Not the Answer

1   Alys the Guide

I am asking you all to consider beginning to think into the unthought, even before I have shared with you the stories from the places that I visited.

The challenge from this whole journey searching for the Ideal School was that I was realising that school and schooling is not the answer and that our current understanding of what is education needs to shift. I realised that the rhetoric, the dialogue that has been continuing in many of the places educating differently, such as Steiner Waldorf and Democratic, is not necessarily our future.

So, although you are very welcome to jump straight into the stories in Part 2, this chapter, although theoretical, helps position the book and the lens through which the aspects of the Alys-we understood the places educating-differently that they visited. Of course, you can also jump into the stories first and come back to this later!

After exploring the terms school, schooling, learning and educating, this chapter puts forward the argument of bringing stories of hope by looking for the gems in the places that I visited. I define this as the edge-ucation. Drawing on work in futurity I was inspired by stories of hope, but I am very aware that this is still within the shadow of now: behaviourism, neoliberalism, racism, hierarchy, privilege. It is still there. I am adamant that I am not coming up with 5 ideas that will make the Ideal School, because that is impossible. That is an oxymoron and all these ideas, and experiences are from a time and a place and my subjectivity as a cis, able-bodied, white-British, middle-class woman.

For it is an entanglement of education, a radical non-binary approach
That draws on the current strengths, the gems, but dreams for the future

For the visions of the not-yet-thought
Made possible by giving young people the freedom to fly.
And to de-school teachers and de-school the system
And chuck out not just the word school
But the institution itself
For there is no ideal school
As school is not the answer
(Mendus, 2017a, from a paper presented at the ICQI conference)

2 The Queering of 'Bad-Alys': The Green School Epiphany Poem

2.1 *Alys the Guide*

The Queering of Bad-Alys speaks for the first time here, following Holman Jones and Harris's definition of Queering autoethnography as "creating dissonance around what passes as 'normal' and 'normative,' ... working against that which passes as stable, coherent, certain and fixed" (2018, p. 4). Bad-Alys is a voice that questions the Alys-we and the status quo. For further examples and development of Bad-Alys and the Bad-Folx, see Mendus (2021).

The Green School is a 'holistic' international school on the island of Bali in Indonesia describing itself on its website as somewhere that:

educates for sustainability through community-integrated, entrepreneurial learning in a wall-less, natural environment. Our holistic, student-guided approach inspires and empowers us to be green leaders. (Green School, 2017)

As a school that is 'educating differently' it has become famous and I am often asked if I have visited the 'Green School.' I found out there was an 'Educators Course' called 'Wall-less-ness' during the last week of February 2016, so I organised my School Tourism research trip to Australia around the course. This poem covers my experience and how that visit became a nodal point of my research.

The heat hangs heavy, creating a wall around me, coating me in lethargy
And I am meant to be in a school of wall-less-ness!
Sweat drips, monsoon rains flow
Rich greens of the paddy fields, wild dogs running by

FIGURE 16   The Green School upper school classroom from above (Bali, Indonesia, February 2016)

So much going on in this strange cocoon
And why am I suffocating in this beauty?
We laugh in the icy pool and put the world to rights, even discussing Deleuze
in the darkness!
And then we are rushed on to the next episode, to eat more food.
The food is delicious but why am I feeling like Hansel, fattened to distract
me?
What is really going on here?
A few weeks later I read my notes and I am confused.
So confused, I share them with others.
For on paper this place is amazing, free thinkers creating free thinkers, such
passion and love for humanity, sustainability, Gaia.
But back there I cried with grief as something was missing.
The money, the energy, my drive to get me there and to not fall in love was a
shock.
"You always see the bad in everything...."
But do I?
And yet here there were many gems, true elements of MacClure's (2010) Data
Glow
But it wasn't enough.

I chastise myself for deep down I know there never will be enough.
My views and ideals are mine alone but...
Can I learn to take a step back and see beauty and not jump to conclusions?
Or maybe just own my stuff and work out what are my compromises?
And then accept me, the place, for somewhere on my journey.
See it as another nodal point?
A clarification that it is societal change that I am after and that education
for sustainability for those privileged few who attend this school is not a bad
thing after all...
Just not enough.

2.2   Alys the Theorist: The Oxymoron of 'The Ideal School'

"What do you mean when you say the Ideal School?"
I know what you are all thinking.
As it was Jane Speedy who sat there, stuck, throughout my whole presen-
tation.
"What is Alys on about when she says the Ideal School
Isn't that an oxymoron?!" (Mendus, ICQI Paper University of Illinois
[Urbana, USA, May 19th 2017])

An oxymoron is defined by the Oxford dictionary as "a figure of speech in
which apparently contradictory terms appear in conjunction" (Oxford University Press, 2021). This epiphany at the Green School began to re-sculpt my
research as I came to realise that the 'ideal' that I was searching for does not
currently exist. I recognized that other academics have also been questioning
the concept of school. For example, Harris asked the question "Why school at
all?" (2014, p. 70) and Gatto wondered "Do we really need school?" (2009, p.
xv). Therefore, I began to problematise the idea that I was looking for a 'school'
after all and I began to question if 'school' and 'schooling' were the correct
terms to be using.

   Horton and Kraftl (2014) see space as a social construction rather than an
observable reality and argue that, for some, the term 'school' covers not just
the approaches to teaching, but also the building itself and the cultural expectations of the use of that space. Wenger (2010) through their work on communities of practice extends this thinking further in relation to people in these
'spaces':

   The landscape shapes our experience of ourselves: practices, people,
   places, regimes of competence, communities, and boundaries become

part of who we are. Identities become personalized reflections of the landscape of practices. (p. 6)

Therefore, by viewing 'school' as a social construction with the cultural expectations of the use of that space, it needs to be positioned in a set time and place. In England and Wales, it could be argued that the understanding of what is 'school' and 'schooling' has continued since the late 19th century and therefore I argue that it is time for the domination of not just the word 'school,' but this outdated understanding of the term, to end. This follows Gray's (2015, p. 75) argument that:

One of the tragedies of our system of schooling is that it teaches students that life is a series of hoops that one must get through, by one means or another, and that success lies in others' judgements rather than in real, self-satisfying accomplishments.

Gray (2015) also argues that traditional 'schooling' and other methods of progressive/alternative schooling that are not Democratic Education are like prison because students are told exactly what they must do and are punished if they do not follow instructions. Hecht (2010) also argues for a new education system (away from traditional education) and found Democratic Education to be his answer. Hecht (2010) searched for a:

New interpretation of the concept of "school" [where] the purpose of a school, after its redefinition, would be to develop in the child the power to choose and create the reality in which he wishes to live, and the ability to see today's reality as multi-faceted and multi-purposed. (Hecht, 2010, p. 40)

However, I struggle with a redefinition of the word 'school' as there is a danger of many misconceptions by using the same term again and I ask why continue to use the word 'school'? (Mendus, Journalling on school [Wolverton, August 2017])

I am aware that this opinion could alienate me from other academics/theorists interested in 'educating differently,' as Kraftl (2013) argues that few people, even those critiquing traditional education, are completely anti-school. However, I do support Kraftl's (2013) analysis that although few people are totally anti-school they may still want to 'de-school' spaces (from seeing school as a "uniform space, characterised by particular smells, rhythms, dress, forms of behaviour and architecture school uniforms, classrooms, corridors)" (Kraftl, 2013, p. 238). I think deschooling spaces is an essential element of a ripple towards change in the future of learning.

The idea of 'deschooling' originated from Illich (1971) who wrote that we need to 'deschool society,' explaining that we have been "'schooled' to confuse teaching with learning, grade advancement with education, a diploma with competence" (Illich, 1971, p. 1). Illich (1971) argues that resistance to deschooling is because it liberates education from society's control. This supports the view that a major purpose of full-time compulsory schooling is about power:

> Classroom attendance removes children from the everyday world of Western culture and plunges them into an environment far more primitive, magical, and deadly serious... (The) ritual of schooling itself constitutes such a hidden curriculum. (Illich, 1971, p. 32)

However, I am interested by Martin's (2002) decision in their work on alternative education to continue to use the term 'school' even though it could be seen as a misnomer because culturally the term is used to imply places where people intentionally gather to learn.

> I am left feeling strongly that school in itself is not the word for the future of learning and that I too want to 'deschool' the system but that I am not just anti 'school,' but anti-institutionalisation of education (see Schaub, 2010). (Mendus, Journalling on School [Wolverton, August 2017])

I wonder if continuing to use 'school' as a term can mean that in these 'schools' that 'schooling' occurs? However, from conversations with adults at several democratic schools that I visited they argued that they may be 'schools' but they are not 'schooling' the students, by which they meant controlling the learning of the students against a set rubric. It is important to mention here the work of Pattison and Thomas (2016) who highlight the importance of an awareness that 'schooling' is the dominant experience of childhood. However, at the same time recognising Holzman's (1997) argument that this dominant experience of schooling is completely outdated and counterproductive. An acknowledgment of the lifelong influences from 'schooling' on our society is essential in understanding the political aspects of societal control that schooling has on society and positions my argument that 'schooling' is not the answer for the future of learning. As Pattison and Thomas (2016) argue that, "through this common experience [of schooling] is a cultural, practical, working definition of what childhood is, what education is, and what it means to learn"

(p. 132). Nevertheless, I feel it is still essential to question the use of the terms 'school' and 'schooling,' even if my questioning of society's current embedded understanding of education and learning may be unsettling to the reader, I feel that needs to happen for change to occur.

One way for this change to begin to happen is to follow Gray's (2015) cry for children to have less schooling and more freedom. I am arguing to take this even further and begin to question if what is needed is not just another term (than 'school'/'schooling'), but another way of looking at learning.

> "I do not think school or schooling is the answer, so I have been using the term 'educating differently' in my thesis," I explained to Phoebe Tickell who was interviewing me for NetworkedU an organisation that connects people with visions and ways of educating for the future.
>
> "Interesting," replied Phoebe, "I have stopped using the term 'education' and only use 'learning' instead."
>
> "I wonder if 'learning differently' would be a better term, than 'educating differently?'" I replied. (Mendus, Interview about my PhD [Cornwall, July 2017])[1]

I began to explore the term 'learning' and found that Harris's (2014) argument seems to support Tickell's use of the word 'learning' over 'education' as:

> To educate" may be obsolete... the notion of 'learning' is perhaps a better or more accurate way of describing a contemporary acquisition of knowledge than is 'educating.' Does anyone really educate anymore? For that matter, did we ever? To save, to educate, to empower – verbs all charmingly out of date to a 21st-century palate. (Harris, 2014, p. 70)

> This left me wondering what is the difference between the definitions of 'learning' (is this something you do by/to yourself?) and 'education' (is this something being drawn out of you... is this by others??). (Mendus, Journalling on School [Wolverton, August 2017])

Smyth (2016) argues that learning is a political act with a social, psychic and emotional investment. However, Biesta (2006) and Burbules (2013) argue that learning is not yet education, giving the example that teaching is more than causing learning to occur. Burbules (2013) continues to say that education is more than mastery, or preparation for work/adulthood, it is about behaviours and the development of a particular type of person. Biesta (2013) called this "learnification," defined by Noaparast as "a dominant trend in which every educational activity is reduced to the activity on the student side, namely learning" (2016, p. 347).

> Is this learning vs education debate similar to intelligence (knowing things) vs wisdom (knowing how to use the things you know)? So, if learning differently is then understood as something that you do to yourself and this research has been exploring predominately imparting the knowledge and skills of life and the pedagogies by which that can occur, then 'educating differently' seems to be a more fitting term. However, continuing to explore 'learning' and where and how that occurs is also important. (Mendus, Journalling about Schooling [Wolverton, August 2017])

2.3 *Alys the Theorist: Developing the Edge-ucation*

2.3.1   The Edge-ucational Gems

Although I argue that 'school/schooling' is not the answer, this book uses the term 'gems,' inspired by MacLure's (2010, 2013b) concept of 'data glow,' to talk about the things that shine-out from performing School Tourism, illuminating gems 'educating differently' in these neoliberal times. This follows Jackson and Mazzei's suggestion of creating stories that seek "connection and recognition in the midst of complexity" (2008, p. 303). Gems can be these complex connections from schools or places of learning, or a teacher, or the School Tourist themselves sharing stories between different educators and schools.

> I visit many of these places 'educating differently' and I see ways they creatively fit our neoliberal society with its high stakes tests and behaviourism and can share ideas, but sometimes I can look a bit deeper to find some 'gems' to play with – to chuck into the melting pot of revolution – towards the utopia that needs a paradigm shift, a societal change to occur. These glimmers and gems are my edge-ucation. (Mendus, PhD Journal [Edinburgh, April 2016])

2.4 *Alys the PhD Student/Theorist – What If the Ideal School Does not Exist?*

> If 'School' and 'Schooling' are not the terms to be used and the 'Ideal does not exist,' where does this position the research? (Mendus, Journalling about Schooling August 2017 [Wolverton, August 2017])

Supporting my argument for the edge-ucation, which bridges the gap between defining education as alternative or mainstream is Singer's argument that the "innovative experiences usually begin at the margins of the state school system" (2016, p. 212). This could be understood further following Ingold's idea of "a zone of entanglement – this meshwork of interwoven lines – there are no insides or outsides, only openings and ways through" (Ingold, 2007, p. 103). This, therefore, positions the stories from the edge-ucation as a 'zone of entanglement.' Figure 17, a drawing by my 20 month old child, playfully shows an example of this entanglement in blue crayon. The red crayon highlights a gem.

FIGURE 17
Entanglement in wax crayon
(drawing by Ginny Connelly-Mendus,
January 2021)

Learning from the 'edge' has been recognised as being a very important concept in eco design based systems such as Permaculture (Holmgren, 2006). Therefore, learning from this edge, for example, by sharing stories of the 'gems' from one system/teacher/approach with another, more people have access to ideas and in turn can choose to be creative and implement them in numerous ways beyond their current understanding, especially within existing mainstream classrooms. This idea of finding and sharing 'gems' is mirrored in Smyth's (2016) argument that, due to the constraints of neoliberalism, top-down changes are unlikely to happen so "bottom-up approaches may enable alternatives to surface" (p. 397).

So, by seeing the value of looking at these different methods and approaches to education as being on the edge and that being beneficial to wider society, my research was refocussed. The edge-ucation learns

> from, as one possible example: the democratic community based model
> in a democratic school and the creativity in a Steiner school, the self
> determination of a Montessori and inclusiveness and alternative teach-
> ing styles of mainstream. Yet it is not stuck in one current mindset or
> paradigm, it is a conversation open to changing, evolving and, hopefully,
> dreaming towards an educational utopia beyond our current neoliberal
> understanding of education, society and learning. (Mendus, Journalling
> on defining edge-ucation July 2016 [Totnes, Devon, July 2016])

Although I am aware that Gray (2015) makes suggestions to improve education which I support and would see as 'gems,' such as "reducing the amount of
time that children must spend at school, reducing homework, and increasing
recesses" (2015, p. 84), it is not the aim of this book to make a list of character-
istics of the 'Ideal School,' as the 'Ideal School' cannot exist. Even a new school
that combined all the 'gems' is not possible as I am aware that all the 'gems'
together could contradict each other in some ways, and they are all temporal.
They are temporal because a 'gem' is for (and from) a specific time and place,
country and educational setting and they are often not generic concepts or
approaches. However, more importantly my argument supports Gray's (2015)
conclusion that you can make changes, or share stories of the gems, but this
does not solve the problem that the current places of learning/schools are not
suitable. It must also be made clear that the 'gems' are a compromise as they
are what, in my opinion, shines in this specific time, mostly in neoliberal countries around the world, but not the answer as I am now aware that in the current world the 'Ideal School' does not exist. I argue that 'school' and 'schooling'
are not the answer, following this it could be extrapolated that home education
is the only current possibility as it would provide full autonomy to the family
(in UK law). Unfortunately, conclusions such as home education/'educating
otherwise' being the answer to 'Searching for the Ideal School' raises the challenge of reinforcing ongoing inequalities (Johnston, Wilson, & Burgess, 2007),
with Seo's (2009) argument that home-schooling is for the middle-classes.

> Is my conclusion supporting home education due to my own middle-class
> privilege that I can choose to make the privileged choice to step outside
> the system? (Mendus, Thoughts on privilege [Suffolk, August 2017])

On the other hand, I could follow Peim (2016) and un-think education as the
solution and step away from exploring what is already out there in terms of
education and look at the bigger picture. Peim (2016, p. 148) argues that:

Both education in general and its paradigm institution, the school, have largely been "unthought" categories that, in their unquestioned positive status, have been taken to be essential components of any good or productive future.

Peim's (2016) claim that we might begin to envision a future that does not see "education as the essential and essentializing grounds of personal and collective fulfilment" (2016, p. 156) begins to step into this unthought aspect of the future of what is learning and it reminds me to think about the 'gems' and the edge-ucation that I had seen in performing School Tourism in a new way, one which looks at the potentiality for hope and change.

3   Edge-ucation, Potentiality and the Utopian Performative of Hope

Positioning the edge-ucation alongside Kraftl's (2013) argument for a utopianism in education that it is not static and Levitas's (2013) work on seeing utopia as a method rather than an end point allows the edge-ucation to have its own mobility as part of the ever-moving nomadic rhizome.

However, I am aware when writing about utopia that neoliberalism has taken onboard utopian language for education which could take the focus away from my argument of using utopian ideas to think into an unthought future. Kraftl (2013) recognised neoliberal utopian terms such as, "aspiration, transformation, promise, [and] legacy" (p. 233). Facer (2016), argues that the current education system projects present anxieties onto children's futures. For example, teachers ask young people what they want to be when they grow up or talk about the impact on their future from their exam results. Even the political left wing, Facer (2016) argues, has called for new stories for the future (see Fielding & Moss, 2010, and in essence the argument of this book). However, Kraftl (2013) defends Fielding and Moss's (2010) work on 'Radical Education and the Common School,' arguing that they may involve utopian impulses, but their work is grounded in current real experiences.

It is in this space of wanting change and being aware of the current situation that I have developed my arguments for sharing stories of the gems in the edge-ucation. Following Facer's (2016) idea that education can occupy a 'distinctive temporal moment':

> The moment of the thick present, the moment between past and future. It might be equated to an ecotone or estuary, where river and sea meet,

> and in which new creatures, novel to both, are created (Odum, 1971). It is
> neither past nor future, neither river nor sea, but its own distinctive time
> and space in which anticipatory practices and lived experiences combine
> and mingle, changing both the past and the future. The challenge is to
> deepen and enrich the awareness of the rich abundance of that distinc-
> tive space and time as a powerful sediment in which new realities can be
> and are being created. (Facer, 2016, p. 71)

I see connections between Facer's concept of 'powerful sediment' and my
edge-ucation as it, too, sits alongside this 'estuary' or 'ecotone.' This also supports the dialogue that there is a need for real change rather than pre-existing
realities and thereby arguing for other definitions of edge-ucation, ones which
include a paradigm shift to a totally new system, not just sharing the current
'gems.' This idea is supported by Gray who argues that we can't change education, "by tinkering with the current system. We have to start from scratch"
(2016, p. 61) and Facer, who extends this further arguing that we "have to be
concerned with continually opening up the possibility of new rather than
pre-existing realities" (2016, p. 71).

The question then becomes about how can this change happen?

Khasnabish and Haiven (2012) argue for the importance of the 'radical
imagination' as the key to radical social change because without it "we lack
the inspiration that motivates resistance" (2012, p. 411) and therefore change.
Khasnabish and Haiven (2012) see imagination as a collective process, further
supporting the idea of the role of the community over the individual which
I see as a common dilemma in many of the places that are 'educating differently.' This collective idea is extended by Amsler (2015) who suggests future
change is possible through courage, not in isolation but with others, including friends, through networks and by Facer, (2016) who argues that it is about
friendship. Khasnabish and Haiven (2012), also argue for a 'collaborative praxis'
as it is not about the 'I,' which builds on Facer's (2016) concept of friendship.
The dialogic nature of this point supports a collective approach to change and
brings the argument for the future of education from "the product of gifted
individuals who contribute the fruits of their genius to a marketplace of ideas"
(Khasnabish & Haiven, 2012, p. 411) to a dialogic process that "allows us to see
how we all contribute to the imagination and how the imagination changes us"
(Khasnabish & Haiven, 2012, p. 411).

Therefore, the sharing of stories of different possibilities of ways of 'educating differently' could allow educators to use their imagination to think the
'What if?' (Spry, 2016). Neuroscience research supports the idea that educational change does not happen if we as a society continue to choose to think

the same way (De Meyer, 2016). If we changed our thinking then educational change could happen. We also need to be aware, as Hauskeller (2014) warns, that although utopian dreams have created progress, they have also contributed to terror and humanitarian disaster. There is now extensive fiction on dystopias to remind readers of the potential dangers of thinking differently (Attwood, 1986; Collins, 2008; Huxley, 1932; Orwell, 1949; Roth, 2012). Keeping this all in mind, then the idea of changing thinking helps me develop another interpretation of the term edge-ucation, as being about potentiality (from Munoz, 2009) and utopian performative of hope (from Spry, 2016).

4 Potentiality and Hope

The 'Principle of Hope' comes from Bloch's (1954/1986) work into the possible realisation of utopia. Bloch's work on the 'not yet conscious' resonates with some of the thinking behind this book, that change in education is possible, it just has not been thought about 'yet.' Macy and Johnstone's concept of 'Active Hope' is about "becoming active participants in bringing about what we hope for" (2012, p. 3). The 'Principle of Hope' (Bloch, 1954/1986) and 'Active Hope' (Macy & Johnstone, 2012) run a thread throughout my research as I continue to search for the 'Ideal School.' Even after I decide 'ideal' does not exist, I continue to visit places of learning/schools and share stories between them because I was aware that, following Munoz's (2009) argument, utopia reminds us that something is missing and through the idea of hope, sharing stories of these places educating differently has the potentiality to lead to a ripple effect of change towards the not yet here. This is further supported by Braidotti's argument for hope being a "vote of confidence in the future" (2012, p. 14) as "the imagination is not utopian, but rather transformative and inspirational. It expresses an active commitment to the construction of social horizons of hope" (Braidotti, 2012, p. 14). This concept of striving forward follows Munoz's (2009) argument that utopia is towards queerness or, I would argue, influenced by Deleuze and Guattari (1980/87), for a 'queering' of identity recognising the mobility of the term. This is mirrored in the voice of the Queering of Bad-Alys in this book, seen as someone questioning society and hoping for change, following Ahmed's definition that queering and queering practices "disturbs the order of things" (2006, p. 161).

Utopia as a possibility follows into work on performance, both the performing of School Tourism and the performative autoethnographic-we as Munoz argues that "performance... is imbued with a sense of potentiality" (2009, p. 99). This book argues that there is a potentiality in sharing stories. Munoz

(2009) explores the concept of potentialities further, arguing that they have a temporality, they are on the horizon (seen as futurity) which builds upon the idea of the edge-ucation, moving towards change and thinking into the unthought.

5 Alys the Guide: Utopian Performative of Hope for Education

It was from reading Spry's (2016) eloquent description of the performative autoethnographic-we and its role in giving visions for the future that allowed me to explore further the concepts of the multiplicities of the Alys-we. I realised that through writing performatively as well as performing stories (at conferences and filmed online) then I too could create my own utopian performatives of hope for education. Spry (2016, p. 96) explains:

> Utopian performatives as autoethnographic labor constitute an autoethnography on the pulses, a redoing retooling renewing, a doing utopia, utopia as a verb, as verve, as sass, as dis and respect, a simultaneous rejection and recuperation of who we can be with Others. The material entanglement of word and body mixed with the transcendent strategies of hope… Utopian performatives respond to Haraway's question, "Who are we?" rather than 'Who am I?' and move us into an embodiment of who we want to be with Others, a hope-filled futurity built with sticks and stones, skin and bones.

Sharing these stories of places educating differently offers answers to the question "Who are we?," and "How are we educating?" It gives this embodiment that Spry is calling out for, for a physical change in the sense-making (see De Jesus, 2018) of what is possible for the future of learning. Sharing these stories develops a utopian performative of hope for education.

6 Summary

- The Ideal School is an oxy-moron and the current approaches to school/schooling even in innovative schools are not the answer for the future of education.
- This book uses the term 'gems,' inspired by MacLure's (2010, 2013b) concept of 'data glow,' talking about the aspects of each school that shine-out even within these neoliberal times.

- Deschooling spaces is an essential element of a ripple towards change in the future of learning.
- There are several elements of edge-ucation:
  - One understanding of edge-ucation is that it accepts that the Ideal does not currently exist but shares the 'gems' of stories of 'educating differently' from this neoliberal world, it is an edge-ucation that occupies Facer's (2016) 'ecotone.'
  - Building on this, the edge-ucation hopes for the future and takes guidance from both Munoz (2009) and Spry (2016).
  - The term 'edge-ucation' bridges the gap between defining education as alternative or mainstream, it can rhizomatically be both and between them at the same time.
- To see the multiplicity of Alys-we and the edge-ucation approach in action, I recommend that you watch this link of a performative piece that I wrote as a 'Utopian performative of Hope' presented at the International Congress of Qualitative Inquiry in USA in 2017 (Mendus, 2017b).

Note

1 This interview can be found at the following link: https://www.youtube.com/watch?v=SGkLdogNH0c

PART 2

Educating Differently

∴

FIGURE 18 A magpie – searching for gems (Lino cut, Yuggera Country, Brisbane, May 2020)

Steiner Waldorf Education

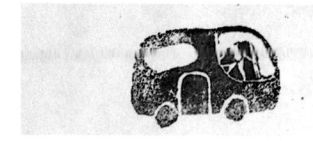

1 Alys the Guide

In Part 2 I share my storying (Phillips & Bunda, 2018) of my nomadology performing School Tourism. There are two chapters for Steiner Waldorf education as it was my first innovative pedagogy that I found as an alternative to traditional education. I describe my initial contact in the essay in Chapter 1. I then trained as a Steiner Waldorf Class teacher (for children 7–14 years old) from 2006–2008, as an Upper School teacher (2010–11), and took extensive Professional Development courses in Kindergarten and Early Years (2008–2019) whilst gaining an additional UK state qualification in teaching and managing Early Childhood settings (EYPS). As a Steiner teacher, after running a home education group for 5–8 year olds three days a week for a year (2008–2009) I worked mostly as a Casual Main Lesson teacher in different Steiner Upper Schools (state and privately funded) in the UK for three weeks at a time, although sometimes it was for as long as a half term (2010–2014). I also worked as a Parent and Child group leader in Sheffield, Derbyshire and at the annual Lifeways festival for one week each summer for 7 years (2010–2017). Since 2002 I have visited over 55 Steiner Waldorf schools or kindergartens in 14 countries.

Chapter 4 aims to show my relationship with Steiner Waldorf education, particularly through the voices of Alys the Theorist, Alys and Steiner and Alys the School Tourist. This chapter gives an overview of what makes Steiner Waldorf education unique, the role of the teacher and the differing approaches for Kindergarten, Class teacher years and Upper School.

In Chapter 5, the second Steiner Waldorf chapter, I critique and grapple with an approach which I love and admire, but which has aspects that I am deeply troubled by, through the voices of Alys the PhD student/theorist, Alys Educating differently, Alys the School Tourist and Alys the Performer). In Chapter 5 I unpick major issues of racism in Anthroposophy (the philosophy behind the educational approach), the focus on Christianity and Eurocentrism even in Steiner Waldorf schools around the World, as well as issues arising with behaviourism. I finally explore the relationship between Steiner Waldorf education and the edge-ucation in terms of state funding and calls for Waldorf 2.0 (Boland, 2017). Throughout both chapters I explore the beauty, rhythm and holistic nature of the educational approach.

2   Alys-We: Why Not Waldorf? A Play-Script from SE Asia

This play-script may include terms that do not make sense to those new to Steiner Waldorf education and Anthroposophy. However, they are all explained throughout Chapters 4 and 5. It has been included at the beginning to offer a snapshot of why this rhizomatic exploration for the 'Ideal School' came about, as although I had found an intriguing way of 'educating differently' with Steiner Waldorf education, it was not enough.

> *One Thursday evening in December 2016, Bozz, myself and three Senior Waldorf teachers from Malaysia met for dinner in Penang. It is a couple of days after I joined them for their annual Waldorf teacher training conference and gave a talk about 'Waldorf Schools around the World.' The conversation flows as we devour smelly Durian cheesecake in a low-lit, mahogany-clad restaurant bestowed with ironic colonial dis-splendour.*

Teacher 2:   So Alys, why isn't Waldorf Primary education your ideal?

Alys: Oh, but I do love Waldorf education! I love how beautiful each place I visit is, wherever I am in the world. The walls are painted pink or pastel colours depending on the Grade and there are always natural materials, home-made resources and the most beautiful blackboard drawings. I love how creative the lessons are and I really appreciate the focus on play. I really love Kindergarten; we think we will probably want our children to go to a Waldorf Kindergarten. Don't we, Bozz?

Bozz: Yeah.

Teacher 1 interjects, looking at Alys questioningly.

Teacher 1:   I'm not sure I understand. So why isn't that enough?

Alys: Well, I have a real challenge with the way that some schools and some places can become so dogmatic about Anthroposophy (see the sections in Chapter 5 What is Anthroposophy? and how to be a 'Steiner Waldorf teacher'), it can become almost religious. Other Steiner Waldorf teachers have told me that Steiner said do not write down my talks, but people did, and he said "Do not follow what I say and make it become a dogma, it must be always changing to meet the children" (see Steiner, 1998). I rarely see this followed, which frustrates me. It seems that change is really hard in established Waldorf places. I think that is what is so cool for you as newer schools, only being 7 years old you have freshness and energy to question everything. I am really interested in how you have been running an enrichment programme after school for the children in your area.

Teacher 3: Yeah it has been great to be able to offer Waldorf to our children, but we were just learning everything at the beginning so only recently are we beginning to question the curriculum and explore ways to make it more specific for Malaysia and our children.

Alys, now on a roll, continues on...

Alys: My other challenges with Waldorf schools I have worked in, especially the upper schools, is the poor behaviour and lack of interest by the students, which really makes me question if it is relevant for them now. And then I see teachers not able to manage their classes and end up using rewards and punishments, which I feel is definitely not what Steiner wanted. I also struggle that most Waldorf schools I visit are fee-paying, so this choice of an 'alternative' education is not available to most children. There are four state-funded Waldorf schools in the UK [in 2016] which is a start, but they have to compromise with teaching for government exams. I had a funny experience in October when I spoke to a German teenager who told me that they used to go to a 'normal-Waldorf' school. Wow, I thought, Waldorf just seen as normal!

Laughter around the table.

Alys: And the truth is I am really not sold on single-age classes.

Teacher 1 jumps in.

Teacher 1: Hang on a minute! You need to have single aged classes as that is linked to Anthroposophical understanding of child development. At each age the child is at a different stage and the curriculum is specifically designed to meet that stage.

Alys: Yes, but I think 10 year olds now are different from 10 year olds 100 years ago.

There is a murmur around the table.

Teacher 1: Are they really that different or do we view them differently.... How much understanding of Anthroposophical biographical work do you have?

Alys: I understand that Steiner saw life in 7 year cycles and that the first 7 years were early childhood, the second were Primary education years (with the class teacher) and then the final 7 years from 14 to 21 were the questioning and developing as an adult stage. I know that at 37 I am in the middle of my 35–42 stage and it is meant to be a significant year. I liked the session you two led on Tuesday morning linking the development/focus of each grade and the Waldorf curriculum.

Teacher 3:   Yes, we thought that would be helpful for everyone to understand the Anthroposophical understanding of the child alongside the history of our country and the current euro-centric Waldorf curriculum.

Alys: I found it a really helpful reminder of what Steiner suggested were the key themes for each grade. It made me think about how in the UK there are a few class teachers I have met who haven't followed the 'yellow book' (Rawson & Ritcher, 2014 – which is currently used in the UK interpretation of the Waldorf curriculum) directly, particularly when it comes to telling 'Old Testament' stories in Grade 3.

Teacher 1:   That is interesting. We had a long look at that one when trying to decide what to suggest here, but we felt Grade 3 needed a strong, authoritarian figure and that those bible stories are perfect for that.

Alys struggles a bit to find the right words.

Alys: Maybe... but I am still not sure as I do not feel the old testament are the only stories that can be told and I feel there must be other stories out there that are neither Christian nor patriarchal. That's actually an issue of mine throughout the Waldorf curriculum. Yes, I know it is about archetypes, but even from Grade 1 I think it is paramount to choose Fairy Tales that are not about rape and control of defenceless, "beautiful," women. I am a feminist and I think Waldorf education can be brought up to speed with the current times.

Alys pauses to breathe and to decide if it is an appropriate moment to share her real feelings...

Alys: So... I think I realise that actually my big problem is the whole curriculum and that it comes from Anthroposophy.

All eyes are on Alys. This is a Waldorf teacher speaking out against Anthroposophy after all.

Alys: I don't believe in Steiner's laying out of epochs and the role of Atlantis in our history. And yes, I know I understand Steiner's views on the seven year cycles of child development. I like 7 year cycles. They make sense to me even as an adult. It is just that I think multi-age learning makes more sense as it is like the real world. Even as an adult I am going through 7 year cycles alongside other people at other stages and we learn from each other. I know this contradicts 'pure' Waldorf education and puts me in a tricky position. It could be the real answer to why I never took a class through... (taught a class from Grade 1 to Grade 8).

In the slightly stunned aftermath someone changes the focus slightly.

Teacher 2: What are teachers like in the schools that you have visited?

Alys: Oh, totally varied... Some teachers are creative and fun and their children love attending their classes. But I've seen some people who are very Anthroposophical and have taken lots of extra training courses but cannot manage with the day-to-day holding of a class, so they resort to behaviourism. It seems to be very subjective and it is hard to get teachers. It is why I often get asked, I think, when I visit schools if I am after a job!

Teacher 3: We have a real challenge here getting teachers too and keeping them as we can't pay them much, they have to have another earner in their family.

Alys: It is a really demanding job to be a Waldorf teacher and I think you need to have not just an understanding of Anthroposophy and the Waldorf curriculum, but lots of other talents such as being able to sing and draw and memorise poems off by heart. That is all before actually teaching and holding a class. Sadly, one thing I often observe which upsets me is that if the Class Teacher does not like Maths or has challenges with understanding grammar, then often the majority of their class will share these issues. Having the same teacher for seven years is tricky and some teachers are actually better with the younger or older grades. I did work at a school in the UK where teachers taught grades 1–5/6 and then different teachers took 6/7–8.

Teacher 1: We have talked about that too. We have also had two teachers for one class. We did this so that the class would have each Main Lesson in a different main language and that seems to work well.

Teacher 3: It also works to support newer teachers as a lot of our teachers started out as interested mothers. But lack of training is a tricky one. If we become recognised by the government then we must employ qualified teachers.

Alys: I did state training first and it was really helpful and I think there is a lot that Steiner Waldorf could learn from mainstream

education. To be a Steiner Waldorf teacher, I think it is not just
Anthroposophy but learning pedagogy as well and mainstream
can be good at engaging students with group work or meeting different learning styles. In Waldorf classrooms I see lots of didactic
teaching, with the teacher at the front and the whole class producing very similar work, and teachers using behaviour/reward
charts as a means to manage behaviour, which really frustrates
me. I suppose this could be a lack of 'proper' training or/and the
art of choosing the right person to be a class teacher.

Teacher 2:   But even after all this you still visit Steiner schools looking for the
             'gems' for your PhD?

Alys: Yeah, I cannot deny that I am very 'Steiner' really and I am influ-
             enced by Anthroposophy in parts of my understanding of educa-
             tion and life. It's just that I am thinking that schooling with a set
             curriculum, particularly one based on a philosopher's ideas from
             100 years ago, is not what I think of as my ideal.

*The dinner finishes, we take a group photo and walk off chatting into the steamy
heat of the evening.*

3   Alys the Educator: What Is Steiner Waldorf Education?

Steiner Waldorf education is based on the work of the Austrian educator, Rudolf
Steiner (1861–1925), who recognised that children interact with the world and
learn in distinctly different ways at different ages. Steiner gave a series of lectures in 1919 which shared his views on a curriculum that would meet the child
at these different stages (see Steiner 1919/1997). A key approach to Steiner Waldorf education which stands it apart from traditional mainstream education
in the UK in the 21st century is that formal learning is delayed until 6 or 7 years
old. However, Avison (2015) argues that by 11 years old, Steiner Waldorf students are often further ahead academically than their peers.

The first school inspired by the work of Rudolf Steiner was opened by Emil
Molt just after the First World War at his Waldorf Astoria cigarette factory in
Stuttgart, Germany in 1919. This school was founded with the desire to "enable
the individual to become not only a balanced and healthy person but one
capable of making a meaningful and socially responsible contribution to society" (Clouder & Rawson, 2003, p. 126).

Throughout this book I will be using the term 'Steiner Waldorf' for clarification because in some countries (particularly Germany and the USA) they use
the term 'Waldorf,' as the first school in Stuttgart was called 'die Waldorfschule'

after the factory, but other places use the term 'Steiner school' after Rudolf Steiner (particularly the UK and Australia).

Steiner Waldorf education began to spread around the world. By 1925 the first English speaking school opened in Forest Row, East Sussex, UK and in 1928 the first in the USA opened in New York (Baldwin, 2009). Waldorf education has continued to spread, with over 1,200 Steiner schools worldwide and 2,000 Early Years settings in a total of 60 different countries. These schools all follow a very similar approach, inspired by Rudolf Steiner's lectures and each countries' interpretations. Baldwin (2009) argues that what all Steiner Waldorf schools have in common is a balanced education for the whole child that engages the child's feeling, willing and thinking, as well as leaving their spiritual nature acknowledged but free. Steiner (1919/1997) wrote about an education towards freedom and how each 7-year cycle was linked to a different developmental area. For example, from 0–7 years the education meets the dominance of the will through the control of the limbs, from 7–14 years the education meets the dominance of feeling through an aesthetic sense and from 14–21 years it meets a dominance of thinking through the unfolding of rationality (Ashley, 2009).

Some misconceptions arise with the use of the term 'educating towards freedom' (see Steiner, 1909/1965) in Steiner Waldorf education that could be understood to mean that the children are free to direct their own learning (as in a democratic school or unschooling). However, this is not the case as freedom is seen to be the end result rather than a pedagogical approach. The concept being if a child is educated at a Steiner Waldorf school then the ultimate goal when they graduate is the development of a fully free human being. Therefore, Steiner Waldorf education is very different from democratic schools or unschooling (both defined in Chapter 7) as it has an established developmental curriculum which is taught by a teacher as it is seen that the "teacher provides the best conditions and nourishment for the child and the curriculum provides the substance for the psychological and spiritual development" (Clouder & Rawson, 2003, p. 30) which in turn, Steiner Waldorf schools believe, leads towards freedom.

4 Kindergarten (3–6 years)

In a Steiner Waldorf Kindergarten (3–6 year olds) the focus is the 'world is good' and on developing physical skills and supporting their 'will' rather than intellectual abilities. Steiner Waldorf kindergarten teachers are trained to be worthy of imitation and to keep a tidy and beautiful classroom and garden (see Nichol, 2016). In Steiner Waldorf education it is not until after the second dentition (adult teeth forming) that formal learning begins. (Masters, 2005)

Vignette 2 aims to share the magic of being a child in a Steiner Waldorf kindergarten and at the same time see important aspects of the approach in action, such as strong boundaries supported by love, song, healthy rhythms and routines.

FIGURE 19
Steiner Kindergarten,
USA, 2013

5   Vignette 2: Alys the Performer – A Poem about a Steiner Kindergarten

A poem about a Steiner Kindergarten through the imagined eyes of a five-year-old written after a 5-week placement as a Kindergarten Assistant in 2012, UK:

Kindergarten children know their teachers
They know their classroom and garden
Where the best hidey-places are and where the fairies play.
They are secure in the daily rhythm
The internal breathing in and out of the day.
We come in and get busy with our play...
With the handmade dollies in the home corner,
Cooking up the conkers to make a feast,
Transporting the same conkers in a wooden cart
Or tying a silk around our shoulders becoming a character from a fairy tale...
I float in 'deep-play' for there is time to be...
Until
"It's time to tidy away," my teachers sings and we all imitate and tidy our
space.

Some children need more reminding or guidance than others...
But our teachers don't speak very much, they don't interrupt our play...
Once tidy, we hear our teacher sing,
"Come and join in my small circle"
And we come and join in.
Sometimes newcomers struggle and watch from the edges
But soon they see how much fun we have singing and reciting poems about
the seasons and the elementals
Or one of our teachers holds them tight if they are upset
It is a cocoon of warmth.
We sing thanks to the world for the food we will eat and our teacher lights a
candle
We collectively breathe out.
After snack, we attempt to put on our over-trousers and zip up our jackets,
Pull-on our wellies and hats and scarves and head out into the garden to play.
There is a pond full of weeds and frogspawn and we search for frogs
There is planting to be done and leaves to be swept or trees to climb and dens
to make.
We play and the teachers are there, but I don't remember what they are doing
They appear when I need them
And I follow their lead.
I follow their voice as I am in this flow of childhood
"Everybody follow, follow..." I hear and I follow the trail of children like the
Pied Piper Out of the garden and back to our classroom.
The room is tidy and reordered after snack
The little chairs in a circle around a table full of lumpy shapes and covered
with a Beautiful blue silk cloth.
Excitedly I pull off my outdoor clothes and, once reminded, hang them on my
peg
I rush to find a seat in the middle if I can
And urge the others to hurry up and sit down
A bell rings
Peace descends,
The candle is lit.
"Come with me to story land..." my teacher sings
They lift the blue silk with a sleight of their hand
And at once we are all spellbound and lost in the magic of
Storyland...
I get to snuff the candle out today
Contented we sing goodbye

I love my teacher.

Coats on, shoes on, bags found we are reunited with our families and the outside world.

FIGURE 20
Steiner Kindergarten, UK, 2014

6   Lower School (7–14 years)

The class teacher years (also called the Lower School) from 7–14 years old empha-sise that the 'world is beautiful' and the task of the class teacher during this time is to represent authority and the world to the child. Each class in the Lower School has their own class teacher who stays with the class over the 8-year jour-ney and takes their 'main lesson' for around two hours each morning, where they study one topic in depth for a series of 3–4 weeks. A key element of the Lower school, Clouder and Rawson (2003) argue, is that it is like a family as the children are taught in undifferentiated year group classes for the whole eight-years.

Vignette 3 aims to share an experience of a Steiner Waldorf classroom, giving an insight into the teacher's conscious role in the environment and creative, yet often quite didactic, pedagogy. It also highlights many pedagogical differences from traditional mainstream education such as a

FIGURE 21   Two images of Steiner Waldorf Lower School classrooms, UK, 2015

three-day rhythm, using movement, verses, skipping and games, the role of storytelling, the use of art and main lesson books created by the children rather than textbooks.

7   **Vignette 3: Alys the School Tourist – An Observation of a Steiner Class 1/2 Main Lesson**

The classroom was stunning, large and airy with a feel that everything had been consciously placed. There were several black boards on wheels at the front that could be moved around, a home corner and a book corner, craft shelves at the edges.

At 8.15 am the children lined up outside and sang the 'Good morning' song. The teacher welcomed each child by shaking their hand and making eye contact as they entered the room. Each child had a hand-made desk and there were 19 children in the class (9 Class 1, 10 Class 2). Each child had a sheepskin (called a "lambie") on their seat so that they were more comfortable. The desks were on a curve on each side of the room with Class 1 and 2 separated and a circular rug in the centre in front of the teacher's desk.

After the good morning circle, the movement routines became more complex with crossing the midline exercises, followed by a variety of speech exercises and some tongue twisters for Class 2.

The main lesson continued with recall. The Class Teacher asked different children to share different parts of the story, told the day before. After retelling the story, the teacher told them they were going to act it out as a play. They loved acting it out although they got pretty excited and had to be calmed down many times and warned that maybe they need to finish it tomorrow. One child decided that they would be a dove as they didn't want to be any of the characters. There was a beautifully serious discussion about the difference between gnomes (friendly) and dwarves (often unkind or mischievous).

Once sitting down and main lesson books handed out, they were led through a guided drawing of a bear from which a yellow capital B was drawn around the outside. Class 2 added Bs to the corners of their pages.

They then all came into the middle, bringing their lambies, for the next story. The story was told very quietly so that I was straining to hear at times, but I could see the attention of the whole class almost all super engaged and drinking in the story.

At the end of the main lesson, they came together for a verse before going to sit outside on the big table on the veranda for morning tea. A blessing was sung then they all got out their lunch-boxes and chatted whilst they ate. Their lunches were healthy, packed with exotic fruits – no crisps or

chocolate. After morning tea, they played outside. Class 1/2 are not allowed
to play ball games as it prevents them from imaginative play.

8   Upper School (14+)

The Upper School is different from the Class Teacher years as it is not until 14
years old in Steiner Waldorf education that young people are seen to be able to
make judgements or form independent concepts (Ashley, 2009), and the teaching changes to include more discussion. There is a curriculum for students up
until the end of Class 12 (18/19 years old). Many Waldorf schools also take the
government exams, so it can be a challenge to combine both the Steiner Waldorf curriculum and the exams from a specific country (see Randoll & Peters,
2015). Some schools (I have visited two in the UK) are adopting the New Zealand Steiner School Certificate as a way of formally accrediting the Steiner Waldorf curriculum (see Steiner Education Development Trust, 2017). Two other
Steiner schools that I have visited in the UK only follow the Steiner Waldorf
curriculum and create their own portfolios of their work which they use to gain
entry into higher education or work. I visited one Steiner Waldorf school in
Australia which had adopted the International Baccalaureate (a school leaving
qualification that is internationally recognised for university entrance).

Vignette 4 shares my personal teaching experiences from the first time I went
to take a three-week Physical Geography main lesson at a Steiner School in the
UK in 2010. Until this point I had only taught teenagers in mainstream state
funded schools. This experience had a profound affect on my becoming teacher
identity and is shared here to allow the reader, especially those used to mainstream schooling, a chance to think differently, but also to see the complexity of
schooling and that being a member of a school community is still challenging
even in an alternative school. These challenges are explored further in Vignette
5, from six years later, in 2016, where I am beginning to have some questions
about current approaches to Upper School teaching in Steiner Waldorf schools
that I visit, particularly in terms of the lack of use of technology.

9   Vignette 4: Alys Educating Differently – My First Experience
         Teaching in a Steiner Waldorf Upper School

What it was like for me to be a Steiner Waldorf Upper School teacher?

> From the first instant I walked into the classroom, I had fun and respect
> from that group of eighteen 14–16 year olds. Some of the students were

exchanges from Germany and France with little English so I had to think about differentiation, but really I was thinking a lot more about how I was teaching. I had answered an advert on the American website of Waldorf Today requesting a three-week main lesson teacher for Geography. I had spent the month before solidly planning what I was going to do, searching the internet for ideas and resources and trying to find exciting, engaging and different activities and lessons. I also needed to think of some games and poems and that was the trickiest; would teenagers really want to sing or recite poetry? And no, they didn't really, but they liked the movement and concentration games. It was the first time I had taught teenagers something that wasn't going to be examined and it was incredibly empowering to see how beautiful their books were and the effort they put in at home to complete the main lesson on top of their GCSE (England and Wales high-stakes tests taken at 16 years old) studies. Most were really into completing book work and virtually all seemed to enjoy the lessons. I used the science lab and accidentally set off the smoke alarms when using a Bunsen burner to demonstrate a volcano. So instead we had a bonfire outside and we made convection currents with golden syrup in a tin can. It was fun. And at the end the students made me a card, said thank you and bought me some chocolates. I was touched and speechless. I left realising that sometimes I really could teach and the work could be fun. (Mendus, 'Memories from my first experience of teaching in a UK Steiner Waldorf Upper School, 2010' [Sydney, February 2016])

10   **Vignette 5: Alys the School Tourist – A Conversation with Steiner Waldorf School Administrator, Australia, February 2016**

A conversation between a school administrator in Australia and myself about Steiner Waldorf Upper schools in the 21st century:

Alys:	As an upper school teacher I have noticed a lot of teenagers not engaged in the current Steiner Waldorf curriculum and feel young people are growing up earlier than in the 1920s when it was designed. I also wonder about waiting for so long to have access to technology. What are your thoughts?
Administrator:	It is down to the teacher. The Teacher needs to set the appropriate work; appropriate to the age the children are, as designated by the Steiner Waldorf curriculum which is designed to assist healthy growth for their age group. Therefore, teachers

should read what Steiner said himself, not just the interpretations from the curriculums. But in terms of computers it is
essential to wait until the Upper School. Here, we do teach
Computing in the Upper School (14+). I think that in Class
7 (12/13 year olds) it is too early as who is the authority, the
teacher or the computer? It should be the teacher, so if you
want to show an image, then print it out and pass it around,
do not project it. Think about what research means with Class
7 – doing it alone is overwhelming. Give a printed handout.

Alys: This is interesting as I visit many schools now that are really
questioning the role of the teacher and looking more at democratic participation of students. Do you think this could be
part of the future of Steiner Waldorf teaching?

Administrator: No. In Steiner Waldorf the lessons are teacher directed as the
teacher is NOT a facilitator. It is about what you are carry-
ing in you, what is living in you and what and how you bring
it to the children. The role of the teacher is essential. It follows that if the teacher meets the need of the child then they
engage appropriately. There is no choice given, but if they
question a task and ask "Why do it?" then the Teacher's reply
is "Because it is worthwhile for your development." Everything that you learn in a Steiner Waldorf school is so that you
can develop an ability to think and make connections. This is
why it is not democratic, nor could be, as if students do not
have the knowledge to make decisions, which I believe they
do not until they have finished the Waldorf school, it creates
a false sense of participation and a want to please the adult...
(Mendus, A play-script written from notes from a conversation in Australia in February 2016 [Cornwall, July 2017])

11   Alys the Guide

Alys the Guide needs to interject into the assemblage here, reminding themselves and the reader that even within exciting and innovative stories about
education there are some people who take an approach or idea too far and it
can become dogmatic. In many ways it can be certain individuals rather than
a whole pedagogical approach that can become dogmatic. However, it is this
possibility of dogmatism that has prevented me from saying that Steiner Waldorf is my Ideal School.

12   Alys and Steiner: The Role of the Steiner Waldorf Class Teacher

> In 2006 when I trained to be a Steiner Waldorf class teacher (for 7–14 year olds) the first question that my tutor asked our group was "Who are you? Who are you who walks into the classroom? and What do you bring with you already?"
>
> I was shocked and excited as no-one had ever asked me such questions when I did my traditional state teacher training in 2004. (Mendus, Steiner Journalling [Sheffield, October 2006])

My experiences from my Steiner Waldorf teacher training are also visible in the Parker Palmer Anthroposophical programme for teachers called the 'Courage to Teach,' whose central tenet is to remind teachers and teacher trainers to question, "Who is the self that teaches? How does the quality of my selfhood form – or deform – the way I relate to my students, my subject, my world?" (Palmer, 1998, p. 4). Following this idea of inner questioning, Steiner Waldorf education has high expectations of the skills and abilities of its teachers and teachers are encouraged to continually be working on their own creative and inner development. This verse by Steiner is often recited at teachers' meetings:

> Imbue thyself with the power of imagination,
> Have courage for the truth,
> Sharpen thy feeling for responsibility of soul.
> (Steiner, 1932/1966, para. 23)

It is important as it reiterates that once a teacher loses their interest to learn more, it is time for them to stop being a teacher. I feel that this is important to be aware of, as the Steiner Waldorf movement internationally has high expectations upon the teacher's skills which when connected with low pay have the possibility of burn-out. For example, Steiner Waldorf teachers need to be able to draw, sing, play an instrument, tell stories as well as plan and teach lessons. Linda Fryer, my tutor on my Steiner Waldorf Upper School training, advises teachers in her book to be "loveable! Be vulnerable, be human, be tragic and comic when you can and it feels good to be so – be firm, but please be real" (2016, p. 1). I think this advice on being real will hopefully encourage teachers to take time out when needed. For example, it is often encouraged for Steiner Waldorf class teachers to take a sabbatical term off after completing an 8 year cycle with one class. Clouder and Rawson describe the teacher as a "role model, authority, facilitator, referee, confessor and, when the children are young, their conscience. In short, the teacher represents social, moral and ethical values" (2003, p. 28). These expectations not only can be quite daunting to prospective teachers, they also include a level of potential personal privilege for teachers to have had such a creative education themselves to have already developed these skills. However, this is also where Steiner Waldorf teacher training steps in, allowing trainees time to develop these specific skills, as well as committing to life-long learning. From my experiences in the UK, most Steiner Waldorf schools do not hire people who have not completed Steiner Waldorf training or who are not enrolled in a course so that the schools know that the teachers have some understanding of the approaches.

One difference to mainstream pedagogy that I have noticed is that Steiner Waldorf teachers plan their lessons to include space for breathing in and out, a time for remembering and forgetting, as well as a chance for students to sleep on the new knowledge presented in one lesson before they work with it the following day. Teachers are also expected to carry out 'inner work,' such as meditation and thinking about particular children's needs, as it is believed to cause educational reform (Palmer, 1998) and lead to a deeper understanding of the children in the class from meditating on their behaviour (Clouder & Rawson, 2003; Moller, 2020; Romero, 2015; Steiner, 1932/1966).

The high expectations of abilities and skills of the teacher raises a question of the danger of there being no time left for the teacher to be 'free.' This can mean that teachers choose to follow what has been done before and comply to a series of norms to be thought of as 'a good Waldorf teacher' (Denjean, 2014). This raises the danger that Steiner Waldorf education can become rigid or dogmatic in its approaches. I have seen aspects of this dogma in my School Tourism and it has been recognised by others arguing for a refocus of what is Steiner Waldorf education in the 21st century (Boland, 2017; Osswald, 2017). I explore this further in Chapter 5.

13   Alys the Theorist: What Are the Main Critiques of Steiner Waldorf Pedagogy?

An important critique is that Steiner Waldorf schools are "antiquated" (Ullrich, 2008, p. 165) in their pedagogy and could learn from traditional schooling and other forms of alternative education (Ashley, 2009). Although Steiner schools that I observed and have taught in include lots of movement, creativity, art and storytelling which is innovative and different to many traditional, mainstream schools, generally the structure of the classroom and the style of direct teaching can be very didactic and formal. For example, as I described in Vignette 3 of my observation of a Class 1/2 main lesson, all the students were copying the same drawing directly from the blackboard. The teaching style in Steiner Waldorf classrooms has been critiqued in research by Randoll and Peters's which suggested that "according to students, lessons – even in class 8 – all tend to be teacher dominated too often, while opportunities for group work or forms of self-motivated study are fairly rare" (2015, p. 41). Ashley (2009) highlights this tension that by continuing to use traditional Steiner Waldorf pedagogical methods, such as copying from the board or dictation, the Steiner Waldorf community does not learn from and include newer teaching ideas such as Gardner's (1983) multiple intelligences and individual learning styles.

Other critiques raised by Ashley's (2009) work uncovered children being held back by the Class Teacher teaching to the lowest ability in the class and the lack of screens until the end of the Lower School has been described as a "fundamentalist tendency" (Ashley, 2009, p. 222). I brought up the issue of later introduction of screens in an interview with an Administrator of a Steiner Waldorf school in Australia shared in this chapter in Vignette 5.

The Steiner Waldorf curriculum is comparable to Piaget's (1972) developmentalism approach, in which it expects children to develop similarly at the same age. So sometimes in smaller schools (such as the one described in Vignette 3) when two class groups of children are educated in the same classroom they are still taught two different curriculums. This is something that I was challenged by as I think multi-age learning allows for different interests and abilities separate from the exact year in which a child was born. Mixed-age classrooms and learning is something that impressed me in Steiner Waldorf Kindergartens where in many countries 3–6 year olds learn in the same setting.

Another challenge for me are the aspects of patriarchal influences on the curriculum which were uncovered by Golden's (1997) three year ethnographic study. My reflections below show my own challenges with the use of patriarchal fairy-tales:

> "As the sisters escaped up the golden thread into the sky, the man grabbed the legs of the youngest sister so she could not escape. He kept her as his wife and they had four children…"
>
> The storyteller said as she spun a tale to a group on a Steiner Waldorf Kindergarten course.
>
> I was not happy.
>
> That is an understatement.
>
> I was fuming inside.
>
> So angry that I raised my hand,
>
> "I could not tell that story to children. I am a feminist. That story is about abduction, rape and no consent. There must be other stories out there?"
>
> "It is about archetypes" the tutor replied.
>
> "Not the sort of archetypes I want to share with young children" I retorted.

And ever since I have spent long hours searching for feminist stories and ones from around the world that do not continue the old patriarchal tales. It is a reason now that I am even more nervous about who teaches in Steiner Waldorf schools – do they have this awareness to choose stories with care? (Mendus, Reflections on Steiner Kindergarten training, June 2012 [Cornwall, July 2017])

14 Alys the Guide: Why I Have Included Two Chapters on Steiner Waldorf

There needs to be two chapters on Steiner Waldorf education in this book as it is my yard-stick by which I compare, contrast and think about each other place of learning/school that I enter. The depth in these chapters is shared for the reader to have an understanding of why differing voices of the Alys-we may be influenced by other innovative schools that I visited. In my PhD I called the chapter on Steiner Waldorf education 'There and back again,' referring to the journey in the Hobbit as my relationship with Steiner Waldorf education continues to be an iterative one, where I am an insider and an outsider, where my homelife is heavily influenced by the ideas and environment of Steiner Waldorf education and, at the same time, I continue to ask questions and encourage Steiner Waldorf teachers and schools that I speak with to consciously re-evaluate their position on race, the patriarchy and eurocentrism.

15 Summary

Steiner Waldorf education is based on the work of the Austrian educator, Rudolf Steiner (1861–1925), who recognised children interact with the world and learn in distinctly different ways at different ages.

- In a Steiner Waldorf Kindergarten (3–6 year olds) the focus is the 'world is good' and on developing physical skills and supporting their 'will' rather than intellectual abilities.
- The class teacher years (also called the Lower School) from 7–14 years old each class has their own class teacher who stays with them over the 8-year journey and takes their 'main lesson' for around two hours each morning.
- In the Upper School, 14–19 year olds, the teaching changes to include more discussion and use of technology. Many Waldorf schools also take the government exams.
- Steiner Waldorf teachers are accomplished in storytelling, art, music, literature and carry out inner work meditating on the children in their classes.

– Some critics argue that Steiner Waldorf teaching methods are old-fashioned. I explore the research into bringing Steiner Waldorf education up to date in the following chapter.

FIGURE 22   Rainbow bags from a Steiner Kindergarten, USA, March 2013

CHAPTER 5

Alys Troubling Steiner Waldorf Education

1 Alys the Guide: Introduction

I see this as a pivotal chapter in this book as it is where I really trouble Steiner Waldorf education, something that I love and am inspired by, but also something that I recognise has many issues that need to be addressed. During my PhD I explored some of these issues but really, with reflection, I realise that I was not brave enough to address the issue of racism and Anthroposophy, therefore I have attempted to address this in this chapter. I see this as the beginning of a more complex exploration and dialogue, but I hope that this chapter will allow people to know more about more hidden aspects of Anthroposophy and Steiner Waldorf education and lead to a moving beyond the current iteration of Steiner Waldorf education around the world to one that is more equitable and inclusive of the country and culture in which the learning is happening.

As well as exploring Anthroposophy and issues of racism, I explore other critiques of Steiner Waldorf education such as eurocentrism and christ-centricism, as well as behaviourism. I also look at ways in which Steiner Waldorf education methods can be used in state-funded settings.

2 Alys the Theorist: What Is Anthroposophy?

> Anthroposophy is a path of knowledge which seeks to unite the spiritual in the human being with the spiritual in the universe. (Steiner, 1924/1989, p. 14)

Anthroposophy, or 'Spiritual Science,' is the name given by Rudolf Steiner to his philosophy which has had a wide-ranging influence including Steiner Waldorf education, architecture, Biodynamic agriculture and the Christian

FIGURE 23   Anthroposophical architecture. Steiner school buildings, Australia, February 2016

Community. Edmonds (2005) states that the word Anthroposophy dates back to 1742 or earlier and that it means 'human wisdom.'

Steiner's Anthroposophy is complex, but aims to understand the human being and discusses the role of the ego (self), astral (spiritual/soul) and etheric (body) aspects of the human (see Edmonds, 2005; Steiner, 1909/1965). Key aspects that influence the thinking behind Steiner Waldorf education are the three-fold nature of humanity (thinking, feeling and willing, or head, heart and hands), reincarnation (including a belief that children choose their families connected to karma), the importance of sleep (at night your astral body works with the angels to process your life journey – or new learning) and an understanding of different epochs of time and their influences on humanity – including a 'belief in Atlantis' (Edmonds, 2005, p. 94). This excerpt from my journalling after working at a Steiner Waldorf school shares my shock at seeing the influence of Anthroposophy within a school for the first time.

> Attending the teachers' meeting was tricky. I've never been a lover of meetings, I've often seen them as a waste of time, but I was fascinated by the religious/Steiner verse and some study of his writings as well as the time for child study, thinking deeply and meditating on particular children. There was a teacher who always liked to play devil's advocate and when I went into their room they were teaching the class about Atlantis as if it was true. I was shocked in many ways by how much doctrine there seemed to be in Steiner. (Mendus, 'Memories from my first experience

of teaching in a Steiner Waldorf Upper School, 2010' [Sydney, February 2016])

Even though Edmonds (2005) argues that Anthroposophy is a way of life, Steiner Waldorf schools are not meant to teach Anthroposophy to the children, although the teachers themselves teach with/from an understanding of Anthroposophy as shown in the journalling excerpt above. As Steiner himself explains:

> You absolutely do not need to be afraid that we are trying to make this school into one that represents a particular philosophy, or that we intend to drum any anthroposophical or other dogmas into the children. That is not what we have in mind. Anyone who says that we are trying to teach the children specifically anthroposophical convictions is not telling the truth. Rather, we are trying to develop an art of education on the basis of what Anthroposophy means to us... how to teach the children something, can only result from a thorough, profound and loving understanding of the human being. This is what is meant to work and to prevail in our Waldorf School. (Steiner, 1996b, p. 79)

Steiner Waldorf teachers are given the task of helping a child incarnate into their body by teaching a curriculum that supports the threefold being of body, soul and spirit. Ashley (2009) raises an important point that the concept of "helping a child to incarnate in the world out of a previous spiritual existence... would be problematic for many secular teachers (and parents) in state schools" (Ashley, 2009, p. 210). This raises a challenging issue of where to place Steiner Waldorf education and if it is also a faith school. Even though Steiner (1919/1996a) argued Anthroposophy is not taught in Steiner Waldorf schools and Masters (2005) argues that Anthroposophy is not a religion, its influence is visible in the curriculum and day-to-day teaching, which has been critiqued by opponents of Steiner Waldorf education (see Snell, n.d.; Lewis, 2012). This is why I have argued in the past (Mendus, 2007) in an MA Module, 'Using Steiner Waldorf methods to teach light to Y8 in a state-school,' that you do not need to be an Anthroposophist to use 'Steiner Waldorf methods.' However, this seems to be a controversial opinion as Lissau (2005) explains that Steiner wanted to create a new educational approach that was not just a 'method' and argues that those who talk about the 'waldorf-method-education' have betrayed Steiner. Lissau argues that by separating the 'method' from Steiner's Anthroposophy a new tyranny begins of "this is the way things are done here," (Lissau, 2005, p. 115). This idea of a 'tyranny' is supported by Gidley, who describes observing teachers and schools becoming "too narrow, dogmatic and even 'cultish' in their interpretation of Steiner's ideas" (2008, p. 25). In my own experiences working and observing Steiner Waldorf schools around the world, I have also observed this dogmatism in action in some places. I think it is worth pointing out that Steiner himself warned, "We cannot afford to become rigid, we have to become broad-minded" (Steiner, 1998, p. 168) and I do wonder what he would have thought of Steiner Waldorf education in 2021 if he was here today?

I am aware that many Steiner Waldorf schools keep quiet about the connection between pedagogy and Anthroposophy, even in my Class Teacher training in the UK we did not cover Anthroposophy in depth. I think this could be because they do not want to trigger people and therefore prevent people learning more about the schools and approaches. This idea of keeping quiet about particular issues is supported by Bast (cited in Frielingsdorf, 2012) who argues that Steiner Waldorf education can be fundamentalist in how it is not keen to critique its founder, Rudolf Steiner. However, I do not condone this. I believe being upfront about the challenges of aspects of Anthroposophy and writing clear statements about how to address inclusivity and diversity in the school and approaches is imperative.

3   Alys and Steiner: Anthroposophy and Racism

'Broad minded,' I argue, is actually essential for anyone to not completely write-off Steiner Waldorf education in 2021, as there are many aspects of Anthroposophy that need to be distanced from today's Steiner Waldorf schools. Steiner's understanding of the development of humanity is racist. His belief that white Aryan people are the most developed, "The white race is the future, it is the spiritually creative race" (Steiner, 1923/1993, p. 67), is horrendously incorrect. Therefore, any discussion about Steiner Waldorf education needs to be aware of the unacceptable, ignorant aspects of Anthroposophy before one can see the 'gems' in aspects of Steiner Waldorf method education.

It was not until the racist murder of George Floyd by police in the USA in June 2020 that Steiner Waldorf schools began to publicly speak out in earnest about the unspoken issue of Steiner's racist views within Anthroposophy. Since then many Steiner Waldorf schools around the world have written statements on their websites and in the USA there have been a series of high profile online discussions. I am also aware of work that is being undertaken by Steiner Education Australia (SEA) to review the curriculum in terms of gender bias and decolonisation and that they will soon have an anti-racist statement on their website. Te Ra Waldorf School in New Zealand has had an important

statement recognising the racism in some aspects of Steiner Waldorf education since 2012.

> Te Ra Waldorf School as a school in Aotearoa New Zealand is uncondi-
> tionally committed to upholding the principles of Te Tiriti o Waitangi –
> The Treaty of Waitangi. Out of this commitment and within the world-
> wide Waldorf school framework, Te Ra Waldorf School does not support
> Rudolf Steiner's statements on race. (College of Teachers of Te Ra Wal-
> dorf School and Kapiti Waldorf Trust, 21 November 2012, Equity state-
> ment, para. 2)

Fundamentally, the challenge as I see it is how defensive the 'Steiner Waldorf'
world has become of Rudolf Steiner himself, elevating him to God-like status
and not allowing anyone to criticise his opinions. This is so obvious in that
racism within Anthroposophy is rarely addressed, even in recent PhD research
such as Haralambous (2016), Moller (2020), and including my own (Mendus,
2017). When reading the limited literature on Rudolf Steiner, Anthroposophy
and racism, it is confronting to see the inability of many academics to acknowledge that what Steiner said is racist and wholly inappropriate (Code, 2020;
Dahlin, 2014, 2017; Rose, 2013). I argue that for there to be a way forward, to be
able to celebrate the strengths of Steiner Waldorf education in the 21st century,
there needs to be an apology for its roots. Rose (2013), and Dahlin (2014) in his
review of Rose's work, extensively argue that Steiner's words have been mis-
understood or translated incorrectly and that it is an issue of semantics rather
than that Steiner had some racist views. Code (2020) even argues that racist
accusations of Steiner Waldorf education "invariably demonstrate a lack of rigorous engagement with either theoretical foundations of WE [Waldorf Educa-
tion]" (p. 17), thereby supporting Rose's analysis that Steiner didn't mean to be
racist. However, the following extracts from Steiner show a very different story:

> The black or Negro race is substantially determined by these childhood
> characteristics. If we now cross over to Asia, we find a point or centre
> where the formative forces of the Earth impress permanently on man the
> particular characteristics of later youth or adolescence and determine his
> racial character. Such races are the yellow and brown races of our time.
> If we continue northward and then turn in a westerly direction towards
> Europe, a third point or centre is reached which permanently impresses
> upon man the characteristics of his adult life. (Steiner, 1910, p. 75)

Steiner then expanded on this further:

This is simply a universal law. Since all men in their different incarnations pass through the various races the claim that the European is superior to the black and yellow races has no real validity. In such cases the truth is sometimes veiled, but you see that with the help of Spiritual Science we do after all light upon remarkable truths. (Steiner, 1910, p. 76)

It is hard to believe that Rose and Dahlin would defend Rudolf Steiner's views, arguing that they were not racist, after reading those two excerpts from Steiner (1910). However, I realise that I am not alone, and others have been concerned about the possibility of Steiner Waldorf education having racist connections (Boland, 2017; Staudenmaier, 2008). I am aware that there was a formal investigation into Steiner's statements (over 89 000 pages of text) in the Netherlands in 2000 which concluded that racism is not inherent in Anthroposophy. However, "of the discussed 245 quotes from Steiner, 16 were of such nature that as isolated statements, they would violate the present-day well-developed and highly sensitive Dutch law on discrimination" (Dahlin, 2017, p. 3). I argue that when Dahlin (2017) and Rose (2013) say that this study shows that Anthroposophy is not racist, they are missing the point and speaking from a position of white supremacy and white ignorance. People need to be aware of the position of Steiner Waldorf education in the wider society and it is beyond the outcomes of this study as, through the media and access to Rudolf Steiner's books, it is well known that certain statements are racist, so the image of the pedagogy and school community has already been tarnished. My critique follows Staudenmaier's conclusions that Steiner's "racial doctrines are nevertheless founded on prejudicial categories and value-laden classifications that have patently racist consequences" (2008, p. 24).Therefore, what is needed is humility, apology and ways to move forward that do not perpetuate the connection between Rudolf Steiner's racist views and Steiner Waldorf education.

Nevertheless, as I read Sapio (2020)'s point that "No amount of organizing diversity conferences for Waldorf teachers will ever fix this fundamental problem in the foundation of the schools' pedagogy" (para. 12), I realise that I have to agree. There is no point to the Steiner Waldorf movement organising diversity conferences or writing equity statements if they do not address the challenging issues of racism and the patriarchy within Anthroposophy which underpin the curriculum. I have to put my hand up and see my role in this issue, as Sapio (2020) further points out (as Sapio also was a Steiner teacher) "we were all complicit in the white supremacist mission that is Waldorf education globally" (para. 15) if we do not critique it now.

It is important to realise that these voices that I am citing, who are arguing that Steiner's views were not racist, are white, European men. Bo Dahlin, a member of the Editorial Board for the main Steiner Waldorf journal, Research on Steiner Education (RoSE) wrote in his review of Rose's book on Steiner and racism that "The thing is that our present cultural situation is actually over-sensitive to the issue of racism" (2013, p. 158). I am so shocked when I read the privilege that speaks in that citation. The voice that says other people are 'over-sensitive to racism' is a white voice. How dare Dahlin (2014) say that society is being over-sensitive? Later in this book I discuss the concept of OWMs (Old White Men with assumed privilege) and Dahlin here, speaking as an OWM, shows the impact that OWMs can have on not giving voice to issues of racism. It is problematic when Dahlin states that when Steiner talked about 'race,' "he did not hold any "principle of harm" towards other races," (2014, p. 156) because in many ways it does not matter what Steiner meant to do, the interpretation of his work is the problem as that has been embodied by the wider community as racist. Dahlin tries to argue that race is such a sensitive issue that no one dares to talk about it in case they are seen to be racist and that all Steiner was trying to do was state purely factual differences and that when he describes races as being more 'advanced' than each other, Steiner is talking about factual differences, not moral differences. I agree this is a fine line to tread and also that it is not one that an inclusive and equitable schooling system wants to be associated with in 2021. However, Staudenmaier would remind Dahlin that:

> unless thoroughly revised or rescinded, the racial doctrines promulgated by Steiner and his followers will remain incompatible with Anthroposophy's self-image as bearer of spiritual wisdom and cosmopolitan tolerance. (2008, p. 24)

Therefore, a change to Anthroposophy's image and a move away from Steiner's racist doctrines is essential before Waldorf 2.0, the vision for the future of Steiner Waldorf education by Boland (2017) and explored later in this chapter, can even begin to be reimagined. This statement on Te Ra Waldorf School in Aotearoa New Zealand based on the Stuttgart Declaration by the German Association of Waldorf Schools (Bund der Freien Waldorfschulen) (2007) is very important and I think needs to be shared on all Steiner Waldorf school websites and country organisations around the world.

> The spiritual science of Anthroposophy, upon which Waldorf education is founded, today rejects all forms of racism and nationalism. The Waldorf schools are aware, however, that there are words, ideas and statements in Rudolf Steiner's complete works which are not in concordance with

> this fundamental direction, are discriminatory, and rightfully regarded as
> offensive in this day and age. (Te Ra Waldorf, 2020, para. 7)

I take hope from my conversations with Steiner Waldorf academics. Drawing from work that has begun internationally, we are attempting to engage with the issue of racism in Anthroposophy head-on, by having those difficult conversations and finding a way to relaunch Steiner Waldorf education as an innovative and inclusive educational approach.

This is where I see the gems in Steiner Waldorf education having the potentiality to keep glowing. It is in spaces such as these where I can allow myself to choose to attend a Steiner Waldorf playgroup with my daughter, aware and rejecting of the unacceptable aspects of Anthroposophy and encouraging a more inclusive space, where in Australia I hope that, through the 2019 Steiner Education Australia Reconciliation Action Plan, Steiner Waldorf education emerges from the Indigenous roots of Country rather than Steiner Waldorf education's Eurocentric history.

4 Alys the Theorist: Anthroposophy – The Elementals and Inner Work

Other aspects of Anthroposophy are more esoteric and unusual and hard to believe, but not racist. For example, as I was not part of a larger school when I trained to be a Steiner Waldorf teacher it took me longer than others to find out about some of the more 'esoteric' aspects. This poem captures the occasion when I first found out about the 'elementals' (such as gnomes/fairies), a realm of beings that exists under the earth, where humans are on the earth and the angels in the heavens above (see Steiner, 1919/1984).

When we found out about the Elementals...

Stunned in disbelief as the conversation darted around the circle
We were ensconced in the womb-like Kindergarten
In a UK Steiner school
It had been a long week and long journey to get here
Friday night
A bowl of soup, some home-made bread and a lot of head-talk
And in the warmth of the space quite easy to drift off
But not tonight
"There are three realms of beings," the experienced Waldorf Teacher told us

I listened on as I had a respectful space for this Teacher
She had, after all, told me off for my dirty fingernails
"A kindergarten teacher shows care for her whole body down to her
fingernails!"
"The angelic realm, the human realm and then the elemental realm"
She calmly drew a diagram for us and passed it round.
I studied the faces in the group
All so serious... accepting?
Then mouths opened and stories flew about their own sightings of
elementals.
Under the tiny child-sized table, our knees knocking together I pinched my
friend's knee
HARD.
What was going on?
We didn't dare look at each other, for fear of fits of giggles erupting...
"There are four types of elementals: the gnomes in the Earth, the sylphs in the
Air, the salamanders in Fire and the Undines by the Water," she continued.
Later...
In the car driving to my friend's parents we had time
(Once we finished convulsing with laughter)
We stopped to think
I love gnomes (My friend was not so sure...) and I tell stories about gnomes all
the time

FIGURE 24
Handmade gnome in bamboo forest

But that these gnomes were real, not just from fairy tales?
And NO ONE had questioned the idea... out loud??
My friend and I definitely were not brave enough to say anything.
The following week
Back at the Steiner Waldorf school where I was teaching, I asked
"Did you know about the elementals?"
A wry smile and a "yes"
My look of shock and frustration was met with
"Just think of them as that piece of grass that manages to defy the tarmac and
peek through"
And that left me placated for a while.
But still struggling with disbelief.
Why had no-one told me before, on my Steiner training four years earlier
maybe?
But no...
The Alys-now in 2010 could hear this new idea, and find her way to under-
stand it, Alys-then of 2006 probably could not.
And Alys-now in 2016, faraway in Chiang Mai in Northern Thailand has little
hand-knitted gnomes in her bag.
Tongue-in-cheek or subconsciously accepting?
(Mendus, Poem about a memory from 2010, Thailand, December 2016)

FIGURE 25
Handmade gnome in a tree house

5   Alys the Theorist: A Dialogue about Inner Work

This play-script was created from a conversation between myself and a Steiner Waldorf class teacher in Australia about 'inner work' and the influences of Anthroposophy on teaching.

Alys: What is the role of inner work for you?

Class Teacher: My own spiritual development has influenced my work as a Class Teacher. By following the inner work and training that Steiner wrote about (see Romero, 2015), I feel that by taking this into my life I have been enabled to aim to be fully conscious with the children in the classroom.

Alys: I was wondering if parents know much about the role of inner work and Anthroposophy and how that influences your teaching?

Class Teacher: I think parents need to know about the four-fold child (the controlled will, the head, the heart and the hands). That the approach is of beauty, imagination and truth and that the curriculum is there to support this. For example, it is not just painting on Mondays but painting with blue to calm the whole class and make them ready to learn after the weekend.

Alys: I have been told that it takes 'time' to understand Anthroposophy when I was doing my training and I was constantly questioning the approach. How are you 'getting' Anthroposophy?

Class Teacher: Well I see Steiner education is not about 'dropping the lens' of Anthroposophy but about being aware of the contradictions. It is about looking, considering and seeing, NOT saying "Steiner said…" and explaining to parents that Steiner education does not need them necessarily to be an Anthroposophist, but they need to be aware that the education is rooted in Anthroposophy. (Mendus, A play-script written from notes from a conversation in Australia in February 2016 [Cornwall, July 2017])

6   Alys the Theorist: Steiner Waldorf Education around the World – The Challenge with Eurocentricism

Following Boland (2017) I argue that a 'Waldorf 2.0' is needed that includes a decolonisation process "to ensure that local, minority and especially Indigenous voices were heard and given value" (Boland, 2017, p. 64). Waldorf 2.0 also needs to focus on social justice and to move beyond the issues connected to racism in Anthroposophy, the patriarchy within the curriculum and gender-normativity that I have observed in Steiner Waldorf schools. The words of Wooltorton, White, Palmer and Collard (2020) writing about working with Aboriginal communities in Western Australia assist those with colonial heritage to be humble and confront the issues, when working with decolonisation.

> Our project required us to decolonise our thinking. We see in hindsight – reflecting upon our place-based reflections over and over again – that this is to decolonise our mental and emotional landscapes at the same time as our cultural, social, physical and ecological landscapes, which feels to us like an application of a relational worldview. There is much to confront, causing distress and anguish, at the same time as emergence of beauty and comfort. (Wooltorton et al., 2020, p. 13)

Eurocentrism is a challenge and critique of current Waldorf education practices (see Boland, 2014, 2015, 2017; Gidley, 2008; Hoffman, 2016; Boland & Demirbag, 2017). Da Souza (2012) argues that Steiner Waldorf curriculum "privileges a certain body of knowledge (it is visibly Eurocentric) and neglects important cultural, economical, and political issues" (cited in Boland, 2015, pp. 192–193). In respect to the dominance of Eurocentrism, Boland (2017) raises a challenging issue: to what degree are the values of Steiner Waldorf education European/Western values? In response to this I argue that Gidley's (2008) ideas need to be followed. Gidley (2008) argues that Steiner Waldorf schools need to use local and culture-specific resources and if eurocentricism continues, the possibility of Waldorf 2.0 is severely damaged. As Gidley (2008) rightly points out, by continuing to use primarily Euro-centric content in Australia and South East Asia, Steiner Waldorf schools are "at best severely limiting the richness of educational experience, at worst contributing to cultural colonisation" (p. 25).

An important decolonisation and Eurocentric issue is the relationship between Steiner Waldorf education and Christianity.

> Although I accept that since completing my Steiner Waldorf teacher training (2008) I have become much more spiritual, particularly following the Celtic wheel of the year and exploring eastern practices such as tantra, yoga and meditation, I am not, however, a Christian, nor do I believe in 'God,' so learning about the 'Christ impulse' (literally meant to educate with love towards freedom) and the Christian (even if esoteric Christian) influences on Steiner Waldorf education made me uncomfortable to

accept the approaches on face value. (Mendus, Journalling about the role
of Christianity in Steiner Waldorf education [Cambodia, March 2017])

The following Vignette 6 (created by me from two different conversations,
one with a school administrator in Australia and another with a Kindergarten
teacher in the UK) aims to show a conversation I had about the role of Christianity in Steiner Waldorf education.

7 Vignette 6: Alys the Performer – An Ethnodrama on the Role of Christianity in Steiner Waldorf Education

Alys: I was excited to hear that there is a specific Steiner Waldorf
                     curriculum for Australia as I often worry about it being too
                     'eurocentric.' How is it different here?

Administrator: Well the festivals should be globally focussed. They make
                     sense in both hemispheres as they are based on 'Christol-
                     ogy' and show spiritual battles, not just the breathing in and
                     out of the earth.... And for example the stories that are told
                     do not need to be 'eurocentric,' it is the quality of the telling
                     and choice of a story that connects to the consciousness of
                     the child. However 'Christo-centric' underpins the philoso-
                     phy of Anthroposophy. That Christ was incarnated and it is
                     a battle of dark and light. It needs to be there, irrespective of
                     culture. For example, in Class 3 by telling a Creation Story it
                     meets the 9 year old child's 'rubicon' and its associated chal-
                     lenges... the abandoned, insecure, creation, rules, journey,
                     spiritual leader – shown so well in Genesis/Moses.

Alys: OK, but what about those people and cultures that do not
                     want to tell bible stories. I know I often chose not to.

Administrator: It is also important to question the dislike by some Steiner
                     teachers/communities to not tell Bible stories as by doing so
                     they are rejecting their own cultural heritage, and to accept
                     that Christianity has had a positive impact on the West – for
                     example abolition of slavery and role of women.

Alys the Guide: What is going on here?

I spent some time deciding if I should include this playscript, but I decided
that it was essential for the reader to see how dogmatic and divisive
some people's views can become. I found the experience to be scary. It

was hugely unsettling to hear someone in power have such outdated and incorrect views and, honestly, it makes me worried about some Steiner Waldorf schools...

The assumptions and use of terms such as 'own cultural heritage' implies that all teachers in Australian Steiner Waldorf schools are of European descent, which is not true. Even if they are the majority, they are all working in schools existing on Aboriginal land, so they need to be grounded on Country. Country et al. (2019) define Country as:

> home and land, but it means more than that too. It means the seas, and the waters, the rocks and the soils, the animals and winds and all the beings, including people that come into existence there. It means the connections between these things, and their dreams, their emotions, their languages and their Rom(Law). (Country et al., 2019, p. 683)

The other assertions, such as Christianity having had a positive impact on the West, such as the abolition of slavery and the role of women is scary and silences the voices of People of Colour and glorifies the Christian slave masters and the patriarchy in the church.

After hearing this Administrator's white supremacist and christian-centric viewpoints I am worried about the future of some Steiner Waldorf schools. I hope that this is just the view of one person, but their power, privilege and dominance has the potentiality to continue this doctrine and poison the future of Steiner Waldorf education. I see this Administrator as an OWM (Old White Man with privilege), a term I explored further in Chapter 10.

(The Kindergarten teacher interjects)

Kindergarten Teacher: Careful! I am finding your words isolating, and not the wording I have been exposed to which is inclusive and non-threatening, particularly when it comes to using the name Christ. I have found that the schools go deeply into the evolution of spirit and that takes them into many major religions and their beliefs, which get recognition whether there are students in the class that have that spiritual path or not. I think more than anything I can see the heart space and THAT is the Christ energy that everyone talks about. I think that if you were to study Steiner's theory on the universal human, he was trying to illustrate that we are looking at the energetic Christ-ness and its unfolding nature within us all, but that we should not get caught up in the names of things within the schools, but rather the meaning behind them. In my own teacher education, I have had mentors say to me that the role of the festival is to be beyond words, which if one was to participate in an advent spiral you can feel it is bigger than the name 'advent'... (Mendus, A play-script written from notes from a conversation in Australia in February 2016 and a social media conversation when I was in Thailand in December 2016 [Cornwall July 2017])

> *Alys the Guide:*
> Even when re-reading this playscript I realise that it seems to be impossible to separate Steiner Waldorf education from Anthroposophy and that it is rooted in Christianity, even if it is an 'esoteric' understanding. Therefore, this in turn comes with a recognition that Waldorf 2.0 may never be able to move beyond its Christian roots as most people in the movement are not troubled by this. I realise that I am and that is part of my challenge with imagining Steiner Waldorf education as my Ideal School.
>
> In 2008 I realised that for me to want to continue in Steiner Waldorf education, I needed to explore this challenge of eurocentricism further by visiting schools away from Europe. So, in the spring of 2008 I travelled overland from Asia back to where I was living in Sheffield, UK and during this journey I spent time with different Steiner Waldorf communities in Kathmandu, Nepal then Chengdu, China and finally Irkutsk, Russia. I have included Vignette 7, from one of the schools I visited to give a flavour to the experience.

8 Vignette 7: Alys the School Tourist (Kathmandu, Nepal, March 2008)

The back streets of Kathmandu are busy with rickshaws and taxis and animals and people and horns beeping and loud music blaring...

My friend Mark and I, fresh from our trek around Annapurna, braved it on push bikes, following directions scribbled on a scrap of paper towards the Waldorf School which had been set up for orphaned Tibetan Children and then had grown as other Nepalese families wanted Waldorf education for their children.

As soon as I walked into the Kindergarten, I felt a sense of peace, not just the circular room, or the soft pink furnishing but seeing in the centre of their nature table a Buddha and a small statue of a Hindu deity.

I could breathe again; Waldorf could meet the country in which it inhabited.

FIGURE 26
Steiner Waldorf Kindergarten, Nepal, March 2010

I was also able to buy a couple of books about using Tibetan and Nepalese culture in Waldorf Kindergarten with examples of ring-times and storytelling ideas with animals such as elephants that the children knew about.

I was able to leave with a sense of hope. (Mendus, Travel journal [Kathmandu, Nepal, March 2008])

With hindsight, I recognise this as one of my first overseas conscious School Tourism journeys. I was looking for evidence of 'eurocentricism' which I didn't see in that school in Kathmandu in 2008, just influences of 'glocalism,' which Patel and Lynch (2013) define as a merger of global and local perspectives. However, as Hoffman (2016) argues, Steiner Waldorf schools began with a strong Christian heritage in European countries and many of the schools around the world were founded by Europeans, taking with them their curriculum, finances and teaching approaches, which meant that quite often Eurocentric Steiner Waldorf traditions were directly adopted. When I visited another Steiner Waldorf project in Kathmandu in 2010, I did see some Christian and German influences which was disappointing as I felt it did not value the local culture. Hoffman (2016) argues that these new schools around the world "often directly adopted [European Steiner Waldorf traditions] rather than adapted or metamorphosed to match the local situation... although local nature and seasons, as well as culture, often diverged considerably from those of their European origin" (p. 89). Unsettled by this, I decided to continue to visit Steiner Waldorf schools around the world to find more culturally appropriate examples. Figure 28

FIGURE 27   Malaysian Steiner Waldorf blackboard drawings

is an excellent example of an amalgamation of Steiner Waldorf pedagogy and Malaysian stories.

My School Tourism has now taken me to over 50 Waldorf schools in 14 different countries, not all of them in Europe, and although Clouder and Rawson (2003) explain that Steiner Waldorf schools are still relevant wherever in the world the school is as the education "aims to develop the universal in the human being, qualities that do not vary in essence over centuries or different cultural settings" (2003, p. 138), I think care needs to be taken into how that is manifested in the classroom. I think it is timely to take heed of the advice of Aonghus Gordon (in Houghman, 2012), for each school (and Steiner Waldorf education in general) to do an audit of influences of the different levels of colonialism. For example, the spread of Steiner Waldorf education around the world could be compared to a type of European colonialism or even a religious 'mission' (Gorden in Sapio, 2020) linking back to my realisation of the deep connection between Christianity, Anthroposophy and Steiner Waldorf education.

This leads me to think the same question that Boland asked, "is it time to speak of the need to de-colonize Steiner education?" (Boland, 2016, p. 5). I see that the challenge is beyond the Eurocentric focus on the curriculum, that it includes the reliance on certain Christian principles and the idea of spreading a set educational approach around the world. Boland's (2014) excellent analogy of a butterfly explicitly points out the need for a paradigm shift or, as he argues, a 'metamorphosis' from the current understanding of Steiner Waldorf education. As Boland argues, you cannot:

> Stick wings on a caterpillar and call it a butterfly. There has to be meta-morphosis. We need the 'traditional,' inherited, Eurocentric caterpillar to metamorphose into a contemporary New Zealand butterfly. (Boland, 2014, p. 8)

Therefore, I think the future of Steiner Waldorf education around the world is not to copy the eurocentric origins, Instead a complete metamorphosis is needed. The challenges with a complete metamorphosis lie in Steiner Waldorf education's need to be able to critique current understandings and examples and to be prepared to make changes. Steiner himself argued for the need to "practice teaching and critique it through discourse" (1919/1996, pp. 30–31). Boland, in response, argues that in Steiner Waldorf education today, "we are really good at practicing teaching, but I believe we are not so good at critiquing it through discourse" (2016, p. 3) and this is the challenge that is preventing Waldorf 2.0 from occurring (see Boland, 2017). For example, Hoffman argues that to liberate countries from the "weight of European influences" they need to create "new Waldorf festivals in accordance with local conditions" (Hoffman, 2016, p. 102) and the whole school community's outlook and understanding of what Waldorf Education means in their country needs to be reviewed. There are some stories of hope in new research at the Honolulu Waldorf School that shows some schools actively exploring their own identity by attempting to "eliminate Eurocentrism from Waldorf education and to decolonise Steiner education" (Boland & Demirbag, 2017, p. 29).

Another challenge I recognise with the eurocentric vision is that not all European countries are the same. Euro-centric is used as a blanket term for what could be also seen more as German, White, Christian, Northern-Hemisphere, Patriarchal influences on the pedagogy. In Germany, school starts at 6, whereas in the UK it starts at 4, so as Steiner Waldorf schools start at 6 it is not seen as radical or delaying formal learning like it is in the UK. Therefore, starting formal learning at 6/7 is not an 'othering' issue of Steiner Waldorf education in most of Europe and Scandinavia, where children in traditional, mainstream schooling also start at this age.

9 Alys the Theorist: Steiner Waldorf Education and the Edge-ucation

Throughout this chapter I have explored my relationship with Steiner Waldorf education and my continual questioning of certain approaches of the pedagogy and of Anthroposophy with a clear search for 21st century Waldorf education or, as Boland (2017) calls it, Waldorf 2.0. Before focussing on this research, and more so on School Tourism, I was passionate about ways that more people – other than those who pay or know about it already – could have access to elements of Steiner Waldorf education and other approaches to 'educating differently.' This section explores something that I originally called 'blended pedagogy,' which I defined as places where different pedagogical approaches are used in the same place (although I later realised that the term has been used by others to define using a mix of face-to-face and online learning, see Bonk & Graham, 2008). I now see this as one understanding of the edge-ucation, where 'gems' in one approach, here from Steiner Waldorf, are used in other (mostly) state-funded or partially state-funded environments. This section also mentions the relatively recent increase in state-funding of some Waldorf settings, particularly in the USA and UK.

Below is a poem sharing my journey into Steiner Waldorf edge-ucation with my colleague and friend, Kath.

Alys Educating Differently: The Alys and Kath poem
We met tidying up the hall
Her husband stepping over other parents who were ignoring the mess
As he put coloured silks in baskets
And I determinedly sang "Time to tidy away"
Hoping the children, if not the parents, would imitate.
I was running an outdoor group for older home educated children
And Kath ending up running the indoor under 3s group
A Steiner inspired education initiative.
There was no local Steiner school or kindergarten and we both were frus-
trated teachers
Wanting change.
The village playgroup gave homework!
Brainstorming ideas of new settings, of helpful parents and outdoor learning
Until
The village playgroup was offered to Kath
She took it – felt like karma, the universe meeting our wishes
But it's not that easy, mate!
The village googled 'Rudolf Steiner'
And got scared
Very, very, scared
I backed away, sad, sick and lonely.
Kath determinedly persevered, transforming from the inside
OFSTED arrived and left gobsmacked at the
OUTSTANDING setting, they left behind

The villages' ears perked up; the school began to listen.
And I began tentatively to appear back on the scene
Together we planned ways to blend new pedagogies
The Early Years Foundation Stage and Forest Schools
Woodland Wednesdays soon became Forest Fridays
Up on the hill on a beautiful site with its very own outdoor classroom
Bringing Waldorf to 3 and 4 year olds In mainstream was very possible (see
Vignette 28).
We took Steiner Kindergarten enrichment courses
Our friendship deepened
And I began a new Parent and Child group
'The Children's Garden'
With policies, detailed plans and insurance
And a nice cup of tea for each adult as they arrived.
As a respite to working with the system, each summer we went to
Steiner-land
To Lifeways Family festival in Forest Row.
At first ensconced in the yurt I made
We ran our parent and child group and parenting course
Discussions, real craft and exploring our model of storytelling
"The world is good."
Enriched we returned to the 'real world'
Grass-roots or inside the system we could make real change
Kath, then Alys, gained the Early Years Professional Status

FIGURE 28   A Steiner Parent and Child group inside the yurt that I built, Lifeways Festival,
Forest Row, UK, July 2010

A government qualification to manage early years
Now becoming experts in the lexicon
Clever to convince the change as 'best practice,' not being 'Steiner'
We had our own lingo and lines
TNVS (That's not very Steiner) we whispered,
Or WWSS (What would Steiner Say) we giggled,
Especially on days we wore black!
And say we were not Anthroposophists but the truth is others say we are
Deep down, inside
We work from our hearts to the children's through love.
Our real challenge was when I ran the neighbouring village preschool
Kath helped mentoring change
We wrote training on how active literacy transformed children's ability to
learn to read
Have you gone to the dark side? I hear you question?
No just back to that lexicon
Let the children have a home corner, uninterrupted play, oral storytelling and
ring time
Yes, you can breathe a sigh of relief
That is the same as the Waldorf Kindergarten model?
Exactly
And I got GOOD from OFSTED after a week in the job!
But the truth was it was not enough for me
I was still struggling with the compromise in mainstream – even when using
innovative approaches in early years
I wanted formal learning to start later
And still loving the Steiner Kindergarten
My wanderlust took me out exploring what else is out there in education in
this world
And Kath had a gap year too skiing in the United States
She returned refreshed for a new challenge
We still continued our annual homeopathic drop of Steiner Waldorf magic at
Lifeways
But we always had a niggling feeling about social inequality and
What about those 4 and 5 year olds?
What about children not from a nice middle-class rural village?
Can we explore the edge-ucation elsewhere?
Once I began searching for what was out there, I couldn't stop
I couldn't compromise again
And Kath took over a mainstream inner-city Early Years department

What is the healthiest way to get 5 year olds reading and writing and ready for
Year 1?
Not do it and let them play is my facetious reply!
But I am talking with privilege
And Kath sees the four-year olds who do not know how to play but who are
part of the system that will write them off if they cannot keep up
And from the inside transcends the challenge
Scaffolds and develops their play
And creatively inspired now by many (not just Steiner) approaches
Kath lets them love learning.
I go in and observe and see their delight in new letters and numbers
And how calm the environment Kath has created is, and the role so clear of
oral storytelling and imagination
And smile, seeing appropriate methods to meet the children, their families,
this area, this school and skills for their lives.
Kath now wonders about the sweet spot for formal learning.
Is it 5.5 for some children and not 7 as we so strongly believed?
As Steiner says??
(Mendus, Reflections on our shared experiences [Sheffield, November 2015])

10   **Alys Educating Differently: Moving from Blended Pedagogy into
        Edge-ucation**

In 2006, when I began my Steiner Teacher Training, I was teaching Science to 11–16 year olds in an inner-city school in Sheffield, UK. At that
point, I was clear there was a set division between Steiner Waldorf Pedagogy and Anthroposophy, so I felt it was quite straightforward to use
Steiner Waldorf Methods as a research project to teach some of my Y8
students the topic of 'Light' – we used a three day rhythm, created our
own main lesson books and the homework was to research and present
biographies of famous scientists. The project was really successful, the
students enjoyed themselves and my line-manager was happy as they all
still got their expected grades in the topic test. I used the same approach
for another project on Food Webs later in the academic year (see Mendus, 2007). At the time I argued that "I agree with Jelinek and Sun (2003)
that many good aspects can be used in mainstream that do not need the
teacher to have an understanding of Anthroposophy" (Mendus, 2007).
(Mendus, Reflections on using Steiner Waldorf approaches in mainstream teaching [Vietnam, January 2017])

However, with hindsight I recognise that there are challenges of bringing new pedagogies into an established system such as English state education with its set policies, curricula, school inspection procedures and expectations that mean that certain compromises need to be undertaken, different language used to explain key terms.

> "It's all about the lexicon," Kath explained.
>
> "Just tell them about the daily routine of the children in your nursery and they will nod their heads and understand... but if you talk about your daily rhythm in your Kindergarten it might trigger them..." (Mendus, Conversation with Kath, 2010 [Sheffield, 2015])

From discussions with Kath and from looking at the strengths and challenges of both the state system and the Steiner Waldorf system, I could begin to see that there were possibilities of change for the 'teacher' already working in mainstream as they could use a mixture of approaches. This could in turn suit both the children and their needs in their class, but also the teacher's own pedagogical understanding of child development, learning, and potentially of Anthroposophy. I was aware that this mix of approaches, or what I was calling 'blended pedagogies,' could incorporate all other experiences and knowledge of other teaching approaches and other pedagogies as well, so in some cases it is easier not to say directly which pedagogical approach is being used to avoid criticism from ardent followers of that method. For example, in the quote below from a document that Kath and I wrote for a training course of Early Years Practitioners in Derbyshire about the changes we had made in our preschools (mostly inspired by our experiences and training from Steiner Waldorf education) we did not mention it in the whole document, but focussed on how our approaches would make the role of the Teacher easier:

> The approach that our preschools have developed is thoroughly researched, and draws on a number of pedagogical approaches to best practice. Its beauty, however, lies in how simple it is to deliver. The child-led independent play allows practitioners the time to watch, listen and learn about the children's development and understanding, whilst the adult-led times involve a minimal amount of planning and preparation once basic resources are collected. The results are a staff with reduced paperwork, and children with the skills and experiences they need to help them make the most of their early years in school. (Bransby & Mendus, 2012, p. 2).

FIGURE 29   Using Steiner Waldorf approaches to classroom layout in a mainstream
             Early Years setting, Derbyshire, UK, 2013

11   State-funded Steiner Waldorf Edge-ucation

Steiner education is state funded or heavily subsidised by the state in most
European countries, as well as in New Zealand and is partially subsidised in
Australia. In the UK, four state-funded Steiner Waldorf schools were established
as part of the academies/free school programme beginning in 2009. However,
by 2020 after unsatisfactory inspections, the only state-funded Steiner Waldorf
school remaining in England is the first school to be state-funded, the Steiner
Academy Hereford. The remaining 31 schools are funded privately. Many of the
schools have fees which are lower than other small private schools and they
have sliding scales of fees connected to income with discounted or free places
for children of staff. However, this in turn reflects the wages, which are much
lower than those working as teachers in the state or private sector.

12   Vignette 8: Alys the School Tourist – State-funded Steiner Primary
           Stream, Australia

An example of Steiner Waldorf edge-ucation from Australia is the option of a
Steiner Waldorf stream within a mainstream school – so families could choose
what type of education they wanted for their children.

> I was shown into the first part of the school for younger children and it
> was just as it had been described to me – a corridor with main-stream

FIGURE 30   Steiner Waldorf stream classroom within a mainstream primary school,
             Australia, 2016

classrooms on one side and Steiner inspired classrooms on the other. The Steiner classrooms having wooden tables and blackboards, 'lambies' (sheep-skins) on seats, natural resources and pastel coloured curtains, with few things on the walls, whereas the mainstream classrooms, across the hall, have interactive whiteboards, bright coloured desks and lots of displays on the walls and hanging across the ceiling. (Mendus, School Tourism notes from Melbourne March 2016 [In the air flying between Singapore and London, March 2016])

I was fascinated by how the teachers in the Steiner Waldorf stream were adapting certain approaches to fit more into a traditional school.

When it was transition time – moving between working at desks and sitting on the floor for morning tea, the teacher used their laptop to play a piece of music that the class immediately recognised was their clearing up song. They got on with the task without the teacher needing to say anything. The class teacher explained that they had been singing a song as traditional Steiner Waldorf teachers would do to signal this change, but the challenge with singing is that often many of the children have questions for the teacher and they cannot answer if they are singing, so with the music playing the teacher is more available for the children. I was interested by this logic and how thinking from the outside had still kept the character of transitions without a teacher 'telling' or raising their voice. (Mendus, School Tourism notes from Melbourne March 2016 [In the air flying between Singapore and London, March 2016])

However, the Steiner steam was not as inclusive as I first hoped when I found out about it as one school I visited had 30% Indigenous children on its books and none attended the Steiner stream. Although this could have been by choice, I was made aware by teachers that it was also connected to the fact that parents were asked to contribute to the Steiner stream – so although cheaper than a private Steiner Waldorf school, it was not accessible to those with no money to pay for education.

> My visit showed me the possibilities of combining many different approaches in the classroom, yet still having one school and playing together at break times helped to show this whole school connection and the importance given for all children (including the Steiner streams) to learn Indigenous history, culture and language. In terms of Steiner education being part of a state school, it was obvious that certain changes had to be made such as the visible learning outcomes and objectives and whole school behaviour systems, however I wasn't in the room long enough to know if these impacted on the class. They may have actually focussed the class in terms of knowing where their learning was heading and held the class with known boundaries. And in terms of Steiner's influence on Mainstream, hearing about some of the beautiful Steiner festivals such as lantern walk being celebrated by the whole school seemed great and yet I wondered if there was more that could be shared? (Mendus, School Tourism notes from Melbourne March 2016 [In the air flying between Singapore and London, March 2016])

In the USA there are now Waldorf Charter schools which are similar to the UK Steiner Academies which do not ask for tuition fees and are often in areas of social deprivation (see Alliance for Public Waldorf Education, 2015). I visited a state-funded Steiner Waldorf inspired Kindergarten in Rhode Island, USA in March 2013 (see Mendus, 2013a). The NOVA institute in the USA was set up in 2000 to use Waldorf approaches in public education by running retreats and teacher training courses (see NOVA, 2021). I saw the founder, Jack Petrash, give a key-note address at the Association of Waldorf Schools of North America conference at Emerson Waldorf School, Chapel Hill, North Carolina in March

2013 and it is interesting to see how the main message from his talk linked back to the need for 'inner work' by the teacher.

13   Alys Educating Differently: Fed up with Behaviourism in the Classroom

13.1   *Alys the Guide*

The following section explores through three different Vignettes (9, 10 & 11) my experiences of behaviour management from a UK state funded Steiner Waldorf school, an observation of a Steiner Waldorf stream classroom in a state-funded primary school in Australia and the final one from my work as a supply-teacher in state primary schools in England. This section is important for this book as how behaviour is managed in schools, something that I explored for my MA Teaching and Learning thesis (Mendus, 2012), influenced my dissatisfaction with traditional schooling as well as my realisation that Steiner Waldorf education as it currently exists was not my 'ideal.' I explore behaviourism further in Chapter 7.

14   Vignette 9: 'Acorn 1, 2, 3'

It was a sunny day and the golden light was glinting off the windows of the newly built Steiner school. Crowds of excited children and interested parents mill around waiting to get a chance to have a look in their children's classrooms. Beauty is a core factor of Steiner Waldorf Education with natural wood furniture and finishings, pastel colours, fresh flowers and carefully drawn blackboard pictures.

I was accompanying my friend's daughter who is in the Kindergarten at the school and her eyes were bright with excitement, wonder and joy, to see what the big children do. She led me through all the classrooms at high speed. However, even though I knew the school and had worked there as a supply teacher in the past, something had changed…

On the back wall across from the blackboard visible to the whole room a beautifully drawn acorn was placed in the Class 1 (6–7 year olds) room. It was surrounded by wooden clothes pegs. Each peg had a child's name and coming down from the acorn were the numbers 1, 2 and 3.

"What's that?" I asked another friend who has a son in the class.

"It's a behaviour chart," they said, "and if they get to number 3 the teacher will talk to their parents."

I stood there shocked. Sick in the pit in my stomach. I had found Steiner Education as my first alternative, a way of educating children differently, with love and respect. Here, in this beautiful held space of Class 1, that illusion had been shattered. (Mendus, A response to a Steiner School open-day [Herefordshire, May 2015])

15   **Vignette 10: "You Can't Sit There!"**

When I came in, I sat on a little chair by the door, so I felt I was out of the way as I observed the class, but as I sat down I heard a child's voice saying,
    "You can't sit there! It is the step...'"
I was a little taken aback but continued to sit there until there was a chance to walk around the classroom.
I saw a sign on the wall which was about behaviour management which I later saw was used throughout school (in the traditional as well as the Steiner Waldorf classrooms); a three step approach – after a warning the next step was quiet time on the chair in the room, then moved into another classroom and then a more serious consequence.
I haven't seen a step approach in a classroom before, only in early childhood settings and it made me think about the impact of visible behaviour management techniques on children's self-esteem. (Mendus, An observation from a Steiner Stream Class in a Mainstream Primary in Australia [Cumbria, March 2016])

16   **Vignette 11: Red on the Traffic Light Means No Playtime**

"Settle down children,
    In your carpet places so I can do the register."
(Voice projected, raised somewhat)
    "Before I count to three..."
    1...
    "Oooh well done Ellie, here's a sticker for you, what lovely sitting."
    2...
    "And well done Charlie, thank you for ignoring the distractions, a sticker for you too."
    3...
    "Robert! Robert!... Why is it always you I am waiting for? I'm moving you down the traffic light to amber for not following instructions... that's

5 minutes off your playtime." (Mendus, A poem to show the language used as a teacher completes the morning register in a typical state Primary School in England (between 2004–2016) [Cumbria, March 2016])

17   Alys the Theorist: A Response to Vignette 9, 10 & 11 in 2016

Parker et al. (2016) argue that "the behaviourist paradigm is strongly engrained in English schools and much of the educational world" (p. 464). For example, in England government policies explicitly endorse the use of rewards and sanctions to control behaviour (Department for Education, 2016, 2018). Behaviourism in classrooms is used to manage compliance and performance through an approach of sanctions and rewards.

Behaviourism stems back to Pavlov's (1927) experiments with training dogs. However, Kozol argues that visual behaviour charts as described in Vignette 10 rely on 'shaming and humiliation' in front of others and have been used in some schools for many years (Kozol, 2006), even though the emotional impact on children was not investigated until more recently. Research has shown that the use of behaviourism can cause negative emotional health issues on children (McEachern et al., 2008; Nesbit & Philpott, 2002; Shumba, 2002). However, as the literature shows (Bettinger, 2011; Chaltain, 2010), rewards and sanctions are effective as a short-term fix to make children abide by the rules and expectations of the teacher, so the approach has continued to be used.

As a teacher and supply teacher, I have observed many state-funded primary schools in the UK in the last twelve years supporting the use of rewards over punishments (see Steer Report, 2005), with the heavy use of stickers and saying 'Good girl/boy' and 'Well done' all the time. Kohn's (1999) work 'Punished by Rewards' and his essays online are very helpful in explaining the challenges of rewards and grading. He explains that rewarding gives, "temporary compliance. They buy us obedience," (Kohn, 1999, p. 161). The use of the stickers in the primary classroom (see Vignette 11 above) is an example of 'buying obedience' which does mean that the teacher can get on with their job of teaching the whole class if students are listening.

As I observed in the Steiner Waldorf classroom described in Vignette 9, the school policy (at that time – it has since changed to a social justice approach) was to use visible behaviour charts for 'unacceptable' behaviour:

I feel that these charts grade the children visibly in front of the whole class. I see this as behaviour manipulated by public humiliation (Kozol, 2006). Those children who are usually pegged up around the 'acorn' and one day end up on 1, 2 or 3 will not forget that day. Speak to an adult about their memories from their school days and unjust behaviour management sticks. But the shame and the disappointment seen in the teacher in their behaviour can 'bully' them back to behave. I feel they are behaving because it is painful/shameful to not behave (Kozol, 2006). This is not building the strength and resilience to behave so that the teacher can teach and they can learn and do fun and amazing things. (Mendus, Journalling about behaviourism [Somerset, May 2015])

Deci, Koestner and Ryan's work on Self Determination Theory (2001) and Adler's (1930) approaches to instil 'intrinsic motivation' in students argue against visible behaviour charts and for relationship building. Steiner class teachers really know their children (as they work with the same group over many years) and if behaviour is recognised as communication (Dreikurs, 1972), then it could be argued that something is not being met of these children's needs. Some argue that 'routine,' as research has shown in Early Years, is fundamental in supporting strong boundaries (Tickell, 2011), but there are still some children for whom school and the daily routine are too much. Parker et al asked "but what happens when it does not work?" (2016, p. 464). These children challenge the peace in the classroom and prevent learning taking place as the teacher spends so much time and energy placating them, and the teacher wants solutions. The 1,2,3 step behaviour process gives a tool for getting rid of the low level unacceptable behaviour from most of the students but those children that were not 'fitting' in the classroom are still on 2 or 3 each day. The teacher has a tool now to say, "if you do that again then I will move you down a step" and reiterate the consequence.

> But is this just manipulation? A power dynamic? Hierarchy? And the child in many cases still behaves 'unacceptably' or creates an inner defiance to the system and teacher. Not a love for learning, a neediness develops. The teacher is acting out of desperation with the lack of alternative skills to handle the class (Benbenishty et al., 2002). (Mendus, Journalling about behaviourism [Somerset, May 2015])

My reflections in my journalling have also been observed in the literature, where behaviourism has been described as 'inflexible' and 'one-size-fits-all' (Harold & Corcoran, 2013; Hart, 2010), as well as Kennedy and Kennedy (2004) suggesting that something different alongside behaviourism is needed that focusses more on attachment based strategies and links back to be aware of the emotional impact.

If the 1, 2, 3 system and the 'step' (from Vignettes 9 and 10) are publicly humiliating students (see Kozol, 2006), causing many to behave to save being shamed and it is still not working for all students, then why is it being used? This is surely not in keeping with Waldorf education wanting to educate with love, respect and in view of the whole child (Steiner, 1932/1966)? What else can be done? (Mendus, Journalling about behaviourism [Luang Prabang, Laos, December 2016)

18   Alys the Guide: Why Steiner Waldorf Education Is Not My 'Ideal'

However much I love and am influenced by many aspects of Steiner Waldorf education, there are still too many areas that need further work for me to be able to declare that in its current iteration it is my ideal school. My continual challenges with Steiner Waldorf education are: eurocentricism, Christ-centricism, the racism and patriarchy within Anthroposophy, some schools using behaviourism, certain dogmatisms, most schools being fee-paying and that there is a lot of didactic teaching with single-age classes and a set curriculum.

Even though Boland (2017) and others call out for a Waldorf 2.0, I am not sure that it could address all of my challenges, particularly my challenge with single-aged classes, although I am aware that this conflicts completely with the Anthroposophical understanding of child development. However, Waldorf 2.0 could be something that openly addresses issues of racism and separates itself from some of Rudolf Steiner's views. It could move beyond the cult of personality to be inspired more by the methodology and teaching pedagogy, rather than outdated aspects of Anthroposophy.

There are many 'gems' that I take from Steiner Waldorf education: the beauty, reverence and magic of childhood, the care and rhythms in the daily routine, the beautiful crafts and quiet confidence of the children and the space to be themselves. The realisation that whatever Steiner Waldorf school I am in, wherever in the world it is located, I feel at home, in the pastel colours, connection to nature and the smell of linseed rubbed into the wood. I continue to visit Steiner Waldorf schools to see their relationships and troubling of Anthroposophy and eurocentricism, but also for an element of 'home-coming,' as I feel safe and secure in their similar warm environments.

In terms of my journey, I may critique Steiner Waldorf education but the approach is special to me as it was my first alternative and I continue to explore its pedagogy and future. I may go and learn about other educational approaches but I return, time and time again, a continual iterative relationship. Even with my troubling of the approach, I am heavily influenced (see

FIGURE 31   Daily influences of Steiner education on my life: A Samhain/Halloween nature table on the front dash of our van, October 2016

Figure 31). For example, my home looks like a Steiner Waldorf kindergarten and I attend the local Steiner Waldorf playgroup with my toddler in Australia. Also, when I finished writing my PhD thesis one of my first jobs was to lecture on the MA Steiner Waldorf education in Norway. However, I continue this unsettled relationship with Steiner Waldorf education fully aware of the challenges and continue to find my place with some aspects of Anthroposophy, alongside totally disregarding and disowning Steiner's racist views.

19   Summary

- Rudolf Steiner's philosophy is called Anthroposophy and it influenced his views on child development and inspired the school curriculum. Anthroposophy is not taught in Steiner Waldorf schools.
- Some of Rudolf Steiner's views were racist. Therefore, a change to Anthroposophy's image and a move away from Steiner's racist doctrines is essential before Waldorf 2.0 can even begin to be reimagined.
- Eurocentrism, christ-centricism and the need to decolonize Steiner Waldorf education (Boland, 2017) are challenges and critiques of current Waldorf education practices.
- It is possible to bring Steiner Waldorf teaching approaches into more traditional settings and there are a growing number of state-funded Steiner Waldorf schools around the world.

- Behaviourism may be common in schools, including Steiner Waldorf schools, but there are other approaches to creating positive learning environments.
- Waldorf 2.0 is possible if people are prepared to step away from many aspects of Rudolf Steiner's Anthroposophy.

CHAPTER 6

Alys and Progressive Education

1 Alys the Guide

Throughout this book, I make sure that I use each places' self-labelled description of their type of school. This chapter covers places that call themselves 'progressive,' however, that does not mean that all of these schools are the same or that they follow the same pedagogies, but that they all identify with the term 'progressive.' I hope the stories that I share will help you understand some of the challenges of terminology, but also see the common threads in Progressive Education of student-centred approaches that,

> incorporate aspects such as learning by doing, valuing diversity, integrated curriculum, problem solving, critical thinking, collaborative learning, social responsibility, democracy, and lifelong learning. An important feature is... actively promoting critical pedagogy and democratic education... social justice. (Bruce, 2013, p. 10)

2 Alys the Theorist: Progressive Education

> From my experience, I have observed that Progressive schools focus on how to teach and often question traditional educational assumptions of hierarchy and gender divisions. For example, teachers are often referred to by first names rather than Mr or Miss, there is not a uniform, they are coeducational and are not following a religious approach. (Mendus, Conversation describing progressive schools to a teacher 2013 [Farnham, July 2013])

Defining Progressive Education has many challenges because of the long history of the use of the term since the end of the 19th century and its differing

© KONINKLIJKE BRILL NV, LEIDEN, 2022 | DOI: 10.1163/9789004506039_007

developments around the world. In the US, Progressive Education is often recognised as beginning after the 1870 child-centred reform act and continues in the work by Dewey (1859–1952). Dewey's influence on pedagogy can be seen in various places educating differently to mainstream approaches, including Progressive Education, Democratic Education, Montessori, Project-Based Learning. Dewey (1900) was influenced by pragmatism, an understanding that philosophy is grounded in the practical conditions of life and, therefore, education should also be connected to society and should be preparing students to be part of the wider social community. Dewey argued (1900, 1938) that children learn by doing and "that children, not content, should be the focus of the educational process" (Williams, 2017). In 1938, Dewey described Progressive Education as the result of discontentment with the current educational approaches as they have adult standards, set curriculum and teaching pedagogies. I find it fascinating that many of my current challenges with education, such as students sitting in rows and didactic, teacher at the front, approaches were what troubled Dewey over 100 years ago! This summary of Dewey's influence by Gibbon (2019) is worth thinking about as you read the stories in Part 2 to see how much they are inspired by Dewey's philosophies.

> Students should be active, not passive. They required compelling and relevant projects, not lectures. Students should become problem solvers. Interest, not fear, should be used to motivate them. They should cooperate, not compete. (Gibbon, 2019, para. 3)

Progressive Education has developed around the world, influenced by different scholars. In France, Freinet's (1896–1966) work influenced the 'Ecole Moderne,' focussing on social activism. In Italy, the work by Malaguzzi (1920–1994) influenced the whole town of Reggio Emilia to transform its early childhood education to include working with professional artists. In Brazil, the work of Freire (1921–1997), engaging the political with power of pedagogical, influenced great changes in education and social reform. Pestalozzi's (1746–1827) work in Switzerland supported children following their interests.

3   Alys the School Tourist: Stories from Progressive Schools

3.1   *Vignette 12: Rural Vermont*
Having got over the initial impression of the austere nature of the buildings and atmosphere, I was introduced to a very grounded and down to earth school community. A strong ethos and vision of service and practical

crafts alongside excellent academic achievement seemed to me tricky to manage. However, as this was a boarding school, service tasks such as the 5.30am milking shift or 7am breakfast-making responsibility was easily made a part of the curricula experience.

This High school – incredibly expensive to attend – seemed to allow for and encourage self-regulation of its students. Perhaps on account of this attitude, every person, staff or student, appeared to see it as a real privilege to be at the school. For new staff and recent graduates, training in 'progressive education' was available to gain a more in-depth understanding of the approaches in cooperation at the school; distinct from three other progressive schools in New England.

Students at the school were involved in the way the school ran by doing daily chores; they also took advantage of the range of opportunities and choice they had in their extra-curricula options: from cross country skiing to pottery to ballet to blacksmithing… Every academic lesson I observed engaged students in a variety of ways from a cross-curricular project-based approach: to the environment and farming in Grade 9 (Y10), to controversial debates around the U.S. Constitution, to creative use of computers to check students' work as they composed essays in English. What really made this school special in my eyes was the inclusive nature of its community. Students come from all over the U.S. and the world for 1–4 years. Every Thursday morning the whole school meets for half an hour and sings. Sings at the top of their voices. Everyone joining in; everyone smiling. (Mendus, 2013a, p. 128)

3.2 *Vignette 13: Reflections on Two UK Private Progressive School Visits*

In both of these schools, the pedagogy, teaching and learning were really exciting. I saw different, conscious and cutting edge approaches with the focus on personal learning alongside a real respect for the community and for the environment. The teachers were more often facilitators or mentors, rather than standing at the front teaching didactically. One school had designed its own comparable courses to state qualifications that included more depth and creativity. They did, however, continue the state exams in key subjects such as Maths, English and Sciences as they did not want their students to leave without their cultural expectations and passports to higher education. The middle school department at the same school had free periods within the time table for children to direct their own learning – they could do their homework, or read a book, or have a music lesson or even play! Another progressive school carried out

FIGURE 32   A progressive school classroom, New York, USA, 2017

an annual project with their Y8 (12/13 year old) students where they built houses and created a village for a week where they had to cook, sleep and decide on activities to do with each other and solve any problems. One of my friends attended this school as a child and he said this Village Project was a transformative childhood experience. (Mendus, Reflections on Progressive Education in the UK from 2013 [London, 2015])

4   Alys the Educator: What Makes a 21st Century Progressive School Progressive?

Stories from the USA and UK show expensive, exclusive schools with a history of self-labelling themselves as progressive schools long after the term was 'fashionable' and directly influencing state-funded education (see Little, 2013). This is important to be aware of, as Little & Ellison argue that some progressive schools are "embarrassed to use the P word" (2015, pp. 196–197), so what makes a 21st century progressive school?

My reflections from visiting big traditional independent progressive schools in the UK have left me feeling that although the building, teaching, creativity are impressive, there seems to be a level of being historically progressive in their ethos rather than innovatively progressive now. When I asked members of senior management why this was, they suggested there is an impact from parent choice. Parents like that there is no uniform, there are friendly relationships with staff and pupils, the focus on outdoor work and the arts, but want their children to still get high exam results and get into top universities. And when they are paying expensive fees it is hard for these established schools to argue. Compared to a regular school these places are 'radical.' but still not enough for me. (Mendus, Blogpost, The concept of compromise in Education is a key area of my interest, November 2013 [Cumbria, October 2013])

It is also worth noting that a school principal (in 2013) shared with me on a school visit that the high-fees mean that the relationship with the parents is interesting in terms of parents-as-consumers and the link that neoliberalism and capitalism has on private innovative schools.

I realised that it was impossible to separate the established progressive schools that I had visited from privilege. This educational opportunity was not available for all children or teachers. But as a School Tourist I recognise the value of visiting such expensive schools as it has allowed me to experience what can be possible if there are no issues with costs. It also allowed me to network, as two big progressive schools I visited in the US had close contacts with two schools in the UK which I visited on my return to the UK and one of those schools then had a contact for a school in Switzerland. (Mendus, Journalling about progressive education [Switzerland, 2017])

Bruce (2013) argues that progressive educators have concentrated on teaching students for the current time as the future is not known. Therefore, skills

FIGURE 33   A different progressive school classroom, New York, USA, 2017

such as critical thinking are taught so the students have the capacity to be able to solve unknown challenges in the future. Following Little's (2013) acknowledgment that 21st century progressive schools are committed to social justice, diversity and equity, I was unsure if this was true in terms of the students that attend. I was aware that it was part of the pedagogy and philosophy, but the high-fees from the first self-labelled progressive schools that I had visited excluded those who did not have the money. However, I found an exception to this rule in a progressive school for 4–13 year olds in New York (which I visited in May 2017), which has a long-established progressive primary and middle school and which has attempted to live its aim for both 'social justice and sustainability' that Little and Ellison (2015) call for 21st century progressive schools to strive for.

4.1   *Vignette 14: Elementary/middle Progressive School, New York, USA*

This progressive school has a farm upstate that students visit throughout the year and a strong focus on social justice and accessibility, with a sliding scale for tuition connected directly to each families' income. This meant that each classroom felt more inclusive in terms of socio-economic background and more multicultural.

The classrooms felt like they fostered many progressive approaches, such as small classrooms, the use of natural wooden materials, block corners, desks together rather than in rows, carpet space in the lower grades and more discussion-based classrooms in the older grades who sat around tables or in a circle.

The school emerged from the civil rights movement as a lab school for integration within New York and the founders had initially hoped that schools would be desegregated within ten years. The new school had to be independent to allow for this desegregation. After three years the notion of equal voice was questioned because the fees were making it not equal. So, over 39 meetings, they created their particular approach to tuition. It is very complicated, but its principle is similar to a tithe where every family pays the same percentage of their income and there are some discounts available such as more than one child or household to support. The idea is that each family has had to make an equal sacrifice to send their child to the school. They have thought about applying to become a charter school but they realised that being truly independent of curriculum and community was more important than the money – also as a charter is a lottery it would not create such a balanced school. The continual question is "How to strive towards equity in New York City when it is so polarised?"

> Although I was happy to visit a progressive school that was attempting to challenge the privilege created by many progressive schools of high-fees

that prevent many children from attending, I would still argue that the tithe approach may still not be fair. For example, if every family pays 10% of their income it will have a very different effect to a rich family where 10% of a large income is not very much compared to 10% of a family income on the poverty line. I know that they had 39 meetings when the school was young to define this approach, but I wonder if it is something that could be regularly looked at to check that the school continues to meet its aims of striving towards equity? (Mendus, School Observations, New York. Friday 12th May 2017 [Uphall, Scotland, May 2017])

5   Alys the Educator: Project-Based Learning

Influences from Progressive Education are visible in a whole range of schools, such as the flexibility to allow students to have wonderful ideas as that leads to intellectual development (from Duckworth, 1987), or those teachers trained at Bank Street College in New York (established by Sprague Mitchell, 1878–1967), or Meier's work in transforming state-funded schools in the US (2002). Another influence on pedagogy is Project-Based Learning (PBL). I visited several places using this approach, which is why there is a designated section within the progressive education chapter of this book.

PBL has been defined by Patton as:

> Students designing, planning, and carrying out an extended project that produces a publicly-exhibited output such as a product, publication, or presentation. It is related to enquiry-based learning (also known as inquiry-based learning), and problem-based learning. (Patton, 2012, p. 13)

> I recognise that Project-Based Learning has continued to be a theme of interest for me (since 2013) as it can connect people of all ages from the school to the wider community and ends up with a final professional, 'real' product. I am also impressed by places that engage with social justice, diversity and inclusivity not tokenistically but with a fully engaged approach even more than first name terms and no uniform. (Mendus, Reflections on Progressive Education [Cornwall, September 2017])

I have noticed that how PBL is carried out is different in each school that I have visited and that there are several dominant models – such as High Tech High and Expeditionary Learning (explored below) and eduScrum (explored further in Chapter 9). I was unable to visit High Tech High in San Diego, USA, but I did visit a school inspired by the approach in the UK.

5.1   *Vignette 15: PBL and Other High Tech High Influences in a UK State*
         Secondary School

This school impressed me by its ability to play the system and float under
the radar. Set in a small northern town, realising that GCSEs (high stakes
tests taken at 16 in England and Wales) are currency to get to college but
that the exams in themselves do not make a whole person or a school community. Uniforms are worn, teachers are mostly Sir or Miss, but no fuss is
made to enforce the dress code. Behaviour is mostly managed by creating positive relationships using Deci, Koestner and Ryan's work on Self
Determination Theory (2001) to develop intrinsic motivation for learning.
Teaching in KS3 (11–14 year olds) is through cross curricular project-based
learning, plus key subject lessons. Teachers collaborate and team-teach
and the recent building extension was designed to avoid having corridors
and create large open-plan learning areas to facilitate group learning. I
was so impressed by this set up and the vision of management, the belief
in teacher teaching and learning development, that I went for an interview for a short term job. I thought I had found an example of the Fielding
and Moss's (2010) utopia here in the UK. My interview lesson was fun, I
did 'worm-charming,' but the interview did not go well once onto my ethics... It transpired I was too radical for the most 'radical common school' I
had found in the UK (I didn't believe in homework, for example...). For the
short term though, I think I could have compromised. I would have gained
from a few months within the system that used PBL and the National Curriculum. It made me think about why although it was offering, in my opinion, a much better education than a regular comprehensive school that it
was not 'radical' enough for me. For example, in KS4 (14–16 year olds) the
school returns to a more traditional exams and grades focus, plus there is
still homework, uniforms and hierarchy and overall it still felt like school.
     Realising this began to scare me; maybe I didn't believe in the concept
of school? (Mendus, Blog Post: The concept of compromise in Education
is a key area of my interest [Herefordshire, November 2013])

6   Alys the Educator: Ron Berger and Expeditionary Learning

Ron Berger, a Massachusetts Elementary school teacher who developed his
own version of Project-Based Learning in his state-school, wrote a book (2003)
'An Ethic of Excellence.' This book influenced my thinking about education in

2013 when I began performing School Tourism in earnest. Berger argues that in his public-school classroom he was able to create a culture of excellence where all students were able to produce publishable work. The curriculum is chosen so that the students are doing real life projects so that the students see the need for the work. The classes focus on quality over quantity, with constant drafting, and redrafting, to lead to an end project that is shareable with the wider community. An example of Berger's work that I often share when I visit schools interested in PBL is a YouTube video called 'Austin's Butterfly' (Berger, 2012), where a kindergarten student is given continual advice on his drawing of a butterfly so that it becomes so transformed in detail and quality that the image is printed on a postcard and sold across the state.

Berger's work has now grown to inspire an organisation called Expeditionary Learning (EL), which combined the ethos of Outward Bound (begun by Kurt Hahn in 1941) and Project-Based Learning. In September 2014, the XP Free school opened in Doncaster, UK following this approach. Here are some reflections from my visit to an EL school in the USA in 2013.

> The kindergarten children were exploring dog sleds and had their teacher sitting on a mat attached to a rope with many handles and were dragging her through the main corridor of the school as I was shown around! Grade 1 were in the process of taking apart everyday machines, so their room was full of computers and old TV parts. The science lab had a large rabbit hopping around and several 'pet monitors' in there to check on its well-being at break time. (Mendus, 2013a, p. 109)

7 The Queering of 'Bad-Alys': The Dangers of Putting Places on a Pedestal – The Green School, Bali

I visited many progressive schools between completing my MA and beginning my PhD, in a time where I was looking 'for a job for me and a school for my future children.' I had not got to the point where I did not want to teach anymore and I was in a space full of hope. Even during my PhD studies, as someone passionate about creative teaching pedagogy I was often excited to visit a new and innovative progressive school. My epiphany at a progressive school, The Green School, Bali, Indonesia in February 2016 (see Chapter 3 and Vignette 16) helped me realise that I too am conditioned that there must be an Ideal School somewhere, even though my reflections and research keep reminding me that it is an oxymoron.

7.1 *Vignette 16: The Green School, Bali, Indonesia*

I had wanted to visit the Green School since it was founded in 2008 and had been following its progress and changes in pedagogical ideals online. I was passionate about sustainability and excited to read about how this influenced the curriculum.

> From attending the week at the Green School, I learnt that the main aim of the Green School is, 'Learning something of value to the world now.' This was explained as being important as it is not the traditional approach of learning, which usually focuses on the future. For example, schools generally encourage students to learn so that they can get a good job, or go to a good University, but I learnt that at the Green School the aim is for the students to be learning for the world, not just for the individual. The curriculum in the Primary school is organised into three frames – the Integral Frame (the Thematic Lessons), the Instructional Frame (the Proficiency lessons) and the Experiential Frame (practical lessons). For example, a topic on Bamboo would include eating it, building with it and making watches from it. (Mendus, Journalling about the Green School February 2016 [Melbourne, March 2016])

FIGURE 34   Two photos of buildings made with bamboo at The Green School, Bali, February 2016

As the poem in Chapter 3 shows, realising that the Green School was not my ideal was upsetting.

> I found it hard to cope with the level of privilege – for example, each classroom has two equal teachers, however, the Indonesian teacher

is paid ten times less than the international teacher. Or how there are scholarship children, but they were pointed out to us as we were shown round which felt like the old approach in the UK, to have separate (and very obvious) lists of children on free-school-meals. Of course, there were 'gems,' the confident and innovative presentations by students about their businesses and projects which showed the authentic importance given to entrepreneurship for sustainability. The fact that the high-school focussed on entrepreneurship over high-stakes tests excited me as it felt like a new vision for the future. However, with reflection, the push of the individual to succeed in business is yet another aspect of neoliberalism and potentially not as radical as I first thought. (Mendus, Journalling about the Green School February 2016 [Melbourne, March 2016])

With hindsight, it is fascinating to realise that the Green School was also the product of neoliberalism. It was too easy for me before I visited to put its sustainable curriculum and lack of high-stakes testing on a pedestal as my 'ideal' and to see it as very different from the traditional, mainstream neoliberal schools which I had earlier critiqued. For example, when Fielding and Moss describe how the neoliberal system requires a very particular 'subject' that needs to be trained from a very young age, one that is "flexible, competitive, entrepreneurial, choice-loving and autonomous, able to thrive in markets" (2010, p. 23), they could be describing very key aspects of the Green School curriculum of 'entrepreneurship for sustainability.'

My experience at the Green School did not just bring me awareness that the 'Ideal does not exist,' it also reminded me to regulate my behaviour and not put somewhere that I have not physically seen on a pedestal as the 'answer.' This again supports my argument for the embodied nature of performing School Tourism, you can read as much as you can about a school or educational philosophy, but it is not until you spend time in a particular place with the people who work/attend there and think deeply about the cultural/societal impact that is it possible to begin to know what is going on. My passion for the environment, sustainability and outdoor learning had rose-tinted my understanding about the Green School until I was able to spend a week at the school. I had been compelled, I realised, by very clever marketing that it was more innovative and radical that it was in practice.

I was greatly disappointed to observe the use of worksheets in the Kindergarten and even though the primary classrooms may have been beautifully constructed out of bamboo, the classroom layout and approaches seemed very similar to what I have worked in and observed in UK

> state-schools. The middle-school seemed more progressive as it began to use entrepreneurship and projects which were extended into the high-school. (Mendus, Journalling about the Green School February 2016 [Melbourne, March 2016])

However, I had naively as a School Tourist presumed that this school would be the answer to my search for the 'Ideal School' – creating a story in my head that the Green School would be a place that combined innovative pedagogy, self autonomy and sustainability – and when it did not deliver I was heartbroken. Even though teachers who we met explained that attending the Green School "inspires creativity and living outside the box," the continual gut feeling that this school was hiding things from those of us on the 'Educators Course' made me wary and ill at ease. If performing School Tourism can be viewed as a feeling journey then my visit to the Green School was very evocative of feeling unwell.

> I feel ill-at-ease to realise that possibly I am a greater part of the neoliberal machine than I think I am. For example, my research continues to see 'choice' as an important factor in education. Maybe this is part of performing School Tourism, thinking like a 'tourist' or 'nomad,' moving on to a better place or what they think is better... this putting on a pedestal... thinking there is always somewhere else in the distance... new options or choice? However, it could also be seen as post-modern, not neoliberal, to be looking at choice and inclusivity, not on a selfish, individual scale, but as part of a bigger picture... (Mendus, Journalling on neoliberalism [Granada, Spain, September 2017])

8 **The Queering of Bad-Alys... Feeling Uncomfortable Realising I Am Too Radical for What I Have Seen**

> My otherness begins to be highlighted as I realise that even within the Progressive Education movement I have not found my home. I am excited by the focus on intrinsic motivation and less time and energy on behaviourism as well as seeing teachers teach varied, creative and pedagogically progressive lessons. However, I feel I am alone. I am definitely too radical for what I have seen. (Mendus, Journalling about attending A New Earth Needs New Schools at Tamera Global Ecovillage Community [Portugal, October 2013])

I asked, "Are we being radical enough? Why are we still using the term 'school?'

If a new world needs new schools then why are we compromising with the old system? Why are we not revisioning education?"

I was asked what my vision was. I spoke of my dream for community learning, beautiful eco buildings (like the yurt I built in 2011) with access to nature and adults with passion for their lives.

> A flurry of people came to talk to me because I had just asked a question on many people's minds. Teresa Mendes, Manager of the Florescer project in Lisbon, a homeschool support group, talked to me of her passion for alternative education, her MA in Progressive Education and her choice to home educate her daughter as no radical school was available. Together we decided to lead a workshop looking at 'Utopias for Education, ideas of how they could be practically implemented and networking across Portugal.'
>
> Our workshop felt very insightful for me as it highlighted the challenges of visioning for a utopian, radical school with a group of 'alternative' educators with themselves holding differing views on what is radical, from unschooling to formal but alternative approaches like Steiner Waldorf, to not being upset by the concept of grades and homework to an abhorrent objection. Also cultural issues appeared, quite 'English' issues like the young school starting age and uniform were not important to others as they start school later and don't wear uniform in their country. Lucky really that we were not trying to create a new dogma of one alternative school fits all. It made me want to visit more schools and to carry on this visioning discussion with others. (Mendus, Blog post [Hereford, November 2013])

9　Alys the Guide

Although I continued to be impressed by many of Dewey's initial aims which underlie many of these schools that define themselves as Progressive, I was still concerned that it wasn't enough and I felt although there were some gems, particularly in the teaching pedagogy, that many places had not been able to answer or even embody Progressive Education in the 21st century. This meant that my search continued and really it was this dissatisfaction with Steiner Waldorf and then my initial School Tourism of Progressive Education that led to me wanting to undertake my PhD to continue my research.

10   Summary

– Progressive Education has several definitions but many focus on student-centred approaches.
– Progressive Education has a long history stemming back to the work of John
  Dewey in 1900 who argued that education should be active and child-centred.
– Different schools address how they make Progressive Education suitable for
  the 21st century and for many this is by including social justice, equity and
  an environmental awareness as a key part of the experience.
– Project-based learning where students explore real life topics for a series of
  weeks is a popular example of Progressive Education.
– Challenges affecting Progressive Education are that often the schools are
  fee paying so the approaches are not available for all children, some schools
  are embarrassed by the term as they see it as outdated and others are not
  necessarily true to their initial aims as they are dictated by parents or the
  culture of a country to comply to outside non-progressive influences such
  as high-stakes testing.

CHAPTER 7

Alys and Democratic Education

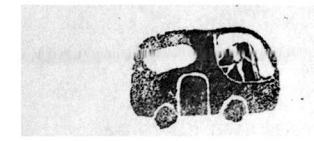

1   Alys the Guide

This chapter explores my relationship with Democratic Education. I recognise that as I had positioned myself as being too radical for Progressive Education, I wondered if Democratic Education could be my Ideal School? My journey took me to explore places that focussed on freedom, intrinsic motivation and autonomous learning which I hoped I would find in Democratic Education. This chapter explores the history and most well-known approaches to Democratic Education; Summerhill, Sudbury and Hecht's (2010) work in Israel. It looks at the role of the adult, rule-making and gives examples of school meetings that I have attended. I then share two examples of Democratic Education that I see as gems as one includes a different approach to decision making (sociocracy) and another focuses on social justice. It finishes with an introduction to unschooling, or autonomous home education, as an example of how these approaches could work in a home setting.

This chapter has been commented upon by first year undergraduate students at Southwestern University, Texas as part of their 'A Place called School' course, taught online during the Fall semester 2020 by Professor Michael Kamen. The students had all read Peter Gray's book, *Free to Learn* (2015), and written an assignment on their own school experiences including finishing high-school during the COVID-19 pandemic. They then read this chapter and gave detailed feedback on google docs, wrote a short reflection and created an artistic response which included poems, cartoons and memes. I have used the feedback to help shape the chapter, refining my writing style, making sure that I was clearer and more succinct as well as drawing to my attention areas that seemed to be most interesting to this group of students, particularly the concepts of freedom, rule-making and student safety. I want to thank this whole class for their time, generosity of ideas and creativity.

© KONINKLIJKE BRILL NV, LEIDEN, 2022 | DOI: 10.1163/9789004506039_008

2   Alys the Theorist: Progressive Education and Democracy

On David Gribble's website (2012) he described Progressive Education was "an old label for what is now called Democratic Education," arguing that the term 'progressive' needed to be replaced as "everyone who wanted to change anything in the traditional system began to use the word "progressive," and in time it lost any specific meaning" (online). It is interesting that Gribble (2012) raises the challenge of too many people using the word 'progressive' for anything other than traditional education as it mirrors my own dilemmas with definition of terms. I argue that there are misunderstandings that can arise from grouping 'approaches' together that are only similar in the way that they are different from traditional education. This confusion can be seen in Gribble's (2012) website where he begins "Progressive or democratic education." By using 'or,' Gribble (2012) suggests that they both are the same. Therefore, I argue that using the term 'educating differently' is beneficial as it covers all of these approaches that are different to traditional education. This is important as I recognise there can be confusion between many places that self-label as Progressive Education and those that self-label as democratic as they can have a different approach and it would be contradictory to be clumped together.

This does not mean I am ignoring the emancipatory roots of Progressive Education, as many progressive schools that I visited, as well as the literature (see Bruce, 2013; Little, 2013), report on the influence of democracy in progressive schools, particularly through including opportunities for student voice such as school councils and the student's being involved in hiring of staff. However, Hecht (2010) argues that democratic schools take this understanding of democracy further because they "realised that democracy was a way of life, a way in whose framework we had chosen to live" (Hecht, 2010, p. 41) which links back to the aims of Dewey (1966). Hecht (2010) explains that it was after the formation of the International Democratic Education Conferences (in 1997) that:

> Many schools changed their definition. Schools which had formerly defined themselves as "open" or "alternative" [or progressive] changed their names, adopting the democratic viewpoint. Changing their names was significant, because language can determine new content and ways of thinking. The use of the concept "democratic education" enabled a clearer framework of thinking about the structure and management of a school. (Hecht, 2010, p. 328)

In my journey 'Searching for the Ideal School' these issues that arose around the use of the word 'democracy' began to fascinate me and, following Waks

(2013), I too began to think about what vision of democracy is suitable for the 'global network era'? This drew me to visit as many schools that self-label as democratic as possible, particularly in the UK and then as I travelled around the world.

3   Alys the School Tourist: My First Democratic School Visit

Questions were already burning in my head.
If children could choose would they actually go to lessons?
What was the meeting like?
What would it be like to teach here?

We were shown around by two older students who seemed so content to attend this school, confident with the visitors, describing the fun games they played as a whole school, the subjects they loved and an aura of being happy now and ready for the world. They showed us the accommo-dation areas and classroom space for the under tens, the 10–13s and then where the older students could have lessons in specific subject class-rooms as well as access to a recording studio, technology/common room and a sunny art room. They explained that students could sign up for classes, but the key element throughout the school was that each child gets to continually choose how they spend their time. It is optional to attend lessons. Teachers are also available for one on one work. We asked our guides if they went to lessons. One who started the school at 11 said for the first couple of years he began going to lessons and then he didn't. After a couple of years he realised he really liked Maths and, inspired to learn, began to go to lessons and has already done several GCSEs (exams taken at 16 in England and Wales). The other explained how when they arrived at 9 that to begin with they felt a little bored until they began to realise all the things they could choose to do with their time. As we toured around, the younger children seemed busy in their outdoor play and in their chess games. Someone asked if children had to get up but it was explained that everyone needs to get up except Sundays and they could stay in their rooms but there was rule 'no screens before 3' so they couldn't be spending their day gaming, but no-one would stop them draw-ing or reading or whatever else they wanted to be doing in their rooms.

At the question and answer session one teacher described the current UK system as having an, 'Obsessive compulsive curriculum disorder' and how here they were honest with how many GCSEs really were needed for

FIGURE 35
Sign in the carpark at Summerhill, Beware
Children Playing, October 2013

college, 4 rather than 10 which many students in the UK take. They aimed to create a place where students could understand and be comfortable with themselves emotionally, were able to learn, were in an environment without fear of failure and being able to understand and to live with others, and academically go into any vein that suits them.

Wow what a radical school. Still going after over 90 years. So where do I fit with this approach? This is the first time I have visited a truly democratic school. I was really interested to hear about the younger children and how many of them really just played and it made me question Primary education with its set curriculum and made me wonder about not just pushing the importance of play for only under 7s but under 10s or, actually, all children.

I am now even more fascinated by Democratic Education and keen to observe and learn more about other approaches in different settings and with different ages. (Mendus, Avoiding obsessive compulsive curriculum disorder Blogpost [Hereford, November 3, 2013])

4   Alys the Educator: What Is Democratic Education?

Summerhill school in Suffolk, UK has been described as the oldest child democracy in the world, fulfilling Dewey's (1966) aim for democracy as being more than an approach to government, it is also a way of living. A.S. Neill, the founder of Summerhill, defined the school in 1960 as:

> Summerhill today is essentially what it was when founded in 1921. Self-government for the pupils and staff, freedom to go to lessons or stay away, freedom to play for days or weeks or years if necessary, freedom

from any indoctrination whether religious or moral or political, freedom
from character moulding. (Neill, 1960, p. 9)

Others inspired by Neill's work (such as Greenberg, 1995; Hecht, 2010) established their own schools based on similar democratic ideals from Dewey (1966)
but with a slightly different focus to each other. It is interesting to recognise that
both Hecht and Greenberg performed their own School Tourism. The impact
of the School Tourism can be seen in practice in the Democratic School of Hed-
era, Israel (see Hecht, 2010). For example, one influence was after Hecht visited
Summerhill he was aware of the importance for him to work with parents and
decided to create a day school (contradictory to A.S. Neill's ideas of a boarding
school). Another influence for Hecht was deciding to introduce a school meeting. Then after his visit to Greenberg's Sudbury Valley School, when Hecht's
own school was in its third year, Hecht decided to get rid of classes altogether.
The focus of Hecht's schools in Israel are on education towards human respect
and dignity... clarity and transparency. Hecht argues that:

> The democratic process seeks to release the child from those 80% of
> subjects apparently important to life (whose?), and to enable students to
> acquire learning tools which will help them to obtain any knowledge that
> is important to them. (Hecht, 2010, p. 166)

Greenberg established the Sudbury Valley School in the USA in 1968 and the
Sudbury 'method' of Democratic Education has spread around the world, with
over forty schools in twelve countries. Gray (2015) describes what makes a Sudbury Valley School:

> The basic premise of the school's educational philosophy is that each
> person is responsible for his or her own education. The school establishes
> no curriculum, gives no tests, and does not rank or in other ways evaluate
> the students. (Gray, 2015, p. 90)

From my observations in Democratic schools, I have seen that students need
to be 'certified,' to show competency to use expensive/potentially dangerous
equipment – computers, kitchens, woodworking tools. If they want a diploma
from the school, they must prepare and defend why they are ready to graduate
to the whole school and key people from the school and wider community.

> I tried so hard to visit Sudbury Valley School in Massachusetts, first in 2013
> and again in 2017, trying to get access through all my contacts I had gained

through my School Tourism, but to no avail. I did receive a generic email saying, 'no visitors allowed.' In May 2017 whilst staying with a friend near the school we did a drive by in the pouring rain and looked in from the outside – it could easily be argued that I was becoming a School tourist addict... I managed to organise a visit for the Tallgrass Sudbury School in Chicago in May 2017, so my stories included later in this section come from that visit. Although it is not the 'original' school, it was built using the framework from the original as they have franchised a handbook (Greenberg & Sadofsky, 2008) to set up and run similar Sudbury Model Schools. I have always puzzled over this idea of 'franchised democratic schools' and saw an analogy with the joke of an 'anarchists club.' However, this 'How to set up a Sudbury democratic school' could be the reason why this approach has spread quickly around the world and in some places (explained later in this section) becomes the dominant model and understanding of what it is to be a democratic school. (Mendus, Journalling on the frustration of Sudbury School Tourism [Uphall, Scotland, May 2017])

FIGURE 36   Alys the School Tourist standing in the rain outside Sudbury School, MA, USA, May 2017 (photo by Barbara Whitesides)

5   **Alys the School Tourist: Different Places That Call Themselves Democratic...**

5.1   *Vignette 17: Tallgrass Sudbury School, Chicago, May 2017*
The motto of the school, "because life is not standardised," made me smile as I walked up the stairs, which displayed lots of art-work and felt welcoming.

FIGURE 37   Tallgrass Sudbury School motto, Chicago, May 2017

The room was light and airy and had a large table with a couple of young people and one staff member chatting about key questions which one young person was reading aloud. I sat down and listened. I looked around the room and saw a student at the signing in table. All students must attend school for five hours a day, for five days a week with a loose sign in time between 9–11 am. I arrived about 9:30am when only a few had arrived and watched the rest of the students straggle in until just after 11. They can go off-site but they must be back for 3pm cleaning chores as there are no school caretakers. I was interested in the off-site regulations – ranging from Zone 0–4. Two younger girls appeared with a bag of sweets and announced they were off to their secret hideout (which one of the Staff members had recently been allowed to visit). They signed out and went off to their place. It was explained to me that they had recently been allowed into the next Zone, which meant that they were in the local area beyond the school 'grounds.'

> *The 'adult' in me watched them go off with a bag of sweets on their own into the neighbourhood. I was not sure if I was delighted at this real freedom or petrified for their teeth or safety! I felt honoured to see how the Sudbury approach works with younger students as I had never seen such freedom being allowed in a 'school' before.*

Most of the students seem to be busy with something – gaming, chatting, phones, drawing, playing in the big room, or going off-site on adventures. One seemed a bit lost, so I asked what he was up to and he explained he was a bit bored as he had forgotten his tablet. Although I had been observing this child during the morning, once they ran through with a water gun and another time I went into the large room and they had been playing a creative game and there were building materials all over the space.

I left around 1pm, happy to feel that I had really embodied a Sudbury school and how different it felt to many of the other democratic schools that I had visited. I think this was down to the role of the adult, it felt more like a Youth Worker than that of a teacher, and the freedom to go off site for even the youngest students.

6 Alys the Educator: What Makes These Democratic Schools Different from Other Schools 'Educating Differently'?

Although these democratic schools, similar to the progressive schools, are child-centred they take a further step. As Neill (1960) explains, a child should live their own life, not what parent or educator wants, to prevent creating a generation of robots. Neill's argument is supported by others who argue that forced guidance is destructive to children (Greenberg, 2014) and that teenagers are as competent as adults (Epstein, 2007). Hartkamp continues further to ask, "How are children supposed to learn to participate in a democracy if they grow up in a dictatorial environment from their fourth until their eighteenth year?" (Hartkamp, 2015, p. 67).

> I am troubled by Hartkamp's (2015) harsh description of traditional schooling when from my observation I have seen dictatorial elements in Democratic schools. Democratic education may insist it is governed by freedom and lack of structure, but there are many rules for which a student or adult is punished if they break them. (Mendus, Journalling on Democratic Schools [Bassenthwaite, Cumbria, June, 2016])

Gray (2009, 2016) draws on research of children in hunter-gatherer communities to argue that children have the ability to educate themselves. Sudbury Valley School, he explains, uses this approach in their school, even though "it's called a 'school,' but it doesn't provide 'schooling'" (2016, p. 52). The challenge of terms such as school and schooling are discussed in Chapter 3.

> Fundamentally, Sudbury Valley is a democratic community in which young people pursue their own interests. The students, who range in age from 4 to about 18, are continuously free to do what they want, as long as they don't break any of the school rules. The rules, which are created democratically by students and staff at the weekly School Meeting, have nothing to do with learning [although I disagree with this as the rules can have an impact on learning choices]; they have to do with keeping peace and order and are enforced by a judicial system modelled after that of our larger society. The school operates on a per-student budget less than half that of the surrounding public schools, and it accepts essentially all students whose parents agree to enrol them. So, this is not elite education. (Gray, 2016, p. 52)

A key aspect of Democratic Education is that it aims to not be coercive (children are not made to do something that they do not agree with). However, it is argued that learning still occurs; it just does not fit the 'traditional' knowledge-based conception of learning (Holzman,1997). Neill argues that learning should come but "after play... And learning should not be deliberately seasoned with play to make it palatable" (1960, p. 38). Whereas Hecht argues that "Play is learning" (Hecht, 2010, p. 67) and Greenberg (1995) separates 'play and talk' as what children and adolescents want to do with their time. Montessori Education (explored in Chapter 8) has been critiqued by Neill because it is "a system of directed play, [it] is an artificial way of making the child learn by doing. It has nothing creative about it" (Neill, 1960, p. 37). Gray (2015) also argues that Democratic Education is fundamentally different to Montessori as, even though Montessori uses more natural approaches to learning than traditional schools, the teachers are still in charge.

Another aspect which makes democratic schools different is that they do not follow Piaget's (1972) idea of child-development, that particular subjects or formal learning needs to begin at a set age. Greenberg (1987) argues that mixed ages are democratic education's secret weapon. It has been argued that single-age classes are an artefact of modern times that have no educational value (Gray & Feldman, 2004; Hecht, 2010). Following Hecht (2010), I too disagree with Piaget's strict ideals that cognitive skills grow in one-year increments:

> The claim that cognitive skills grow in one-year spurts, at a uniform pace for all of the same age, is not grounded in any research. In fact, the division into grades is merely a simple organizational tradition. Why aren't the children divided by two-year groups – or half year groups? There is no real reason. (Hecht, 2010, p. 182)

These questions that Hecht raises are very important when trying to trouble the traditional educational assumptions and practices. It was the idea of mixed-age learning that drew me to investigate Democratic Education further as it was one of the challenges that arose for me with Steiner Waldorf education, which has similar single-age classes based on a curriculum that presumes similar uniform yearly growth.

Hecht (2010) argues that the reason Democratic Education works is due to 'pluralistic learning.' Pluralistic learning argues that curriculum designed by different countries can be understood as a tiny square within an entire world of knowledge. This makes it easy to visualise how much potential knowledge is capped and controlled by using a curriculum. However, Hecht (2010) argues that the aim of Democratic Education is to encourage people to step outside the square. Therefore, this stepping out of the square creates 'pluralistic learning,' where students are in charge of their own learning, but also realise that they live in a society where everybody has their own talents and that working together to share these different skills is the way to create a winning team and a democratic culture (Hecht, 2010).

> I realise that any approach (even those that are 'educating differently') that imposes a curriculum is creating its own 'square,' even if that is a different or bigger square to one created by state education or for high-stakes tests, which in turn limits the possibility of knowledge and the growth of pluralistic learning. Steiner Waldorf is another curriculum, so another square. (Mendus, Journalling Stanmer Park [Brighton, August 2017])

7   Alys the Educator: What Is the Role of the Teacher in Democratic Education?

In democratic schools the adults are not called teachers, their role is re-envisioned as a facilitator or mentor. In Sudbury Valley Schools the adults are called 'staff members.' Gray (2015) explains this is because, "students learn more from one another, and from their own play and exploration, than they do from the adult school members" (p. 90). It should also be noted that staff members are seen as equal to the students so must abide by the same rules as students and are tried in the same way if they break a rule. As Gray states "Nobody is above the law" (2015, p. 90). For example, if a student is disrespectful to an adult they are reprimanded by the community, not for being rude to an adult per se, but for being rude to another community member and therefore breaking a rule on respect.

Throughout my journey of 'Searching for the Ideal School' I have been fascinated by pedagogy, particularly the 'how' to teach a lesson. I think this is why
I was first drawn to Progressive Education after Steiner Waldorf, as the 'how'
is a key focus. As a School Tourist visiting democratic schools, I was surprised
that once a child chose to attend a lesson then the teaching that I observed
was mostly of a traditional text-book based or didactic style. This was very different from the new pedagogical approaches seen in progressive schools such
as including different learning styles (Kolb, 1984) and multiple intelligences
(Gardner, 1983) or project-based learning (see Chapter 7). However, my experiences are similar to Holzman's description of their observations at Sudbury
Valley School in which they describe the Sudbury method as a "rejection or
negation of pedagogy [more] than a positive creation of a new educational
method" (Holzman, 1997, p. 101). Further reading shows that Neill himself did
not actually value creative pedagogy, arguing that:

> We have no new methods of teaching, because we do not consider that
> teaching in itself matters very much. Whether a school has or has not a
> special method for teaching long division is of no significance, for long
> division is of no importance except for the child who wants to learn it.
> And the child who wants to learn long division will learn it no matter how
> it is taught. (Neill, 1960, p. 21)

However, Hecht (2010) argues that the 'learning experience' is different from
traditional education as the class is not focussed on if a new concept is going
to be in a test or if they will be set an assignment on something, but now coming from curiosity and interest. It is interesting to note that some democratic
schools that I visited (particularly in the UK) were very focussed on high-stakes
tests and the classes may have had aspects of "curiosity and interest" but were
mostly concentrated on how to pass the exam. In contrast, at De Ruimte democratic school in the Netherlands, although the classroom set up could be seen
to look like 'school,' some of the staff members were also interested in pedagogy which this piece of journalling from my school visit shows.

> One of the approaches of the younger years was connected to some
> research by the staff members into the time it can really take to learn.
> The 6–12 year olds Maths curriculum, for example, is possible for some in
> three months, not over 6 years. The children know this, so when they are
> ready to learn maths they can agree to a three month, three times a week
> with homework/work to do between classes programme to cover all the
> maths in the curriculum and then choose to stop or to keep going with

FIGURE 38   A small classroom in a democratic school, Netherlands, June 2017

extension work or move to a higher level. This concept interested me as I felt it is something that is worth reflecting on for mainstream education – if it is possible to do 6 years' work in three months then if schools could trust the children to decide when they are ready it would not need to be forced/coerced upon them when they are not ready or interested. (Mendus, Journalling from visit to De Ruimte, Netherlands June 2017 [Oslo, Norway, June 2017])

I have never taught in a democratic school and when I first visited one in 2013, I was unsure if I ever would be able to work at one. For me, planning creative lessons was what I really loved about being a teacher. The idea of not knowing how many students would turn up had really annoyed me when I ran a home-education support group. With hindsight, I see myself 'schooled' as a teacher, able to talk-the-talk and teach from the government stated script.

I was fascinated to visit my friend who I had trained to be a teacher with and who had worked in the same school for 12 years and realised I was observing outstanding government teaching following a script very similar to one that we were trained in. I realised that I could also teach like this but that mainstream teaching would not negate the feeling in my stomach that it was not the way to educate.

I would never happily be a 'traditional' teacher again. I knew I could also teach 'progressively,' meeting different learning styles and using multiple approaches including group and project-based learning to meet the students, but could I really let go of control of 'my' classroom? Gribble (personal communication, 2015) explained to me that often in democratic schools the new staff needed to be 'deschooled' (Illich, 1970) themselves before they could become effective staff in this new environment. (Mendus, Journalling – Alys though the ideal school looking glass [Uphall, Scotland, November 2016])

8   Alys the Theorist: Democracy-in-Action?

Neill (1960) explains that at Summerhill not everything is covered by the governance of the students as the menu, bills, administration and hiring of teachers is organised by the principal (A.S. Neill himself, then his daughter Zoe Readhead and now more often by her son, Henry Readhead).

> The Neill-Readhead dynasty at Summerhill school has concerned me as I can see tradition preventing true democracy in action. (Mendus, Journalling about Democratic Education [Finland, June 2016])

> I heard criticisms of Summerhill at the International Democratic Education Conference (in Finland in 2016) by Sudbury enthusiasts for not really being democratic because at Sudbury schools self-governance takes a further step to include everybody, as staff and children are all equal.
> My gut feelings help me understand my positionality, further questioning the role of the adult in learning. I disagree with the Sudbury 'democratic' model that children, even as young as 4, are equal to adults. I feel there is a role of adults in children's learning and growing to become adults themselves, but not the current didactic teaching role that I see in many schools that I visit.
> One particular skill I think that adults can share is how to communicate effectively and compassionately. I feel this needs to be modelled by people with experience of this approach, which could be older children/ teenagers and adults. I saw this effectively modelled in a team-work skills session at Koonwarra Village school in Victoria, Australia in February 2016 (Mendus, 2016b) and Chapter 9. (Mendus, Journalling on Democratic Education [Cornwall, September 2016])

FIGURE 39
Sign from the wall at a democratic school,
New York, May 2017

9 **Alys the School Tourist: Observation of Democratic School Meetings**

One of the defining factors of democratic schools is the hosting of whole school meetings (Neill, 1960) to decide on all aspects of the school life. I have had the opportunity to observe several of these in different settings. Vignette's 18 and 19 share my observations, feelings and reactions from being present at two different school's meetings.

9.1 *Vignette 18: School Meeting 1*

> *A boy of about ten stands up and addresses the meeting,*
> *"I am bringing up Billy as he keeps banging the bedroom door."*
> *The Chair, taking all incidents seriously, replies*
> *"Have you asked him to stop?"*
> *"Yes, loads of times but he keeps doing it. I want him to be fined."*
> *"Billy, is this true?" asks the Chair.*
> *Billy hides under the table, looking uncomfortable, but refrains from speaking.*
> *Someone else raises his hand and, looking at Billy, says*
> *"I've heard him slam the door too. I think he should be fined."*
> *The Chair looks back at the boy making the complaint.*
> *"What do you think? A jobs fine or money fine?"*
> *The first boy looks a bit uncomfortable himself now and mumbles*
> *"Money fine, It's not that big a deal..."*
> *"Oh, but it must be, you brought it up here... Anyone have anything else to add??*

Right, let's have a vote. Who agrees with 50p off Billy's pocket money?"
Hands are slowly raised around the room.
"Well, that settles it," the Chair concludes.
"50p fine for Billy... what's next on the agenda?"

I am sitting here shocked at what looks to me like the punitive aspects of 'behaviourism' in action in front of my eyes and that no one in the audience seems at all upset – a radical school 'normalised' to behaviourism? (Mendus, An observation of a meeting at a UK democratic school [Cumbria, October 2013])

Stronach and Piper's (2009) research into whole-school meetings at Summerhill recognised the use of sanctions and a deeply complex web of interrelations. They argue:

Summerhill school has invisible boundaries, powerful inspections, binding agreements, and redemptive rituals, as well as a set of public punishments that prompt and enact acceptable ways to live together. These all act as an "outside-in" pressure that frames and disciplines interactions while developing identities and relationships, yet always with the possibility of change or resistance. (Stronach & Piper, 2009, p. 54)

Neill, however, does not see the meeting as using rewards and punishments but one that differentiates between 'freedom' and 'licence,' arguing that "in the disciplined home, the children have no rights. In the spoiled home, they have all the rights. The proper home is one in which children and adults have equal rights. And the same applies to school" (1960, p. 105). Neill (1960) argues that punishment is morality and through having set rules (Stronach and Piper recorded 174 laws at Summerhill in 2005) and the school meeting to sort out misdemeanours then this is not punishment.

9.2 Vignette 19: School Meeting 2

At a different democratic school, I observe an interesting meeting which has a special focus to decide if an excluded boy can return to the school or must be permanently expelled. The boy turned up at the meeting and asked the meeting if he could return to school one day a week to go to his technology classes as he got on well with the teacher. The accused then left the room whilst the discussion began.

It seemed that those students who shouted the loudest got to control and manipulate the discussion. A few adults spoke up, saying that his behaviour had been unacceptable and that he was not the sort of student that the school wanted and that they would only be able to support his return if he could agree to obeying school rules and accept if he broke one again then he must leave. And one girl did speak up trying to get those who had been bullied to voice their opinions but, not surprisingly to me as an observer, they did not. However, I realise that it is hard to stand up and speak out against someone who has bullied you or made you uncomfortable, especially when there are louder and more popular voices.

The vote passed that he could return one day a week. At lunch there were whispers about those who had been bullied being devastated that he would return and there were grunts of complaints amongst the adults.

> I am puzzled, trying to step away from my traditional hierarchical view of school procedures and thinking about the long-term effects of expelling children from school and how some of the children saw potential in their peer. However, I have concerns for the children who were bullied. By allowing this student to return, their safety was overlooked and not protected by the adults who just seemed to support this student led approach to decision making, even if they disagreed with the outcome. (Mendus, An observation of a meeting at a UK democratic school, December 2014 [Cumbria, December 2014])

I am still concerned when writing this book about essential issues of child protection and wellbeing which seemed to be overlooked by the adults in this example. I argue that there needs to be a line drawn between autonomy and freedom with safety of the whole school community and that it is the role of the adults to ensure all students are safe when they attend school.

It is also the level of surveillance noted by Stronach and Piper (2009) at Summerhill and at Sudbury schools that caused me concern. When speaking to a staff member at a Sudbury school in the USA the staff member mentioned that students do say, "I will bring you up" if someone has obviously broken an agreed rule – such as tidying up. However, it is not deemed necessary to point out to someone that they have broken a rule, it is also perfectly ok to write the infringement on a piece of paper and put it into the file/box for the Judicial Council to work with the following day. The concept that everybody is equal and everybody is able to be 'brought up' for breaking a rule sent shivers running down my spine. I was not sure if I could live, let alone work, in such an environment. However, I do live in a country with a long list of laws with serious penalties if I break one. Yet, I know if I do choose to break (a minor) one I can do it without getting into trouble, whereas in a small school community I do not think there would be anywhere to hide. Thinking with Klaus (2016) who used to teach at Summerhill:

Intimacy is an interesting issue in regards to Summerhill. There are not many private spaces, for pupils or staff, and so one is constantly implicated in everybody else's daily life. (Klaus, 2016, p. 35)

I am also worried that I would not agree with all of the rules anyway, so I would feel they are arbitrary – what sort of 'adult' would I be in that community who does not support many of the rules agreed by the community? I began to realise that this particular method of democracy of rules, meeting and fining at Summerhill and again (although slightly different) in Sudbury school was not my preferred understanding of democracy. (Mendus, Journalling about democracy [Brighton, August 2017])

Concluding this section, I reiterate that I am still left wondering about the role of safeguarding and where the role of the adult lies and can self-governance in this approach keep every child safe? As one of the student's reviewing this chapter for me asked, "What do they do to ensure a child is not ganged up on by their peers, falsely accused, or more?"

10 Alys the School Tourist: A Discussion with an Experienced Democratic Educator

Alys:	What do you think is the aim of Democratic Education?
Democratic educator:	The aim is not to coerce children into learning a set thing like they do in Montessori, where there is always a set outcome to the task. I think that coerced learning can be even more dangerous than explicit didactic teaching.
Alys:	I have just returned from the International Democratic Education Conference in Finland (2016) and I have begun to realise that there are many different versions of what a democratic school is. For example, the differences between Sudbury and Summerhill... Some Sudbury people I heard argue that Summerhill is not a democratic school but one that uses democratic approaches... And then I get stuck on all the rules at both of them!
Democratic educator:	That is an interesting question. From my experience at Summerhill, I actually told the new teachers to look at all the rules and only be a stickler to a particular rule if it really meant something to you – for example

	stopping the children from hanging out on the fire escape is only worth bringing up at a meeting if it makes you feel unsafe seeing children there…
Alys:	Now that is an interesting approach which I hadn't thought about before. But what about those people who are pedants??
Democratic educator:	Well, the culture is designed to prevent people from being like that.
Alys:	Really, how?
Democratic educator:	Well, if someone keeps bringing people up for breaking the slightest rule then they become unpopular and eventually they stop.

11   Alys the Guide: Reflections

I am wondering now about the popularity contest that is going on here and wonder about the point of rules that are not strictly adhered to? For example, in the example above of the fire escape different people will have different levels of risk and safety, therefore so much is left to the personal interpretation. How 'fair' is that within such a 'democratic' system??

> I have had challenges with some democratic school models as their defi-
> nition of 'democratic' creates a school where although all students and
> adults have a voice, they are residing within an environment of rules. In
> these schools I have seen behaviourism being enacted in the sanctions
> (such as the fine in the poem in Vignette 18) and in my opinion it is
> because the students have not come across other models of communi-
> cating, so were repeating cultural norms. However, as the school was run
> by choosing to attend classes or not it would be difficult to make a change
> if the young people did not want to attend sessions on new methods of
> communication. (Mendus, Journalling on Democratic Education [Corn-
> wall, September 2016])

12   Alys the School Tourist: Gems from Democratic Schools

Through performing School Tourism, I have (by August 2017) visited 4 democratic schools in the UK, 2 in Australia, 3 in the USA and 1 in the Netherlands.

FIGURE 40
Art classroom,
Netherlands, June 2017

This chapter has explored key approaches of Democratic Education. However, as I visit more schools, particularly those choosing not to follow the dominant Summerhill or Sudbury tradition, I keep getting glimpses into different understandings of what 'democracy' means to each democratic school. I offer two examples here that I see as 'gems' for new understandings of Democratic Education. School 1 in Vignette 20 from the Netherlands uses sociocracy, a different method of self-governance and School 2 in Vignette 21 from New York, USA really troubles Social Justice in action.

12.1 *Vignette 20: De Ruimte, Netherlands*

Law in the Netherlands means that school is compulsory and home education is illegal. Although they are able to run a democratic school, it has not been an easy experience to convince the government that their approaches are justified. An impact of this law is that students must attend school for a certain number of hours each week and they must turn up before 10am unless they phone school in advance. De Ruimte also has its own understanding of what is democratic education and they aim to create a community built around consent rather than consensus (the method used in Sudbury schools and Summerhill). Following St. Pierre (2016), I recognise that consensus approaches can be connected to power and that often those who disagree with what is happening are silenced, I am therefore fascinated to learn about a democratic school using a consent based approach and hope that this includes all voices.

We spent time in the daily meeting room where a core group of students and a staff member meet each day to discuss any issues that have arisen. There are about 23 different meeting groups that students can choose to be part of,

FIGURE 41   Outdoor space at De Ruimte, Netherlands, June 2017

plus the weekly whole school meeting. I was interested to hear that actually not that many students, particularly not younger students, attend the weekly meeting and that it is mostly the adults. When I asked why, I learnt that as students could be part of a small meeting group that was more relevant to them, they felt that their voice was already being heard and that they would only come if it was an important subject. For example, there are meeting groups for money, hiring staff, new students, keeping the internet and computers in order, looking after the animals, the time table, caring for the environment, fundraising and the school shop (where they can earn some money), computer gaming... and then each age group has a weekly meeting as well. All meetings have agendas so people know what is going on and can pick and choose which sections of the meeting they attend.

Consent means that all people involved in the meeting agree to the final outcome. It is not about a vote which could lead to 6 people voting for something and 4 against but it would still happen as the greater number had voted for it, even if it could affect the lives of the other 4. With consent, all would accept and be happy with the outcome. This does mean that meetings take a long time and the student who showed us round admitted that it can be a bit frustrating sometimes. Our guide also told us that they had joined the school because they had been bullied at their previous (regular state) school and that bullying is less likely to happen at De Ruimte as issues are recognised and talked about. However, due to consent approaches it was interesting to hear about how the original philosophy is at risk of being changed. For example, for a while there was a teacher keen to have more Sudbury-style approaches in the school and he managed to convince a group of students to run a Judicial Council (JC), as well as the daily meetings. The staff member and group of students involved in this approach have now moved on from De Ruimte, but it seemed to have caused some challenges in identity over the last few years.

> I left wondering more about the concept of freedom. The stories that were shared during this school visit made me aware that even a Democratic school could get stuck in a rut and that the approaches were always being challenged, especially through the power of popularity. For example, if someone has a loud and pervasive voice then they can change the future of the school. It also made me think about having some set foundations on which the school was built on and I felt that consent rather than consensus was one of them and felt sad that this strain had been on the community for 3 years and there had not been a chance to say – NO! We are a consent school, if you want consensus you are welcome to go elsewhere. It also made me more wary about the Sudbury model as it rises to become a dominant force in the Democratic Education movement and is giving the impression that Sudbury is the 'only' way to educate democratically, a sentiment with which I disagree. (Mendus, Journalling about De Ruimte [Oslo, Norway, June 2017])

It is important to note that the consent approach has spread within the Netherlands and there are now four schools using this approach. Two filmmakers have made a movie on sociocratic schools in the Netherlands called the 'School Circles: Every voice matters' (Shread & Osorio, 2019) and it will be interesting to watch the effect this has on the culture of other schools (including consensus based democratic schools).

12.2   Vignette 21: Embodied Social Justice in Action, New York

The walls were decorated with students' work and with signs reminding students of their active participation in their school, for example – "We need to hear you" and "Do you want someone else to call the meeting for you?" or "Anyone can call a meeting at any time." However, although it was possible to call a meeting at any time, when we asked it was quite rare except for one particular semester when one student was finding the school challenging. There are also mediation guidelines on the walls suggesting using these approaches to solve problems rather than directly going to a School Meeting.

One of the major themes of the school is Social Justice. Outside the upper elementary classrooms was a display about 'Charlie and the Chocolate Factory.' The children had written their reflections on the book – one wrote "We noticed

FIGURE 42
Classroom in a democratic
school, New York, USA, May 2017

there were not any black people and the Oompa Loompas ideas seemed racist because they are orange and dancing around and singing..." Another wrote "We noticed that the Oompa Loompas reminded me of slaves because they had to work and work and work and they were not being paid fairly..." Alongside the display were definitions of key social justice terms – poverty, privilege and entitlement. Inside this classroom was a vocabulary sheet that showed evidence from a discussion about gender and around the classroom was an alphabet of inclusive language. In another classroom there was a poster display on Marches, Boycotts and Rallies and in another, signs for 'LGBTQ+ allies group' for students 12 and up. There was also signs for workshops for White Parents on 'The Role of White [Name of School] Parents in Anti-Racist Work.'

> What impressed me about this place was how Social Justice was a key framing of the identity of the school and from observing some of the teaching and the arrangement of the day I think that this came initially from the adults working in the school, however it seemed to be authentic and to have permeated to the students as well. I felt this was a gem as it showed a way that adults could have a formative influence on a democratic learning environment. (Mendus, Journalling from New York [Champaign-Urbana, Illinois, USA, May 2017])

13   Alys the Edge-dweller: Democratic Education and the 'Ideal School'

Hecht (2010), and Gray (2015), argue that Democratic Education is the education of choice for the future. Vignette 22 below shares an experience from Alys the edge-dweller at the International Democratic Education Conference in Finland in 2016 where, when running a workshop on the 'Ideal School,' many people voiced opinions that they had already found it with Democratic Education.

13.1 Vignette 22: "Where Was the Singing?" My Surprise at Not Feeling 'at Home' at the International Democratic Education Conference!

After attending the International Democratic Education Conference (IDEC) in Finland in June 2016 I was fascinated by my strong reaction to Sudbury. With reflection, I see a connection between the 'evangelical' Sudbury supporters and the dogmas that Wenger (2010) argues can happen when "a community becomes too much of a community, too strongly identified with itself, prone to groupthink, closed, or inbred…" (p. 10). Wenger's (2010) words mirror my inner frustration that I felt that the Sudbury-ites were blinded by their view that Sudbury is the answer.

When I led my session on "What is the 'Ideal School?'" I saw that some of my groups were controlled by people using the 'Sudbury' method of talking, which is very different from usual group work discussion. In a Sudbury meeting, there is a chair and each person raises their hand if they wish to speak and their name is put on a list. The discussion follows those who are on the list rather than the natural flow of conversation as people must wait their turn to speak. I have observed this in a large meeting and although it felt slightly disjointed, I could see it as a method that allowed all people to have a voice. However, in a group of 7/8 people sitting around a table it was painful to watch as it became dictated by the person who had decided they were the chair of the group rather than a free-flow of voices and ideas about the topic of the ideal school.

> When a college student read this section of this chapter in October 2020 they responded with an important critique that using this discussion approach, "seems really entitled that in a Democratic Educational setting that someone gets an almost tyrannical position" and I agree there is certain irony in a democratic approach becoming dogmatic. (Mendus, Journalling on Democratic Education [Gubbi Gubbi Country, November 2020])

Another group having a more 'traditional' group discussion had many opposing views, which I had hoped, but at the same time had one person write 'Sudbury' on their sheet as they felt that was the answer. Another person came in and once hearing what the session was about smiled at me and told me their school was the 'Ideal School' and headed out the door. The joy of an open space session meant that the other 'Sudbury' people who chose to stay in the room chose to be there and offer their input into the group – I wonder if they were either there to listen to what others had to say on the ideal school, or as "missionaries" of Sudbury?

The truth is I felt lonely at IDEC at times, surprised that the people I had hoped to connect with were somehow too busy with meetings, or energetically realised quite quickly that I wasn't a Sudbury-ite after all. Max Hope, my PhD supervisor who also attended the conference, made a comment that I was at home here – maybe more so than the British Educational Research Association conference in 2014 with its traditional papers about mainstream education. But without the daily singing and crafts of a Steiner conference I was still a bit lost and not fully 'at home.'

In Israel, Hecht (2010) has worked hard to democratise public education. The International Democratic Education Conference was held in Israel in 2017 and if I had attended I would have had the opportunity to visit state funded democratic schools (as so far all that I have visited are privately funded). However, although I chose not to attend because of the political situation. I am aware that by not physically visiting these schools I do have 'gaps' of embodied School Tourism experiences within this book.

Hecht suggests that Democratic Education for all is not "an unattainable utopia" (2010, p. 319) but common sense for a democratic country to follow the approaches of Democratic Education. Gray (2015) supports this further claiming:

> I predict that fifty years from now, if not sooner, the Sudbury Valley model will be featured in every standard textbook of education and will be adopted, with variation, by many if not all public school systems. In fifty years, I predict, educators will see today's approach to schooling as a barbaric relic of the past. (Gray, 2015, p. 88)

> A college student from Southwestern University, Texas read one of the drafts of this chapter in October 2020 and responded to this idea that Democratic Education is the education of the future, "This is an interesting assumption, it is definitely true that the approach to schooling will shift. Especially since COVID-19 has proved that you don't even have to attend school in person." I hope that there will be international learning from the impacts of COVID-19 on education and hope that today's schooling will be recognised as a 'barbaric relic,' but I do not think the future is the current version of Democratic Education either. (Mendus, Journalling on Democratic Education [Gubbi Gubbi Country, November 2020])

Gray (2015) and Hecht (2010) both argue for a shift in society's viewpoint. Gray sees this as relatively straight forward, "When adults see that coercive schooling isn't necessary for success in the culture, they will find it hard not to choose freedom for their kids, and the kids themselves will demand it" (2015, p. 233). In my journalling below I show my challenges with these ideas in August 2016 and later in this section my journalling from August 2017 shows how my thinking has moved again:

> And why am I back at the edge, not jumping for this evocative option of children roaming and playing in these (inter)nationwide 'Sudbury model' schools? I am aware that, like the example of Steiner Waldorf, once a system spreads there are major chances of it becoming dogmatic. But more so, it is the self-management through rules and meetings that I am unsure about, not autonomous learning. Democratic schools are still schools, still institutions and I realise that I am challenged by institutions. Maybe unschooling is the answer? (Mendus, Journalling on Democratic Education [Devon, August 2016])

14   Alys the Educator: Unschooling

Democratic home education has been called unschooling (Holt, 1967) or autonomous home education (Pattison & Thomas, 2016). Unschooling is where home-educating parents allow their children to direct their own education and is similar to Democratic Educational approaches as the parents do not give set lessons or tests but follow and support the interests of their children. Kirschner's (2008) doctoral research on unschooling families argues that parents were driven to follow their children's intrinsic motivation. So, for many families this manifests as a busy daily schedule, meeting other home educated children and giving value to learning from everyday life experiences. This follows Gray who argues that in unschooling most learning occurs incidentally when someone has a "real-life need or desire for that knowledge or skill" (Gray, 2016, p. 54).

Being aware of this idea that unschooling covers learning in all aspects of family life, it is interesting to note that Pattison and Thomas's research shows that "with home educating families... often what is being learnt and how it is being learnt cannot be identified with any degree of clarity" (2016, p. 136). It is therefore not surprising that Gray and Riley's (2013), work explains that parents in unschooling families often have to go through a "deschooling" phase in which they consciously learn to stop worrying about their children's progress and learn instead to enjoy and interact with their children as they might with anyone they love and respect.

The role of the parents to choose/allow/know about unschooling or to send their child to a democratic school arises here and Gray (2015) argues there are different types of parents with 'trustful' being the most compatible with unschooling. Gray defines trustful parenting as ones that:

> understand that today's successful adults... are assertive and independent and that children today should be so trained – "trained" not by directing them, but by allowing them to guide their own development and make their own discoveries about the world. (Gray, 2015, p. 210)

> Warning bells begin to ring for me when I read about 'trustful parents' as I often find myself in a challenging position with unschooling families – on one side thinking that this approach to learning is the future and on the other side being presented by wild and sometimes quite rude children. I remember a Forest School session I was running in 2009 one Easter time where my group of home-educated children had been making nests in the woods. We went off to have a snack and story and, magically, chocolate eggs had appeared in the nests. One child (from an unschooling family) had decided not to join the group that morning but once hearing that there were chocolate eggs had a massive tantrum and would not give up until her parent asked me to give her chocolate! This reminded me about the importance of boundaries for children and that following unschooling approaches needs to be within a held, safe environment with clear boundaries. I know of some families that have family meetings and use sociocratic approaches but total licence, in my opinion, does not make pleasant children to spend time around. (Mendus, Journalling about unschooling [Cornwall, September 2017])

Riley (2020) argues that there are three main examples of unschooling families; relaxed home schooling, unschooling and radical unschooling. Knowing about these categories has been helpful for me to understand the different home educating families that I have worked with. Relaxed home educators are families that loosely follow a set curriculum or framework and this is often because of the regulations for home education in their state or country. It is important to be aware, as Riley points out, that "Relaxed homeschooling is not school at home. Instead, relaxed homeschooling allows for the child or teen to take control of their own learning, with some focused facilitation organized by the parent" (2020, p. 54). This is different to unschooling which is total freedom and autonomy in how a young person spends their day. Riley (2020) describes the role of an unschooling parent to be similar to a librarian assisting in finding resources that are guided by the child or teen. Gray and Riley (2013) reiterate that unschooling families, "do not send their children to school, and they do not do at home the kinds of things that are done in school" (p. 7) so they are different to relaxed home educating as they do not have a curriculum, framework or assessments. Radical unschooling takes this further and applies unschooling to daily life. As Riley explains:

> In some families who engage in radical unschooling, children and teens have full autonomy over when they eat, sleep, watch television, play video games and engage in household tasks. Rather than rules, families live and learn guided by familial principals or basic ethics (2020, pp. 56–57).

Olsen (2020) argues that radical unschooling is not "unparenting," although for some it can be challenging to observe and I realise that radical unschooling was part of what I was observing in my journalling extract above.

Following Riley (2020), I see connections between unschooling and the Democratic Education movement. Riley (2020) argues that unschooling has a key role to play in educational reform, similar to Hecht (2010) and Gray (2015)'s argument that Democratic Education is the future. However, it is interesting that Riley describes Democratic Education in a physical school as a "more structured unschooling-like school environment" (2020, p. 146). This could be seen to be positioning unschooling as having greater potential to be less structured and possibly truer to the original ideals of Democratic Education as it only focusses on one family so can be much more child-led than a larger school environment. Nevertheless, both Unschooling and Democratic Education have arisen on the premise that "Life and learning do not occur in a vacuum, they occur in the context of a cultural environment, and unschooling parents [and democratic schools] help define and bring the child into contact with that environment" (Gray & Riley, 2013, p. 7).

15   Alys the Guide

I found Democratic Education even harder to position than I expected. This chapter explored my journey of observing different approaches to 'democratic,' from the original 'Summerhill' school in the UK to other versions of democratic schools and home-education projects in the UK and abroad. This included a visit to a 'Sudbury' model school, which is becoming one of the dominant approaches. This chapter explored my challenges with the Sudbury understanding of democracy (shown by examples of school meetings in different democratic schools) and then gave an example of De Ruimte in the Netherlands that is using sociocracy (an approach that reaches mutual consent rather than consensus). From my experience of Democratic Education, I realised that I resonate with Hecht's (2010) suggestion for 'pluralistic learning' and stepping outside of a government/curriculum designed 'square' of knowledge, aware that many places that I visited limit the possibilities of learning.

I also realised from this chapter that I have still not found my home and wonder if unschooling could be a future possibility as a self-designed approach to learning.

FIGURE 43
Open-plan democratic school, dress up area, New York, May 2017

16 Summary

– Democratic Education came from Progressive Education wanting to focus further on democratic approaches such as student voice.
– Key examples of Democratic Education that this chapter explores are Summerhill, Sudbury, examples from Israel, sociocracy in the Netherlands and Social Justice in New York.
– Democratic Education is different to other places educating differently as students are in charge of their days and of their learning experience. They can choose to attend a lesson or to lead their own activity in, for example, the art room, in technology, or outdoors. This means that there are often multi-age groups learning together and they have the chance to learn outside the set box of a traditional curriculum-based school.

– The democratic meeting where students and adults have equal say is used to decide upon rules, to penalise those who break rules, to discuss key issues and to make essential decisions for the whole school.
– Unschooling and autonomous home educating is where children follow their own interests at home rather than a set curriculum or learning pedagogy.

Alys and Montessori Education

1 Alys the Guide

This chapter explores Montessori as another well-known approach to 'educating differently.' I recognised that I was visiting many schools/places of learning that were combining their approaches with some Montessori elements. I explored my relationship with Montessori through the mindset of originally being a Steiner Waldorf teacher and then actively visited places using Montessori from early childhood to teens in England, Scotland and Portugal. Through the voice of a friend who is a Montessori teacher I was able to explore what it means to be a Montessori Primary teacher in practice and begin to get an idea of some of the real gems within the approach, particularly in places following very closely to Montessori's original guidance. I was left impressed by the maths resources, seeing the potential of these manipulables as a gem particularly with Primary aged children (6–12 year olds in Montessori education). However, I was still missing the imaginative play with the younger children (3–6 year olds) that I have seen in Steiner Waldorf, Progressive and Democratic schools.

2 Alys and Steiner: The View of Montessori

(My thoughts are indented and in italics throughout.)

> *"Ugh, Montessori, that is even worse than mainstream" is a comment friends and I have used in the past.*

As a person heavily embedded within the Steiner Waldorf educational approach it was easy to become dogmatic in my 'othering' of different educational approaches, particularly Montessori. Our voices (myself and close

© KONINKLIJKE BRILL NV, LEIDEN, 2022 | DOI: 10.1163/9789004506039_009

Steiner Waldorf inspired friends) were made up from fleeting visits to the local Montessori nursery or friend's reports from their children about how there isn't free play, which is seen in Steiner Waldorf or even Mainstream Early Years education.

> *My daughter, one friend told me, went and picked up the beautiful wooden blocks and began to pretend that one was a telephone, only to be redirected to putting the blocks on top of each other to build a tower. Horrified, we did not send her to that nursery.*

What my friend had observed here (I later learnt from reading more about Montessori and observing a nursery) was that the children are free to choose from a large range of 'age-appropriate' set activities that all have a learning objective that the child is encouraged to attempt and, once finished, tidy away before moving on, mostly solitarily to their next chosen activity. Montessori wrote about the 'Absorbent mind' (1949/1995), recognising that children absorb information from their environment and so the classroom is designed "where a child can learn to read, write and calculate in the same natural way as learning to walk or talk" (Wolf, 1995, p. 1) and where the hand is the chief teacher of the child.

> *"Steiner and Montessori are the same thing, right?" is a comment I would regularly hear.*

Annoyed, I would always reply they are about as different as you can get, they are just lumped together as the known-about alternatives to traditional schooling.

> *I once heard a great comparison – just imagine it is 1919, the First World War has just ended and there needs to be deep healing in Europe. Maria Montessori and Rudolf Steiner meet up to discuss education for the future of Germany and Italy.*
>
> *"What the Italian people need," Montessori said, "is order and structure, they have heart and play."*
>
> *What the German people need," Steiner replied, "is heart and play, they have order and structure."*

Creating this binary of ordered Montessori Education with its set activities in comparison to play based Steiner with it free-flow of play was not helpful to my lens of looking for the 'Ideal School' and it prevented me from possibly incorporating some of the Montessori approaches into the heavily Steiner influenced lens that I was looking out into the world through. It also prevented me from truly realising that I was already guided by aspects of Montessori Educational methods and others visible in Montessori such as emotional intelligence (Goleman, 1995) and flow (Csikszentmihalyi, 1990). One of the Montessori approaches I had used in Early Years was teaching independence as children are encouraged to put on their own coats, tie their shoes, close their buckles and to pour water or milk into a cup.

3   Alys the School Tourist – What Is Montessori Education?

According to Lillard (2019) Montessori education is "very different from, even incommensurable with the conventional school system most people know very well" (p. 958) and this has meant that for some it has become more attractive as they wanted an alternative for their children but for others it has been shunned. Maria Montessori, the founder of Montessori Education, initially trained as a doctor specialising in paediatrics before founding her first 'Children's House' for 3–7 year olds in Rome, Italy in 1907 (Marshall, 2017). Montessori developed her pedagogy based on child observation and her approaches have been copied internationally and there are many Montessori Early Childhood centres, Primary schools and some Secondary schools around the world.

> My vision of the future is no longer of people taking exams and proceeding from [one level of school to the next], but of individuals passing from one stage of independence to a higher [one], by means of their own activity [and...] will, which constitutes the inner evolution of the individual. (Montessori, 1948a, p. xv)

In the quote above Montessori (1948) argued that children pass through several stages of development and within Montessori schools this can be observed through adults providing students with a specially prepared environment from which they can engage with self-directed activities (Marshall, 2017). Therefore, the central tenet of Montessori education is the relationship between the teacher, the child and the specially prepared environment. As Lillard (2019) explains, the role of the teacher "is not to impart information, but instead to connect children to the environment where self-guided learning occurs" (p. 940). The specially prepared environment has key learning materials including manipulable objects to help children's learning of key areas and the environment is different for children of different ages. So, in Montessori Education the classrooms are set up, for example, for 3–6 year olds, 6–9 year olds and 9–12 year olds. This environment supports learning as the:

> children learn by engaging hands-on with the materials most often individually, but also in pairs or small groups, during a 3-h 'work cycle' in which they are guided by the teacher to choose their own activities. (Marshall, 2017, p. 1)

The essential part of the nature of learning in a Montessori classroom is that the children have freedom to choose what activity they are doing and where in the room. However, each activity does have a set way in which it is meant to be carried out although, as Lillard (2019) argues, there is space for different ways to explore the manipulable to get to the same end point. This is because the manipulables are designed to be self-correcting, therefore allowing students to make mistakes and only need minimal teacher support (Marshall, 2017). However, within this freedom of choice to work with an activity there are "set ways to remove them from the shelves" (Lillard, 2019, p. 953) and they must be returned to the shelf in the correct order. Another important role of the teacher is to guide students to find an activity to explore or to introduce small groups of children to new materials to keep them on track. Lillard (2019) explains that Montessori gave guidance to teachers to how to behave with students, asking them to be sensitively responsive following a secure-attachment parenting approach and at the same time following an aspect of authoritative parenting by giving children autonomy within set boundaries. This freedom within set boundaries is what has been critiqued earlier in this book by key proponents of democratic education (Gray, 2015; Neill, 1960).

Another link between Montessori Education and the key themes of this book and my journey searching for the Ideal School is that in the Montessori classroom there is no system of extrinsic rewards or punishments. For example, there are no grades in the Montessori school and teachers are advised not to praise or openly evaluate children (Lillard, 2019, p. 950). I see this conscious lack of extrinsic rewards as a gem. For example, as Marshall (2017) argues, the goal of Montessori education is to "allow the child's optimal development (intellectual, physical, emotional and social) to unfold" (p. 1) rather than constrain it within set grading systems. Lillard (2019) argues that the central aspect of Montessori education is self-determination through free choice which is not directed by any extrinsic rewards. Lillard (2019) extends this further saying that to have free choice and learn then, most importantly, the activities need to be interesting. Lillard (2019) argues that the Montessori learning environment is designed to be interesting, "one that inspires deep attention, which develops executive function, that then assists self-determination" (p. 953). This can be understood further that there is no need for extrinsic rewards nor punishments in the Montessori classroom as the students want to learn and explore the activities but also, they have a strong relationship with the teacher who helps guide their journey.

Lillard et al. (2017) carried out an important study into Montessori education. They compared children in Montessori and non-Montessori education and from two age groups – 5 and 12-year olds – on a range of cognitive, academic, social and behavioural measures. Lillard et al.'s research raised an interesting point that when Montessori ideals are strictly followed then the social and academic skills of students were equal or superior to similar students in mainstream schools, but what is particularly interesting is that Montessori children scored higher on executive function when they were 4. This could be because Maria Montessori argued that the education was aimed at development of the whole child through integrating social and cognitive growth leading for healthy independent functioning (1994, p. 2). Marshall (2017) also argues that there is evidence to support success for Montessori education that is faithful to its founder but not necessarily for those places that have adapted the approaches. In terms of my research, reading the outcomes of the papers by Marshall (2017) and Lillard et al. (2017) was fascinating as many of the schools that I visited used a Montessori inspired approach that often was also incorporating other innovative pedagogies, so I was left wondering if this blended approach was actually successful? Lillard (2019) described these places as "pseudo Montessori" (p. 959), for places that call themselves Montessori or Montessori inspired but often have no training or use the approaches with poor fidelity.

4   Alys the School Tourist: Combined Pedagogical Approaches

Early in my school tourism in 2013 I visited a progressive school that was for 5–11 year olds based on the teachings of Krishnamurti (1953) on educating the whole person by freeing themselves from any conditioning, with Montessori. See an image of the classroom in Figure 44.

I wrote a recount of my visit for the parenting magazine Juno, some of which is in the excerpt below:

> The child-led free-flow learning was a new progressive approach for me within a school environment... I was impressed to see how the teacher

FIGURE 44   A Montessori inspired primary school classroom, UK, 2013

was able to oversee that each child was following a balanced curriculum and how older children helped the younger ones, for example, with writing the date. The real child-led element made me step out of my comfort zone of 'Teacher' to become 'Facilitator.'

I thought about what it would be like to be a new teacher here? The key thing I recognised was the strength of the community of the school, seen in the relationships between staff, students and parents. It was one based on an ethos of respect, and not using rewards and punishments to engage students in learning or activities. Quite often a child would be playing alone outside and then come in to rejoin the group or continue with their chosen activity. The magic in this approach seemed to be the creative "how"? That the teacher held the space or taught the lesson in such an interesting or engaging way to different learning styles or needs that allowed the child autonomy to be involved or to step out into their own space when needed. (Mendus, 2013b, pp. 14–15)

It is interesting to read my awkwardness in the teacher relinquishing their "power" and my questioning of the teacher having the role to enable the student to follow a 'balanced' curriculum. However, as Goertz (2001) explains, a balanced curriculum happens for a child in a Montessori classroom if there is a correctly prepared environment which is inviting, attractive and not cluttered.

I feel with hindsight there is a level of ignorance on my part, an inability to see, or to ask further questions about the approach as visiting the school very strongly through the eyes of a Steiner Waldorf and Mainstream teacher prevented me for many years from exploring Montessori Education further. I now recognise that there is a key role for the teacher, someone who demonstrates the correct use of materials which the children have individual freedom to choose when to use them. The teacher also keeps careful notes and observes a child's readiness to work with a new material and when to divert a child who is choosing an activity beyond their ability.

As I began to extrapolate Montessori Early Childhood Education from their Primary education, I began to see some strengths in the Primary classroom. I also observed a multi-lingual blended Montessori classroom in an eco-village community in Portugal, that was trying to combine Portuguese, German and English into the teaching. See Figure 45 which shows a photograph of this multi-lingual Montessori classroom in a yurt.

> The natural wooden tables were placed in a semi-circle, in the middle of the yurt was a candle which burnt for the time of the class. On the other side the two teachers worked together to hold the lesson. The teachers spoke to each other in English and to the children in their own native language. The lesson was about the water cycle and they were shown the results of an experiment with a glass bowl, water and cling film. The children joined in, encouraged to speak in Portuguese. The task of the lesson was to draw the water cycle on paper/for some in their workbooks and to label it in Portuguese. (Mendus, Multi-lingual Montessori journalling [Portugal, October 2016])

FIGURE 45   Inside of a yurt-based Montessori primary school, Portugal, October 2016

5 The Queering of 'Bad-Alys': Seeing Montessori with New Eyes

I recognise that these combined pedagogical approaches were not really helping me to understand the Montessori method as Lillard et al.'s research argues that places that do not have trained teachers following closely Montessori's original approaches are not necessarily good examples. So, I decided to visit an early childhood and a primary Montessori setting that closely followed Montessori's guidance. One of my oldest friends is a keen proponent of Montessori Education, her children are educated in Montessori and she has trained as a Montessori Primary teacher, so I contacted her about visiting her Primary project and her children's Early Years. I knew how well respected and experienced the teachers at the Early Years were and I felt that would help me position myself within Montessori Education.

> *As soon as I entered the door, I felt like I had stepped into a magical place, with a swing, hiding places, a little house and leaves waiting to be swept up.*

I was pleased I had asked what the etiquette for observing in a Montessori setting was so that I felt secure just sitting and watching. Sometimes when I observe I float around and ask questions and help children, but to get a real feel of such a well-established Montessori environment I really wanted to just watch. The children had been trained that visitors just watch so they didn't come up and ask who I was, they went on with their work. Luckily, I asked what to do if they asked or tried to engage me and was told to tell them that they had work to do, as did I; watching was my work.

> *And then I sat for three hours, totally spellbound by the hive of activity. For the first hour, most children were in their own self-directed bubble. As I was new to the environment it took me a little while to see how much was actually going on. Each child is in charge of their own learning and the teachers have provided a learning environment rich with activities that Montessori's research suggested are needed for the 3–6 year old child. I was able to observe how cleverly designed each activity seemed to be and I was not surprised to learn that each activity (on a child accessible tray), carefully laid out on shelves around the room, had a learning objective/outcome.*
>
> *As I watched I was fascinated by the most popular activities, which included ways to explore fine motor skills as well as understanding basic scientific approaches, for example a tray with two china bowls, one with a little water in it and a sponge. The adults in the room will demonstrate a tray's activity to the children either alone or in groups so they know the*

learning activity of each tray – however, this is not done in a traditional mainstream approach of explaining why and how you are doing it, but often nonverbally through demonstration and then copied via imitation. Another popular activity was again two containers, one with blue liquid (food dye in water) and a pipette. This one, from the expressions on the children's faces, seemed to be incredibly satisfying.

I learned later that having these separate activities can prove to be controversial with other non-Montessori settings. It is often asked why the children cannot combine these activities, as that would be fun. However, the idea is to learn the separate, concrete skills and then to move on and that when outside there are water and sand trays where they could combine the skills they have expertly learnt inside.

Behind the science shelves was a larger space. When I arrived, a small group of children were trying to build a very tall tower using two sets of blocks (brown and pale pink), they were using a chair to get to the top and had to ask an adult to put the final block on the top.

I learnt later that they were actually combining two different learning activities together, here following their own experiment which is normally allowed after they have completed the single activities. Soon this activity felt complete to the children, so they tidied it away and moved on.

FIGURE 46   Montessori literacy material, Scotland, January 2021 (photo by Emma Hughes)

One thing that fascinated me was the quiet, studious environment that was created and it felt that especially for the first hour there were barely any voices as the children were working alone. Adults, I observed, only spoke when they needed to and then only in low tones. Even when things went wrong, no disturbance or raised voices occurred. For example, a child dropped a container full of small items all over the floor and, after a moment of silence, the child breathed, put down what they were carrying and began to pick up the small pieces. They were soon joined by an adult, other children helped if they were passing. There was no issue made of what was happening. Occasionally one of the younger children raised their voices or felt a bit impatient about waiting for an activity and an adult would be there and calmly sit the child down, talk through what was happening and redirect.

After picking up time, I had a good walk around the classroom to see all the beautiful resources in more detail and to have further chats with the teachers. One thing that I had been wondering about was why there was no 'home corner' in the room and it was explained to me that actually within a Montessori Children's House the whole space is the home-corner and the children get to experience living and using a real home rather than a pretend one.

6   Alys the Guide

After my visit to the Montessori Early Childhood centre I wrote down my reflections on my visit, concluding that:

> *I had a really nourishing morning and it was such an honour to see such a careful and high-quality example of Montessori Education. I wondered where my own journey in my search for the ideal school would have taken me if I had seen them as my first alternative?*

This final question still leaves me troubled. I saw Montessori for many years as the shadow side to my journey within Steiner Waldorf education and my search for the 'Ideal School.' But here, after watching such a carefully planned, presented and articulated example of Montessori Education, I was wondering where my journey would have gone if I had found Montessori first. However, I think my love of unstructured play, fairy tales, home corners and creativity may have never matched up directly with Montessori and there was a feeling of a memory of the Team-Teach (see Hayden & Pike, 2004) approach for children with additional needs in schools in which I have taught. There was an aspect of silent little robots in a beautiful space that I know does not sit happily with me.

However, I am now able to see many of the strengths in the approach, particularly in the Maths resources and the independence skills, and I have been talking to teacher colleagues about incorporating some into their mainstream schools.

> *Aware of my continual troubling of Montessori Early Years I also began to realise that I was fascinated by the Primary teaching ideals, so I reached out to a friend who was an experienced Primary Montessori Teacher to learn more about what it is actually like to be a teacher.*

7   An Interview with Emma Hughes, Primary Montessori Teacher, July 2021

Alys: You teach six to twelve year olds. Can you explain why Montessori grouped students of this age together?

Emma: From age six upwards, they won't just take their parent's or teacher's word anymore – they argue. A lot. They won't just do what we ask them to, they want to understand the *reason* for our request. This developing ability really is one of the most amazing and miraculous features of what Maria Montessori termed 'the second plane of development.' The second plane of development takes place between the ages of six and twelve. During this time Montessori observed that the children's developmental focus shifts from individual formation to development as social beings. She also noted that children begin to interact with and explore the world around them in increasingly abstract terms rather than just through the concrete. She believed that all the children's behavioural inclinations function to serve these new purposes.

Alys: This is really interesting. How do you as a teacher, or the curriculum itself, support the student's development of reason?

Emma: Well, the answer, I see time and time again through my teaching, is that the materials are guiding the children and scaffolding their ability to both identify problems and to solve them. They become problem solvers, not merely problem doers. The development of the reasoning mind is essential in the process of becoming a problem solver, it allows the children to make connections between things – they can deduce (from the general to the specific) and they can infer (from the specific to the general). Montessori said that in the second plane, "*The world is acquired psychologically by means of the imagination. Reality is studied in detail, then the whole is imagined. The detail is able to grow in the imagination, and so total knowledge is attained*"

(1994, p. 18). It is imagination which powers the ability to infer as well as the ability to invent and problem solve.

Alys: It's so interesting to hear the perspective of a Montessori teacher. What is your favourite part of the curriculum?

Emma: My favourite aspect of the curriculum is what Montessori called 'Cosmic Education.' First and foremost, Montessori was an empirical scientist, thus the organisation and implementation of her cosmic education is based upon her understanding of the psychology and developmental needs of the child between six and twelve. Of paramount importance to her was to centre children in their world and connect them to it in a meaningful way, only then could they develop and begin to find answers to the questions 'who am I and why am I here?' For her the best way to do this was to give the child *"a vision of the whole universe"* (Montessori, 1989, p. 8). However, trying to convey to a 6-year-old the whole of human knowledge is an impossibility and so she came up with 'The Great Lessons.'

Alys: What are these Great Lessons and how are they taught?

Emma: The Five Great Lessons are impressionistic stories which outline the history of the universe from its inception to the modern day. The first story, *The Story of the Universe*, takes the children through the beginnings of the universe and origins of the solar system and earth; the second – *The Story of Life*, tells of how life came about and takes the children up to the rise of the hominids; the third tells *The Story of Humans* through to the Iron Age; the forth, *The Story of Language*, explores how writing came about, its importance and impact; the final story, *The Story of Numbers* tells the children about mathematical development and the importance of geometry.

Alys: I can see connections to the use of storytelling within Steiner Waldorf schools where the teacher will use story to share moments from history and the lives of scientists to Primary and lower Secondary aged students. Do you know of any research that has been carried out into this approach?

Emma: Angeline Stoll Lillard (2007), a Psychology Professor who devotes much of her research to detailed and careful scientific analysis of the outcomes of Montessori educational practices, believes that that the efficacy of the great lessons may lie in the fact that it is well known that humans find meaning in narrative, because these stories are told with such attention to the interconnectedness of things and because they are accompanied by practical demonstrations which connect the abstract of the story and the children's imaginations to the concrete world around them.

Alys: Fascinating. I have been reading the work of Lillard (2019) as well. I was interested in her evidence-based research into the efficacy of Montessori Education and the great challenge that many places using the approach around the world use the term 'Montessori' but do not always follow Montessorian approaches. I can tell from your passion that you are following Montessori's guidance and having success in your teaching, but also see it as a worthwhile pursuit.

Emma: The reason this approach makes sense to me (both philosophically and in practise) is that, I believe, the ability to reason things out for ourselves has never been so important. The world our children are growing into needs adults who can think for themselves. It needs people who can look at the world around them and see the things that could be made better and then be able to work out how they can do it. That is why, I believe, supporting our children's developing ability to reason through Montessori Education is one of the most important things I can be doing.

8   Alys the Educator: Gems within Montessori Education – Exploring Montessori Maths Resources

Through my journey exploring Montessori Education I have become aware of the strength of Montessori methods in the teaching of Mathematics (see Figures 47a, b & c), allowing students to really understand number and to allow a student to continue with a subject for as far as they can take it, intrinsically extending their learning. As Marshall (2017) explains, the theory behind the approach is the importance that is given to conceptual knowledge being the foundation for children to be able to understand fractions. For example, in Figure 47b, the Montessori fraction circles, are designed to "provide a sensorial experience with the fractions from one whole to ten tenths" (Marshall, 2017, p. 6). I asked an experienced Montessori teacher, Emma Hughes (personal communication, 2021), to share her thoughts on using the Maths resources in her Primary classroom.

> *As a Montessori teacher, it is the developing ability to reason things out for themselves, that I believe must be nurtured just as carefully as other parts of their lives… and something that traditional education often fails to do. For Montessorians it is the passage into abstraction that is being marked by the child's increasing ability to reason things out for themselves. How the Montessori materials and method support this ability is something I never fail to be mesmerised by as a teacher.*

Traditionally, maths is taught by rules and formulas which, all too often, leave out reasoning and understanding. However, to use an example from geometry, the Montessori Equivalence Metal Inset Squares enable even the youngest children in the primary classroom to discover the precise geometric definitions of congruent, similar, and equivalent for themselves. By comparing the various figures, the metal insets contain, the children are able to test for shape, line length, angles, proportions, and area. From these comparisons they arrive at the correct definitions, write them down and illustrate them. The importance and effectiveness of concrete materials like these, in aiding the passage to abstract comprehension, cannot be underestimated. It is because of the didactic nature of the materials that they reveal their 'truths' to the child gradually and according to the child's own developmental journey. See Figure 47a.

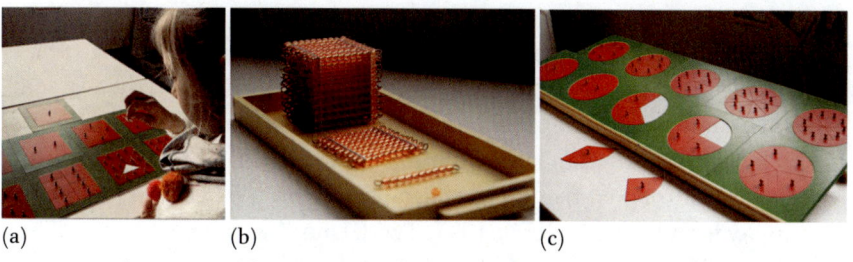

(a) (b) (c)

FIGURE 47 Three images of Montessori maths resources, Scotland, January 2021.
(a) Montessori Equivalence Metal Inset Square, (b) Montessori Golden Bead Material; (c) Montessori Fraction Circles (photo by Emma Hughes)

In contrast to traditional education, the emphasis in Montessori is to make rules and formulas the point of discovery, not the point of departure. Nowhere is this better illustrated than the formulae we use for calculating the area of various polygons. As adults our familiarity with these formulae might be taken for granted and never questioned. 'But where did they come from?' I ask the children I teach, and 'who discovered them?' And most importantly, 'how do we know that they're accurate?' Enter Euclid, 4th century BCE father of maths and geometry. So, I introduce the children to the idea that they are going walk in Euclid's shoes, working with seven of his theorems, to understand for themselves how he came to discover that knowledge, and to prove whether it is still as true today as it was nearly two and half thousand years ago. Carefully, and accurately they work with the materials and find two ways they can calculate the area of any regular polygon. They never cease to be awed by how ancient people discovered these things without the benefit of our modern materials… and they remember what they have learnt, simply because it makes sense to them on a deep level having worked with the materials. "How many teachers have actually proven these formulae for themselves?," the children ask... The answer, I fear, may be less than we would like.

I wanted to see these Montessori maths resources in action so I observed a maths session in a Montessori Primary home-education group in the UK in November 2016 and I am beginning to see these resources and the whole pedagogical approach to Montessori Primary education as a gem.

> I enjoyed seeing how the maths resources made learning 'times by ten' much more real and concrete than purely abstract. There is a real difference between learning a rule that when you times by ten you add a zero on the end, and physically getting out the number cubes and making the shapes. Also, there was real sense and order of where to place the blocks that was the same method used as when writing down a sum. I also observed the children doing the sum with the blocks on the mat and at the same time writing them onto a sheet. These sheets also were colour coded for the Thousands, Hundreds, Tens and Units columns which are the same throughout, really establishing continuity. There was still a possibility for mistakes if a child rushed with counting, but if they took time, which I felt the Montessori approach suggests, then they had the scope to really love and understand number. (Mendus, Montessori 6–12 year old home-education group observation, November 2016 [Uphall, Scotland, November 2016])

9 Summary

– Montessori early childhood education allows young children to freely choose set age-appropriate activities organised by the teacher and put on accessible shelves in the classroom. These activities promote independence and skills for life, such as tying shoelaces or pouring a cup of water to drink.
– Montessori early childhood is different to Steiner Waldorf as the focus is not on unstructured play and home corners and they do not tell fairy tales. Montessori early childhood is often called the 'Children's house' as it is viewed that the whole learning space is a home, with a real kitchen that the children use to help prepare real food, so they do not need a pretend home corner.
– The role of the adult is to prepare an age-appropriate learning environment and then to guide the students in how they access the materials.

- This chapter shares stories of places that have combined Montessori approaches with other approaches such as Krishnamurti and holistic education.
- This chapter argues that the Montessori Maths resources are a gem as they allow a deep understanding of number and can also be used in mainstream primary settings.

  Montessori Early Childhood and Primary settings that closely follow Montessori's ideals have been shown to be the most successful (Lillard et al., 2017).

CHAPTER 9

Alys and Edge-ucational Gems within the System

1 Alys the Guide

This chapter liberates the story from the constraints of 'Searching for the Ideal School' by accepting the oxymoron that the 'ideal' does not currently exist. From this place of liberation it allows the new understanding of how performing School Tourism has allowed the 'gems' within the current neoliberal world to glow and offers some examples of places that are practically re-patterning the understanding of what is education within the system through their own grass-roots changes, even within more traditional places.

This can be seen in these stories, chosen as examples of autonomous approaches within more traditional settings, including schools, individual teachers and home education, that often have to follow a set-curriculum. I see the stories in this chapter as gems, part of the edge-ucation, as places that do not necessarily fit under the heading of a set alternative pedagogical approach but are places making innovative changes, focusing on social justice, new ways of communication and learning environment. There are also examples of places that have modelled ways of succeeding without high stakes testing. This chapter, written as a series of vignettes, is just a selection of the many schools I have visited that were not included in the earlier chapters to help the reader to realise the possibilities that are currently available, even within more traditional settings.

2 Alys the School Tourist: Using Autonomous Approaches with a Set Curriculum

2.1 Vignette 23: eduScrum, Netherlands

Ashram College is a large public high school in the western Netherlands. The students come from a wide range of backgrounds, they wear their own clothes and call the teachers by their first names.

FIGURE 48   Looking out of the classroom window, Netherlands, June 2017

One of the teachers, Willy Wijnands, created the eduScrum (eduScrum, 2021) pedagogical approach, which he uses in his Chemistry classes. eduScrum is defined as:

> An active form of collaboration, with which students in teams complete assignments according to a fixed rhythm. They plan and determine their own activities and keep track of progress. The teacher 'determines' the assignments, coaches and gives advice. (eduScrum, 2021)

Wijnands explains on the eduScrum website that they learnt from the Scrum approach, "a well-developed method to let people work together intensively, pleasantly and with great results" (eduScrum, 2021). Scrum was being used in IT and Wijnands realised that similar approaches could be possible in teaching. Spending one day in the school helped me observe several classes using the approach for both the core Chemistry curriculum and for self-designed Chemistry-based projects.

The students sit in their groups around tables and the first thing they do is to pick up their big chart and pin it on the walls of the classroom. A large A0 sheet is used to guide the eduScrum with columns of what is to be done, what is being worked on and what is complete. There are also agreed (by the

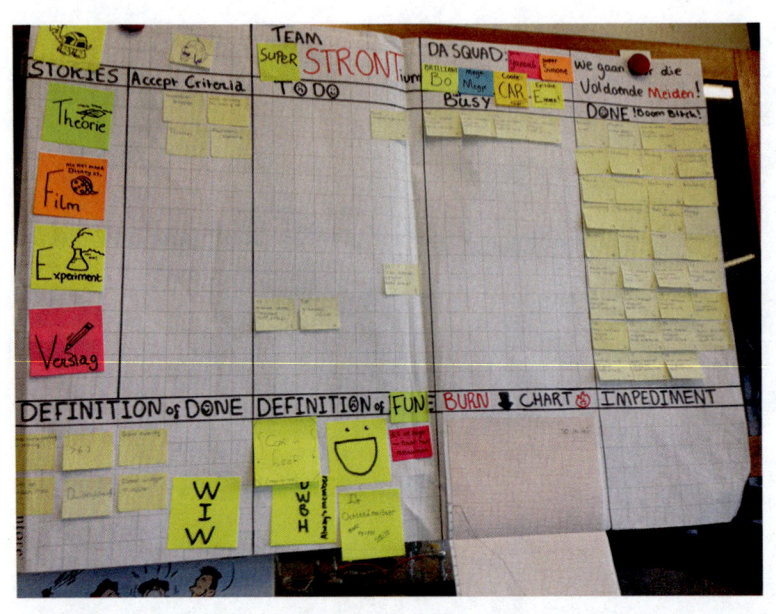

FIGURE 49   eduScrum task sheet, Netherlands, June 2017

group with the possible influence of the teacher such as achieving a particular exam grade) the success criteria (called in eduScrum the DOD – Definition of Done), the happiness criteria (the DOF – Definition of Fun) and a Burn Chart (diagram of how much work has been completed). By filling in the Burn Chart and keeping it visible, the teacher is able to see if they are doing too much or not enough. For this Chemistry project the target was to get a 6.7 on the test, but also for one group DoD included working together and enjoying the experience.

> *First thoughts on eduScrum – it really can be used for anything...*
> *To be sitting there in a complex Chemistry lesson on moles*
> *And they have used eduScrum for that*
> *Made me think differently*
> *I had seen it as a tool for project-based learning*
> *But here is was being used as a tool for curriculum-based learning*
> *Group autonomous learning.*
> (Mendus, Journalling on the Netherlands [Amsterdam, June 2017])

I left feeling that I had observed another key example of my edge-ucation, a gem, in terms of educating differently, bringing more autonomy and group skills into public education. I was also aware of a theme that often arises, that of the individual and the collective, and from my reflections at the beginning of this piece I saw eduScrum as 'group autonomous learning,' trying to step away from the binary of an alternative approach being either purely individual or purely for the collective, as there were aspects of both. In terms of the role of the teacher – when eduScrum is used for a set curriculum, in this case Chemistry, then Willy was still the expert and 'teacher' at times, then 'Scrum Master' or 'Mentor' at others.

2.2 Vignette 24: Florescer Home Education Support, Lisbon, Portugal

2.2.1 A Walking Interview with Co-founder Teresa Mendes

Teresa and I met at the 'A New Earth Needs New Schools' conference at the eco-village Tamera in Southern Portugal in October 2013. I returned to stay with her and visit her home-education project in Lisbon in October 2016. This section of the interview is included to show how Florescer has been able to be influenced by a broad range of innovative pedagogies whilst creating links with the local community centre and woodland area, as well as covering the state-mandated curriculum. The interview was carried out as we moved between the different settings and buildings, indoor and out, inspired by Springgay and Truman's (2018) Walking Lab, hoping that we would be engaging with a 'critical mode of walking-with that engenders solidarity, accountability, and response-ability" (p 15).

Teresa: Florescer is not a school, it is a tutoring centre for home-educated children. The adults who work there are called by their first names and see themselves as facilitators or tutors, not teachers. In Portugal,

FIGURE 50 A display at Florescer, Portugal, October 2016

all children must take exams at 10, 12 and 15. It does not matter where or how you are educated; each child must take and pass the exams in Maths and Portuguese to be able to progress to the next grade. This affects home-educated children. So Florescer, although free in how it educates, must follow the state curriculum so that the children can pass the tests.

Alys: That sounds like a real challenge. How do you make it as creative and autonomous as possible?

Teresa: This has been really tricky as there is a very broad curriculum, so it is hard to cover all of the subject matter. Self-autonomy is one of the key areas of Florescer. The partner of one of the other founders works in IT and has designed an App. The idea of the App is that each child has the whole curriculum that needs to be covered broken down into manageable chunks and can show each week that they have worked on different areas and given evidence for meeting that objective – this could be by completing a project or pages in a workbook, they tick a box so that it changes colour when they think it is completed, then one of the adults checks this and ticks it so that it changes colour again. It also gives a visual way for the child and adult to see where there are larger holes in the children's learning and what they may need to spend more time on.

Soon it was time to go to the forest. As we leave the building and walk through the park towards the community centre, we continue chatting.

FIGURE 51   Florescer classroom, Portugal, October 2016

Alys: How do you start each morning?

Teresa: Each morning starts at 9am with a circle which lasts about half an hour. When the weather is nice, we do it outside, sometimes members of the community join in. The circle begins with meditation and then is more or less directed by the interests of the children; they may play a game, sing songs, or do some timetables. In a way this is similar to the beginning of a day in a Steiner school main lesson, but with more democratic elements.

As we walked through the park, other people using the park said hello and recognised the children.

Alys: What do the local people think about Florescer?

Teresa: We are well respected as one of our main aims is to be really part of the community. For example, the local community centre was needing some love so the Florescer group and others in the community repainted the building and brought natural resources into the space. The building was transformed and is now full of different community activities, from yoga and wellbeing to martial arts and a community cafe and guerrilla knitting groups. We have a permanent room there which was set up very similarly to a Steiner kindergarten with simple toys, a calm beautiful space, a nature table and a rocking chair for storytelling. A group for younger children and their parents is held here daily and they meet the older children in the park or the woods for lunch. You will notice when we get there that the older children enjoy coming to the younger children's room and playing with the toys and dressing up materials, so there is much crossover between the groups.

After visiting the community centre, we go into the woods and as the children play we continue our conversation...

Alys: What has happened to the interest for a group of alternative educators in Portugal since 2013? (See Chapter 6 for more information about when this group was established.)

Teresa: A network of alternative schools/projects has been set up with 16 different partners with the agreement of the overlying principles of 'Autonomy' and 'Integral.'

Alys: What do you mean when you use the term 'integral?' Do you mean holistic?

Teresa: No, they are similar, but we are avoiding the term 'holistic' as it is not
            always taken seriously and seen as too 'hippy'. And, in practice, not
            all the projects agree with each other as each has their own focus,
            this in itself has caused some challenges for the network. However,
            the network is thriving and other groups of people interested in
            'educating differently' are finding out about us.

Alys: What other approaches influence your work?

Teresa: I did my Master's thesis on Ecole d'Ponte near Porto in Portugal,
            which was the school set up by Jose Pacheco. It was a radical demo-
            cratic state school, but since Jose Pachecho has gone to live in Brazil
            and has started a more radical school over there, unfortunately his
            school in Portugal has had to make changes to fit the mainstream
            system, including becoming part of a super-school – lots of high
            schools joining together. (Colleague) Teresa and I went to visit Jose
            Pacheco's new school in Brazil last year and it was really inspiring to
            see a school not controlled by the state and able to meet his vision.

Alys: So, you are a School Tourist as well! I remember when we met you
            had been over to Brockwood Park School in Hampshire, is that influ-
            encing your work here?

Teresa: Yes, I am very influenced by my experiences of Krishnamurti's work
            and my visit to Inwoods and Brockwood Park school. For example,
            Krishnamurti's view is that it is not the pedagogy of a school that is
            important, but that the adults in the school are doing personal spir-
            itual developmental work on themselves. And 'Flourishing' is what
            Krishnamurti suggested would be a good name for a new school –
            one that is flourishing... So Florescer is a mix of many different peda-
            gogical approaches – Steiner, Montessori, Democratic, Krishnamurti
            and community-based learning, underpinned by staff who are con-
            tinuing to do work on themselves as well as making sure that the
            children also cover the state curriculum.

Writing this several months later, now on a beach in Thailand, I reread my
notes and reflect; is this also part of my edge-ucation? An 'Ideal School'
is not just about finding 'gems,' pedagogical ways to work within the current system, but also about the adults doing work on themselves. Perhaps
this then segways into the question I was asked when I trained to be a
Steiner Waldorf teacher. "Who are you who walks into the classroom?
And what stories do you bring with you?" (Mendus, Reflections on the
edge-ucation [Thailand, February 2017])

2.3   Vignette 25: Koonwarra Village School, Victoria, Australia

Koonwarra Village School is included here as an example of a relatively new school (established 2012) where autonomous learning and a state-curriculum can co-exist symbiotically.

> At Koonwarra Village School, the students have learning contracts where they are in control of a great proportion of their own time. They must reach agreed learning goals each week as well as attend focus groups with children of a similar 'ability level' – regardless of age – on particular subjects, thereby ensuring they meet the requirements of the Victoria State Curriculum. All students are aware of their level and progression, which is similar to the expectations in UK schools. This approach is underpinned by John Hattie's (2008) work on Visible Learning in terms of clearly displayed learning intentions and outcomes. (Mendus, 2016b, p. 385)

Koonwarra Village School is a clear example of my edge-ucation, a school polishing its 'gems'; there is freedom for students to learn autonomously, even when they must follow the local state curriculum. Another aspect that interested me was how, even within a traditional school environment, they challenged the typical role of the teacher.

> Koonwarra Village School is different from many mainstream schools that I have visited as the school views the 'teacher' as a 'mentor,' helping with the learning process. Sarah was getting the group of nine children to think about skills needed for inquiry-based learning by introducing a group work activity. The children split into two smaller groups and one group chose to work outside. It was really interesting to see the children visibly grow as learners as the group inside realised that by not writing anything down they forgot their ideas. The group working outside realised (with a little help) that their group dynamics had been challenging, as they had not sat in a circle, but at different levels and distances from each other, thus making it easier for one person to take over or another to remain silent. (Mendus, 2016b, p. 387)

FIGURE 52   Koonwarra classroom, Australia, February 2016

Koonwarra Village School has been critiqued as 'not a democratic school' by self-labelled democratic schools, however, I saw real strength in the way the school scaffolded self-autonomy in the Upper Primary room with the development of skills in Working Together:

> Teaching group work skills seemed like a really sensible idea as it made me think about the line between self-actualised learning [the top level on Maslow's Hierarchy of Needs] (Maslow, 1943) and democratic learning (Neill, 1960; Greenberg, 1995), understood in this context as child-centred learning. At some 'democratic' schools that I have visited, the idea of offering a formal lesson on developing a particular skill, such as inquiry or group-based skills, might be seen to contradict the philosophy; this is because the students might not have suggested this lesson or even chosen to attend it. I know that Democratic Education can be implemented in many ways, but I am wondering if by giving the students the skills to work effectively in groups it could be seen as actually being more democratic as they are then able to make a choice to use those skills, thereby achieving a higher level of self-actualisation and freedom. (Mendus, 2016b, p. 387)

FIGURE 53   Koonwarra sandpit, Australia, February 2016

2.4   *Vignette 26: An Innovative State-Primary School, Melbourne, Victoria, Australia*

Usually I find out about schools by searching on the internet or through word of mouth, but this school I found myself by my curiosity of looking over the school fence at the piles of wood and other outdoor play equipment in the school garden. I contacted the school directly and visited a few days later.

The school is over 100 years old and has always had a progressive history, adapting to the children in the area – there were lots of Greek migrant families. I was interested to be told by senior leaders that as the school is inspired by many approaches it does not want to be known as 'that Reggio school,' although it is heavily influenced by Reggio Emilia practices (Edwards, Gandini, & Forman, 2011). I observed other progressive approaches such as no uniform and everyone being on first name terms, including with the principal. (Mendus, Journalling on a School Visit [Melbourne, Australia, February 2016])

I was excited to visit as I had never been into a primary school that uses the Reggio Emilia approach throughout.

The first room was an open-plan classroom – a combined Y1/2/3 space for 66 children and 3 teachers working together. The space was divided into areas with a stage, tiered seating, small group tables, little cubby spaces for small group work and book corners. The timetable on the wall was very different from a typical primary school as it included time like ILT (independent learning time) and Curiosita, which was arts-based subjects, as well as Italian and music. It also included Inquiry as the whole class were involved in Inquiry-based projects. Philosophy was a taught subject, as was 'Earn and Learn' where they ran small businesses. On the wall were lots of ideas of everything they knew about a subject before they did their inquiry project. Teacher's work and writing was not visible on the walls. I was told that all things put on the walls were there consciously and from the children's work. This is very different to the teacher led, assessment focussed displays seen in many mainstream classrooms.

We then went on to have a detailed look at the Kindergarten, which was beautifully set out with veg growing in planters outside. Inside there were lots of different cubby areas and a central area with sofas for sharing books and displaying home-made books. There was a well-equipped art space with displays of the children's art, as well as photos and information on how projects were made. Lots of books were available to take home, including books written by the children. The young children are encouraged to see themselves as an author and 'write' books. The spelling is not corrected at this stage, just 'published' with a 'translation' written underneath when needed. There was an area for the current project. So far a small papier-mache volcano had been built and some cotton wool clouds were hanging in the sky. The next area had a light box and was for quiet and reflective manipulation of the resources, then a home corner with lots of space and small tables and

> *chairs as well as wooden kitchen equipment. The next space had shelves of*
> *maths resources and a large carpet area for getting them out to manipulate*
> *them.*

I was feeling really impressed by how a state-funded school could choose to change the classroom layout and learning environment and create a very different atmosphere for more independent learning. Once I saw on the wall in the Kindergarten a display of drawings of butterflies and a link to the YouTube video of 'Austin's Butterfly' by Ron Berger (2012). I was really impressed as I was seeing in action Ron Berger's work (2003) on the first draft is not the completed project, as discussed in Chapter 7.

> *The Principal and I returned to her office and I learnt about the school*
> *golden rules, the two rights and two responsibilities that made it possible for*
> *learning to occur: Right to learn; Right to be safe. Personal Responsibility to*
> *look after yourself to be the best you can. Community Responsibility to make*
> *the community work. I also asked about a poster the Principal had on their*
> *door which really promoted inclusion and equity. 'Faith. Culture. Gender.*
> *Race. Ability. Sexuality. Age. XXX Welcomes You.' Above the words are a pic-*
> *ture of legs showing all sorts of shoes and clothes, including religious dress.*

This school shows edge-ucational 'gems' by transforming its environment, timetable, role of adults and whole community for learning, even though it still must offer the state curriculum. It shows real effort at inclusion, including gender-inclusion, aiming to meet the needs of all students and staff. It also attempts to step out of the dialogue of privilege as this state funded school has a wide catchment of socio-economic backgrounds and nationalities.

2.5   Vignette 27: A Public High School That Uses Its Own Assessments and Teaches through Inquiry, New York, May 2017

This inner-city state-funded school has multi-aged classes, so it runs more like college than a high school. The real gem here is that their students are able to follow their own assessment courses and only need to do one high stakes test to gain the New York Regents Diploma. They also use the city as a classroom and half a day a week they volunteer locally.

The school has 160 9th–12th grade students. The school follows an inquiry approach to its teaching and learning. The school website describes this as:

> Inquiry teaching requires the teacher to frame questions in a way
> which challenges students to examine often conflicting evidence, draw

FIGURE 54
Poster – No cookie cutter education, New York, USA, May 2017

conclusions and support these conclusions in thoughtful discussion with others who, using the same evidence base, reach divergent conclusions. (School website, 2017)

I visited this school as part of a group, which I explore further in Chapter 11. We observed several lessons and had a discussion with a group of students. When observing lessons, we were able to see the inquiry approach in action. The courses, particularly in literature and social studies, are discussion based. This means that they are not all about the facts, but more about how they are interpreted. I observed a fascinating lesson on Civil Rights, the class all sitting at desks positioned in a circle. The class were discussing the Black Panthers, a member of the Black Panthers was coming in to talk to the students later in the week.

The curriculum is designed by the teachers, but with influence and discussion with students. The courses look at depth rather than breadth. This means that the classes are often more hands-on. For example, in Math, students work in groups of 3 to solve a problem together after the teacher presents the topic, then talk about the answer and look at the different ways to solve the problem. Then in the next class they build on this progress. Or, in Science, the students choose a question to study in groups or alone and then research the subject and design an experiment to test the question. After writing a lab report they present the findings to others. Students seem to really appreciate the approach, particularly ones who have been elsewhere. Here, they have freedom to go out

FIGURE 55   Small classroom set up for discussion-based classes, New York, USA, May 2017

of the school for lunch as well as the freedom to choose which courses that they take.

When we spoke to a group of students, they could find few negatives about the school, but one was the lack of variety of sports or art on offer. In terms of the lessons, the Students said that the more creative approach to classes meant that they had a lot of essays to write. They did not use textbooks, sometimes there were worksheets, but they did not describe the lessons as tedious. The amount of homework depends on the class you take, often reading and essays (like college). For example; one class called "Looking for an argument?" sold itself as having no homework, but it involved a lot of reading and discussions in class and the writing of essays in class time.

The group of students seemed to be relaxed and honest when they spoke about their school, really reinforcing that they all "wanted to be there" as there "was always something interesting happening." We asked about grading and they explained that at mid-term you get comments which are honest, and they won't go on your transcript for college and then at the end of a semester they get a grade. They described the respect they had for their teachers and how they liked using first names as it meant that they could "talk on an even level and build good relationships." They also mentioned if there were any disciplinary issues then mediation was used, but that the school does not tolerate fighting and the consequence for fighting was being expelled.

> *I was excited by our visit to this school and many of the other School Tourists were equally impressed. One person in our group exclaimed that this was definitely their favourite school and they would love to teach here! I was*

pleased to observe the level of diversity and inclusion, and that this publicly funded school offered a real alternative to traditional state-funded education. There were some issues on the lottery attached to getting a place, but once students had a place they had free access to an inquiry-based curriculum that respected the students' viewpoints and allowed them to show their own success in ways that did not include the pressure and narrow focus of high-stakes testing. This is also an example of schools working together to show a unified approach to question the education board's assumptions that their high-stakes tests are the only way to assess students' progress. This school, since 1997, has been working with 47 other schools in the district to organise alternative assessment approaches. There were many signs up around the school from education marches that had important activist slogans such as 'No cookie cutter education' (Figure 54) and 'One test does not fit all' (Figure 3). If one publicly funded high-school can make this massive difference in the schooling experience then I am sure that by sharing the successes of this school many other places could be inspired to do the same.

2.6 Vignette 28: Woodland Wednesdays and Forest Fridays: Running Forest School Sessions in a Mainstream School Nursery UK

"The wheels on the bus go around and around" the children sing merrily as the minibus takes them the fifteen-minute journey from school to the Forest School site. The bus drops them 300m down the road and holding hands they walk along the quiet road, still singing. There is no gate, so the children all take turns to carefully climb over, some needing more support from the adults than others, all growing in confidence over the school year.

The site, a patch of established beech woodland in the Peak District national park, took a while to find and needed continual discussion with the local park ranger. The boundaries, known by all the children, are the dry stone wall on one side, the outdoor classroom on another side (three big poles lashed together with a tarpaulin wrapped around the outside), where the branches to the trees get thicker on another side and the path down to the porta-potty on the other. Within this space there is a swing hung from a tree, small trees and branches to climb, mud to dig and a designated fire pit and cooking area.

The children joyfully put their bags down and energetically move over to sit around the empty fire pit.

FIGURE 56
Kindergarten children hugging trees, UK, 2012

These children are 3 and 4 years old, the nursery class of a local Primary school, and come regularly once a week over the academic year. Several members of staff are Forest School practitioners (Knight, 2016) and the teachers are inspired by many different innovative pedagogies, such as Steiner Waldorf early childhood and Montessori. However, as a state funded setting they must also meet the Early Years Foundation Stage. The lead teacher established a planning cycle where observations from children's play from the session before influence the planning for the following week. Due to the young age of the children, most weeks begin with a scaffolded activity or game from which open-ended play often develops. Each session has a supportive rhythm, with a beginning safety talk and introductory activity before free play, then a coming together for snack and songs before going on a walk or another game and then coming back together for a woodland puppet show. This is very similar to the rhythm used in many Steiner Waldorf Kindergartens. All adults in the space are trained to redirect unwanted behaviours. Also, therapeutic storytelling, which is inspired by the work of Susan Perrow (2012), is built into the weekly rhythm (see Figure 57). For example, there was one child who was biting other children so a story was made up about an ant in the forest who none of the other animals would play with until it stopped biting. As another example, a child who was frustrated that other children would not join in the games they wanted to play, so a story was created about a gnome who lived on one side of a river and one day there was a flood and they needed some help so with their

FIGURE 57   Alys the Educator telling stories in a woodland, Australia, June 2020

neighbours they built some stepping stones so that they could have help but still live in their own house.

> *What was so inspiring about this setting introducing Forest Schools was the impact on the local community. The school began a Forest School afterschool club and then began to offer sessions throughout the primary schools. Other local early years settings also began to offer Forest School sessions. This meant that the gem was that many children who would not have had the opportunity for nature immersion experiences now had them throughout the year. Another breakthrough was one teacher had their Early Years Practitioner assessment at the Forest School site, proving to the examiner that the whole of the Early Years curriculum could be met in an outdoor setting, opening future possibilities for more children to gain outdoor experiences.*

3   Alys the Guide

This chapter has shared stories of hope, places and people that are making change within the current neoliberal system and it is my wish for you as the reader to have a feeling of empowerment, that taking small steps for educational change is possible and available not just to those with more privilege. I hope that you are ready, if you haven't already begun, to become a School Tourist yourself!

4 Summary

- This chapter has shared gems, several examples of places that are educating differently within more traditional settings. The examples show that changes made by individual teachers, homeschooling families, and whole school transformation, as well as using different learning environments, can bring more autonomous learning opportunities for young people.
- The stories included:
  - Using eduScrum, a collaborative approach to completing set assignments.
  - Using an App to help collective home-educated children follow their progress against expected government standards.
  - Using learning contracts in a primary school to help develop autonomy and intrinsic motivation in students.
  - Transforming a whole state-funded primary school to have mixed ages classrooms and to follow a Reggio Emilia inspired approach.
  - A public high school creating its own assessment that were accredited by the local council so that its students could graduate, therefore avoiding most high-stakes tests.
  - Introducing weekly outdoor Forest Schools sessions into Early Childhood settings and realising that all the set standards can be met in the outdoors.

FIGURE 58   Alys the School Tourist. Alys' large bag hanging up next to the children's small bags at an outdoor kindergarten, Massachusetts, USA, March 2013

PART 3

Towards a Paradigm Shift

∴

FIGURE 59   A wet-felt rhizome. From a home-made felt jacket, Cumbria, August 2015

CHAPTER 10

Performing School Tourism

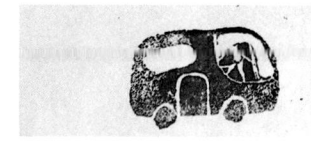  

1 Alys the Guide

This chapter aims to answer theoretical questions about performing School Tourism. There will be a section on the theoretical positioning of performing School Tourism as well as a critique of the approach and a discussion of the ethical stance. If you would prefer to miss the more theoretical discussions in this chapter, I suggest you jump to Chapter 11 where I will share with you how to become a School Tourist yourself!

2 Alys the Theorist: A Theoretical Discussion of Performing School Tourism

2.1 *Overview*

This section builds upon the nomadology of this book, the multiple voices of Alys-we and their intra-action (Barad, 2007) with performing School Tourism which was developed in Part 1. Conceptually this 'live method' (Back & Puwar, 2012) of performing School Tourism rhizomatically intertwines many theoretical approaches. It recognises the importance of relationality from the new mobilities paradigm (Sheller, 2011, 2014; Sheller & Urry, 2006; Urry, 2000, 2002; Urry & Larsen, 2011); the role of performance and importance of emotion (Zembylas, 2003) with an ethic of storying (Phillips & Bunda, 2018), linking performing School Tourism back to its autoethnographic roots; alongside Deleuzian (1980/87) thought on nomadology and rhizomatic theory; with Braidotti's (2012) work on 'nomadic inquiry,' seen as an unsettled dialogue between the ever-changing-peripheral and its centre, and Barad's (2007) ideas on feminist new materialisms to look at research differently.

2.2   *Discussion*

School Tourism stems out of curiosity (Stagl, 2012) of 'What is currently out there in education?' The School Tourist decides to take a journey to visit schools and places of learning. This follows Crouch's idea that tourism is "a process of seductive encounter" (2005, p. 23) and Bauman's (2011) concept that tourists are consumers. Following Bauman, who said that tourists are "seduced by the true or imaginary pleasures of a sensation-gatherer's life" (Bauman, 2011, p. 22), has helped to develop an understanding of School Tourism.

> I visit schools and observe, sometimes I teach or share a story of other schools that I have visited, but mostly I consume... I take photos, think and reflect on what I have (in my opinion) observed and add those thoughts and assumptions to my 'bag-of-tricks' of knowledge about places 'educating differently.' (Mendus, Alys the School Tourist Journalling [Isle of Skye, Scotland, April 2017])

By reflecting on the spatiality of School Tourism, its rhizomatic iterative nature of continued journeying, possibly from a home location away to an unknown/new location and back again, can be seen to be influenced by the mobilities paradigm. Sheller and Urry remind the School Tourist to change their viewpoints and understandings of space, scale and "existing linear assumptions about temporality and timing" (2006, p. 214). Therefore, it is worth recognising that School Tourism, following the 'New Mobilities Paradigm,' is moving beyond what has been seen as "a clear distinction... between places and those travelling to such places" (Sheller & Urry, 2006, p. 214). For example, the school building and the visiting school tourist. Sheller and Urry (2006) argue that "Places are like ships, moving around and not necessarily staying in one location" (p. 214). This develops an understanding of more-than-human influences, where places are about relationships with peoples, materials and images (Sheller & Urry, 2006). Therefore, understanding that these 'places' and 'people' are situated within a complex rhizomatic entanglement connected via performances (Sheller & Urry, 2006) helps develop the role of performance when visiting schools. I applied these more-than-human understandings to an arts-based response to my PhD journeys living in a van by running 'Come Dance my PhD' workshops and making two films (Mendus, 2019) which can be viewed on YouTube (Mendus, 2018a, 2018b).

The visit, and all aspects of School Tourism, can be seen as a performance (see Adler, 1989; Gingrich-Philbrook, 2014; Goffman, 1959). School Tourism draws on the Deleuzian concept of 'becoming' (1980/87), which sees 'becoming' as dynamic, as a verb and with a consistency of its own, therefore

FIGURE 60   Alys the Performer dancing at the British Autoethnography
              conference, Bristol, July 2018 (photo by Tessa Wyatt)

supporting the reframing to 'performing School Tourism.' The idea that the act
of physically visiting a school could be envisioned as a performance follows
Gingrich-Philbrook (2014) who states that performance happens when "crossing the thresholds of performance spaces" (2014, p. 83). For School Tourism this
could be from initial emails and connection to websites, to the physical visit
and, afterwards, to thank you emails and reflections, as well as filmed papers
shared on the internet. Another way of looking at the connection between performance and School Tourism is through Goffman's (1959) concept of 'front-
stage' and 'back-stage.' For example, the front stage, less open, more guarded
conversations that happen often with Senior Management and in correspondence, in comparison to those back-stage, much freer, conversations over a cup
of tea in the staff room, or with a student being shown around without observation by teachers. The idea of performance can be developed further, following Adler's (1989) argument that the performance is not just visiting the school,
but also includes the travel (linking back to the work of Sheller & Urry, 2006,
on the New Mobilities paradigm). In this case, the travel to/from a school can
be viewed as a 'performed art' which involves anticipation and day-dreaming
about the journey, the destination and also who/what might be encountered
on the way (Adler, 1989). Following Wunderlich (2010) that when one "dwells

through time in place" (2010, p. 47) they rely on the body (the School Tourist) as performer.

Performing School Tourism also builds on Massumi's (2017) argument of 'embodied encounter,' giving space for the emotional body of the performer to speak. This encounter includes the School Tourist, those who work/attend the school as well as the "non-human environment – objects that characterise that school identity" (Mendus et al., 2020, p. 220). Emotions, as Zemblyas (2003) states, "connect people's thoughts, judgments, and beliefs" (p. 222). However, it must also be argued that there is a relational matrix (Massumi, 2017) between "the multiplicity of emotions likely to be experienced in any one event" (Zemblyas, 2003, p. 222) and by any one person at that event, or school visit. Wenger's (2010) term, "multimembership," explores this so that when we travel/move through these different schools/places of learning that each person has differing emotional responses where, "Some we only visit, merely catch a glimpse of, or ignore altogether. With some we identify strongly, with others lightly, and with many not at all" (Wegener, 2010, p. 6). Nevertheless, the emotional aspect of performing School Tourism is an essential part, as the role of emotion in power, agency and potential for self-transformation (Zemblyas, 2003) are given space to be explored. This also highlights the struggles in the concept of becoming-identity where lived emotional experiences, here from visiting schools, might have "antagonistic, multiple meanings" (Zemblyas, 2003, p. 223).

Performing School Tourism is also a temporal practice. For example; when physically in a school/place of learning "one experiences place-temporality by being in touch with the place, listening to its sounds, and observing what goes on" (Wunderlich, 2010, p. 47). Place-temporality has been important throughout this book as the stories that I shared from particular school visits are connected to a time and place in the place of learning/school's timeline and in the timeline of the School Tourist, especially realising that "places are not experienced in a similar manner by everyone" (Jiron, 2010, p. 131). I would argue that through gaining these mobile new experiences performing School Tourism we continue to be developing our becoming identity (see Mendus et al., 2020) as the School Tourist continues to reflexively respond to the differing school visits. As Edensor argues, "places are always becoming, and a human, whether stationary or travelling, is one element in a seething space pulsing with intersecting trajectories and temporalities" (2010, p. 7). Therefore, there is potentiality for change from hearing stories from School Tourists and there are even more possibilities from individuals visiting schools themselves as everyone will have a different experience and come with their own preconceived views about education and what they would observe to be a 'gem.'

By connecting performing School Tourism to rhizomatic theory, the visit itself can be seen as a nodal point from which the stories that are shared can spread throughout the rhizome to unknown (beyond the self) ends. Sharing stories can also be seen as a political act (Freire, 1970; Labonte, 2011; Spry, 2011), as giving new ideas can thereby enable others to be mobilised for change. This change can be supported by framing performing School Tourism through the lens of Massumi's (2015) understanding of affect that: "When you affect something, you are at the same time opening yourself up to be affected in turn, and in a slightly different way than you might have been in the moment before" (p. 4). Therefore, the affect of School Tourism can be seen to be rhizomatic, with some changes happening immediately, others at varied times and others not yet known when or if they will have an affect, but an awareness of their potentiality. For example; the School Tourist can be seen as becoming a 'Cultural Broker' (Giroux, 2005), through sharing stories they have the potentiality to make change by filling a gap in the understanding of approaches to 'educating differently.' Whereas the corporeal spatial practice of School Tourism, the 'literal act of travelling' (Braidotti, 2012) somewhere and then not just observing with your eyes but emotionally (Zemblyas, 2003) by "physically walking or seeing or touching or hearing or smelling a place" (Urry, 2007, p. 261) is very much present in the now. Sharing stories from the embodied experience is part of the future whereas embodying the feeling journey within the school is very much about the present.

All these theories combined create a conceptual framework of Performing School Tourism as a mobile method, an ever moving rhizomatic dance between periphery and centre (Braidotti, 2012; hooks, 1984). However, there are certain aspects within this theoretical stance that need to be troubled and critiqued.

3   A Troubling of Performing School Tourism

I have recognised several critiques of performing School Tourism that will be discussed in this section. These include issues such as hierarchy, patriarchy, the dangers of volun-tourism and a critique of the term 'tourist' and 'school.' I am aware that one of my conclusions (see Chapter 3) from my research is that 'school' is not the answer, nor does it cover all places 'educating differently' as some do not even use the term 'school.' My hope is that by beginning to trouble into performing School Tourism, it can live beyond this book and be something that can be developed, disagreed with and understood in new ways.

Although I consciously use the word 'tourist' in this book, assumptions around this term need to be critiqued. Professor Michael Kamen, fellow teacher, academic and, in my opinion, 'school tourist' wrote me a thoughtful response explaining why he was reluctant to embrace the term 'school tourism' as he never liked to be associated with the negative aspects of tourists when he travelled. Particularly he had a, "worry that "tourism" may be associated with outsiders changing a place, pushing interactions away from their cultural fidelity" (Kamen, personal communication by email, 2017). Reading Michael's words made me question my terminology, maybe I was not a 'tourist'? Michael asked:

> Is Alys... better described as an ethnographer, or on a quest, or a story-teller, or an explorer, or an educator, or critic (as in restaurant or theatre or film)? (Kamen, personal communication by email, 2017)

I hear what Michael is asking and realise that that is why I carried out the research through the lens of multiple identities of the Alys-we, as there I could give voice to the person on a quest, the ethnographer, the explorer and educator. Therefore, the 'tourist' in performing 'School Tourism' is multifaceted and I argue that 'tourist' is positioned not as a negative term, but one that is empowering as it is through the 'tourist gaze' that I, "view a set of different scenes, of landscapes or townscapes [or schools] which are out of the ordinary" (Urry & Larsen, 2011, p. 3). I do not see myself as a school inspector, taking on the 'critic' hat that Michael suggested, as that involves a different approach altogether, one that is comparing each school to an 'Ideal School' rubric which, I argue, is impossible as we all have our own subjective understandings of schooling. However, as the School Tourist I am able to share stories between different schools, settings, educators and parents in the UK and abroad that can cause a ripple effect for personal change, rather than top down hierarchical 'school improvements' from an inspector.

Michael Kamen raised a further point about School Tourism, "I am thinking what Alys is doing is much deeper, more important, and more interesting than the image of a tourist provokes in me" (Kamen, personal communication by email, 2017). I agree with Michael that my work hopes to be deeper overall. So, in a way, I like the 'grittiness' of School Tourism, that it creates a rise and a raise of an eyebrow. However, I am aware of the level of privilege and colonialist history that accompanies 'tourism' that I must continue to trouble into.

Colonial privilege can be seen in 'voluntourism.' This is where people travel to different areas in the world to volunteer in education, environmental and community projects and I do not want performing School Tourism to be described as 'voluntourism.' Stanley's important work (2013, 2017) critiques the troubling nature of colonial privilege in 'voluntourism':

> Like backpacker tourism, 'saving the world' is one of the discourses among foreign teachers. This motivation type, of 'helping,' carries overtones of the 'White man's burden' in which imperialism was justified as a noble purpose in which Western expertise could help lift non-Western peoples out of poverty and ignorance. (Stanley, 2013, pp. 27–28)

This reminds the School Tourist to be aware of their position within a school visit. They are a guest of the school and, culturally, that brings with it polite interactions but also an awareness that your visit is taking up time within the school day and a redirecting of those showing you around from their usual activities. I have learnt that those in the school may not be interested in your experiences of how other schools have approached similar problems, they may not want to be 'helped' nor see your opinions as valid or needed. There can also be an unsettling position where the School Tourist can be seen to be doing something that the observed teacher would like to do, but cannot. I have learnt for a need to be aware of the "power relations between gazer and gaze within tourism performances" (Urry & Larsen, 2011, p. 15) as I am able/choose to do something that the other teachers in a school are not as likely to be able to do. The concept of motility supports this further, seen as "the manner in which an individual or group appropriates the field of possibilities relative to movement and uses them" (Kaufmann & Montulet, 2008, p. 45). Or, in other words, motility is a measure of a person's ability or access to be mobile. Kaufmann and Montulet (2004), discuss a 'mobility capital' where different people have different levels of access to motility. For example, I have chosen to have a high level of motility and thereby travel the UK and abroad to visit many schools. However, many educators that I work with have a low level of motility as they are bound by contractual agreements to be in their own school throughout the year, so do not have the time to visit other places.

Another critique of 'voluntourism,' particularly for people on gap years in developing countries, is the unofficial "position of expert, or at least as knowledgeable by locating them in roles such as teachers" (Simpson, 2005, p. 51). Stanley rightly questions that the "hiring of unskilled Westerners in jobs that would normally require qualifications may be of questionable ethical standing" (2013, p. 28). In my research, as well as being a School Tourist I am also a qualified teacher. So, when I visit schools I come truthfully in the position of a trained teacher, but not necessarily an 'expert' as I only taught full-time in a state-school for 2 years before spending the next 10 years as a self-employed educator. I have become an 'expert' in different types of schools from the sheer number and variety that I have visited, but each country is different and there are huge gaps in my work.

I displayed a power-point slide to the group of teachers showing a map of all the countries around the world that I had visited and the number of schools (see Figure 14).

"I notice that there are large gaps of countries that do not predominantly speak English. How do you choose which countries to visit?" Asked one teacher.

"That's a great question. I have been wondering about that as well. I think it has been mostly due to ease, in places where I speak the language, I can have more in-depth conversations and speak to both adults and children. I have visited some places where I do not speak the language so I have organised a friend or someone at the school who will translate for me but this does mean that I don't have as many 'back-stage' (Goffman, 1959) more informal conversations" I replied.

My monolingualism has also limited my access to literature on educational alternatives. There are several key texts in German, Spanish, Portuguese and French that have not been translated into English, so as I do not understand these languages this work is not included in this study. My hope is that someone will work with these texts in the future. (Mendus, Reflections on a teacher training session [Germany, June 2017])

School Tourism is not trying to create a rose-tinted view of research, as there are many aspects that could easily be overlooked. For example, the role of patriarchy and hierarchy in the schools that are visited and the role that the School Tourist has themselves, as well as the School Tourist's prior knowledge of an educational approach or having known contacts at that school. The role of the School Tourist has been described as an insider/outsider (emic/etic) position. Naake, Kurylo, Grabowski, Linton and Radford (2011) describe emic perspectives to be those taken by a researcher who is a member of the community being studied, etic perspectives are those taken by a researcher who is an outsider to the community being studied. However, extending the importance of rhizomatic theory in performing School Tourism, this book follows Hellawell (2006) who argues that instead of stressing a binary that the researcher should use an insider/outsider continuum as a heuristic device. For example, when I visit a Steiner Waldorf school, as a qualified Steiner Waldorf teacher I enter into a different relationship (that of somewhat insider), but also I am a visitor to that particular school and a researcher with my own list of critiques to Steiner Waldorf education (so also partially an outsider). Thereby, following Reed-Danahay's (2017) arguments that autoethnography lies at "the intersection of insider and outsider perspectives, rather than setting up a dualism that privileges the insider account" (p. 1), this book attempts to use reflexivity to prevent a dualism of positionality being established. The dualism is also prevented by viewing the rhizomatic movement between insider and outsider reflexively, following hooks' (1984) use of margin and centre as descriptors of positionality. This adds to Braidotti's (2012) concept of the nomadic movement between the centre and the periphery, as an awareness of power and change to positionality within different relationships as I recognize that I move from the margin and centre several times, even within one school visit.

It is also essential to be aware of aspects of visible privilege such as age, gender, physical ability and skin colour. Privilege needs to be examined, especially when visiting places in a different country or culture of your own, as there could be a level of assumed hierarchy and potential colonial privilege. Writing this book in Australia, as a 'settler academic' (Country et al., 2019; Rowe & Tuck, 2016) on stolen Indigenous land, reminds me again of my place of privilege and urges me to follow Lupinacci (2020) to not think being an activist scholar is 'enough,' but to also constantly question and trouble my assumptions and privilege. This reminds me again to ask: Who is Alys when she walks into the classroom? The question can also be put to the reader to think about when they too walk into a classroom, what stories, what privileges and assumptions do they carry; visible/invisible, spoken/silenced...

> *Who is Alys-we?*
> *My positionality positions me away from the others*
> *The others being my colleagues... the teachers*
> *Often people like me who did well in school*
> *But for some reason I just don't fit*
> *The Queering of 'Bad-Alys' unsettles this*
> *Yet still I have entered a hierarchical career*
> *How when I thought I was an anarchist?*
> *Is there hope for me?*
> *For teaching?*
> *For education?*

I argue that performing the nomadology of rhizomatic School Tourism is one way of stepping away from current patriarchal educational patterns. As Braidotti says:

> Nomadism is an invitation to disidentify ourselves from the sedentary *phallocentric* [emphasis added] monologism of philosophical thinking and to start cultivating the art of disloyalty, or rather that form of healthy disrespect for both academic and intellectual conventions that

was inaugurated and propagated by the second feminist wave. (Braidotti, 2012, p. 24)

Reading this idea of 'phallocentricism' reinforced my awareness of something that I had coined OWMS (Old White Men with assumed privilege), which had been troubling me as I visited places that aim to be educating differently and I saw hierarchy, status and privilege given to the older white men in that place of learning/school. It also began to give me the bravery to bring the concept of 'OWMS' into the dialogue of the research. I am also aware of the term DWEM (Dead White European Male), used to think about the number of dead, white, European men who continue to influence the academy (Gale, 2017). Gale's (2017) comment adds to observations by Phillips and Bunda (2018) who speak of the issue of academia pushing the work and giving adulation to individuals, "especially white male scholars" (p. 64) who are the dominant voices that are heard in academia. For example, "The Foucault fan club, Bourdieu fan club, Deleuze fan club [create] academic idolation of these white male scholars [which] is widespread and disturbing" (Phillips & Bunda, 2018, p. 64). This reminds me to be more conscious about my responsibility of who I cite in my work and that by continuing to cite dominant scholars I perpetuate the silencing of less known academics, particularly women, LGBTQIA, people of colour, people with disabilities and other silenced groups.

There was only one time that I needed to stand up to my host, a school principal, and leave before the visit was over. This experience highlighted white-privilege, patriarchy and a patronising attitude in action. For the School Tourist it shares an example that not every school visit plays out as expected and acts as a prompt that the School Tourist is temporally engaged in the visit, not always as a placid observer but as a political being. It is a reminder to be responsible to stand-up for one's own rights and of others, again drawing back to Lupinacci's (2020) call for activist scholars to be responsible in calling out their privilege and anyone who uses their position against others.

"You need search no longer" he says
"For we are the 'Ideal School.'"
And something inside me clenches
And my hackles rise
What is going on here?
The 'Ideal School' is an oxymoron!
The tour of the school shows classes so silent the doors can be left open into the
hall
For no one is disturbed

By the silence of 'Obedience.'
Our guides, so happy to be here,
So passionate about learning and achieving
Futures destined to academic High-Schools.
I felt proud of our guides
Knowing little about their lives except the stories told on the website
Children from families of 'lowest income and highest values'
Later, I dared to ask the Principal about 'values'
How did I know I would agitate the
HORNETS NEST?
B U Z Z ZZZZZ ZZZZZ ZZZZ ZZZZZZZZ
Accusations and theories about me and my life followed...
"Doctorate students this..."
"Your Professors that...."
"I've never had anyone not be impressed EVER...."
My attempts to interrupt stopped with sarcasm
"You will never hear but maybe you don't want to...
"You want my answer to write your thesis..."
How can this man make such judgements about me?
He knows nothing about me at all.
Heart racing, anxious tension
(Whilst, in the background, bloody strong incense is burning and itching my eyes
and throat)
He does not know that my whole thesis is about a feeling journey...
I hate being patronised.
I sat there lost
Feeling stripped bare
Violated even...
Later he mentions 'kindness' as a value and 'loyal' and 'hardworking' and
'agile'...
"Thank you" I say
"Thank you, that was what I was looking for earlier."
He continues to talk more, answering questions, waffling on and I find myself
writing
OWM on my page in front of me
Wow an (old) white man in action!
True privilege, arrogance...
I mentioned I felt uncomfortable
He said, "not my problem"
I said, "my emotions are my own, so I shall leave..."

And now in the lobby I sit
Shocked…. Alone…
Thinking about all the schools I have visited
I have never had to leave before.
Across from me a 12 year old girl is ringing her parents
A teacher and receptionist beside her
"Mom, I lied to my teacher," she explains in a small voice
My stomach tightens at the shame.
Our guide had just agreed this was his
'Ideal School'
"REALLY?" I shout silently inside.
And it is not for me in my position of privilege to judge
Knowing that for one of our guides the opportunities from this school are likely
to have transformed his life.
Yet the OWM in charge speaks sarcastically and judgmentally
to visitors
Which makes me cry out at this hypocrisy.
(Mendus, Poem written in the school lobby [New York, May 2017])

FIGURE 61
A classroom where the Principal
described the school as 'Ideal'

4   The Ethics of Performing School Tourism

The agency of School Tourism can allow for consent to be asked for a story to be shared, but once a story is told it takes on its own agentic level of 'aliveness' (see Sheller, 2014, p. 804). Calls to celebrate the "living state" (Phillips & Bunda, 2018, p. 13) of a story remind me that those who share and those who tell do not have control of where it ends up, as whoever comes in contact with that story interacts with it from their own rhizomatic story of existence. By positioning this concept that sharing these stories is theoretical through the verbification of the term 'story,' to becoming 'storying' (see Phillips & Bunda, 2018) acknowledges the power, potentiality and "emergent meaning" (Phillips & Bunda, 2018, p. 7) of each story arc.

Therefore, the stories in this book from the experiences of each separate school visit or conversation are more fragmentary and less accountable to one person or single opinion. It can be argued, following Barad (2007), that these stories are becoming diffracted (Barad, 2007) and that these diffracted stories can be viewed to have their own 'agency' and potentiality for change as, "through storying, we come to live, breath and feel deep penetrating understandings of identity and place" (Phillips & Bunda, 2018, p. 39). Therefore, by ethically viewing School Tourism as beyond the single "I," beyond the person that has visited, to an intra-action between multiple shared other-than-body experiences rhizomatically together, I argue that there is a composting that occurs after an intra-action; the many layers that come from new thoughts, feelings, smells and ways of looking at the world that are beyond the original school visit. This can materialize as the taking on and the letting go of other ideas to decompose, nourishing existence both human and non-human.

However, although I am arguing that the stories and the experiences are beyond traditional understandings of consent, ethical research practices are still needed to be followed. Most of this book came from my PhD research and as a student at the University of Hull, UK I gained ethical approval for visiting schools and for anonymising those places where consent was not formally granted (because of visits prior to the PhD or non-return of forms). That being said, I am aware of Ellis's (2007) argument that gaining ethical approval in itself does not make your work ethical, you have to continually be reflexive to be ethical. Therefore, this book includes the names of schools where informed consent was given or where I paid to attend a visit or course at that school. This journalling excerpt explores that ethical dilemma.

> As a PhD student living on a student bursary I lived well in our van, with just enough money to travel and visit schools around the world. I have

my own ethics that I do not pay to visit schools but ask and if they say yes then visit and then send a write-up about my visit which the school can choose to share in school newsletters. Both the Green School (visited in 2016) and Tamera Ecovillage Community, Portugal (visited in 2013, 2016) were exceptions to this rule and it is interesting to reflect how much on a pedestal I had positioned the outcome. For both, I joined an expensive week long course; at the Green School the 'educators course' and at Tamera, where even though I had been in extensive discussion with the school teachers I was asked to join their Introduction week (similar to the Green School) to be taught about the philosophies and approaches of Tamera before I could visit the school.

With reflection, paying for School Tourism makes the performance closer connected to actual tourism – a buying in of a service not usually part of your life. Being aware of the different interactions and power structures that are put in place (even if hidden) once money is added to the equation is interesting and I hope that in my future School Tourism if I choose to pay to visit a school that I am also aware of the imbalance and avoid putting a particular school/place of learning on a pedestal. (Mendus, Journalling about paying for School Tourism [Brighton, July 2017])

In other cases, schools have been anonymised and described only by their 'self-labelled pedagogy' and location. In all cases I argue that assent was gained for me, as a researcher, to be visiting the school and carrying out research for my PhD. Before visiting a school as a solo School Tourist, I emailed each school, including in the body of the email an overview of my project and my wish to visit their school as part of my study. After each visit, I sent back my observation notes to each school, asking for consent and to check the details from my writings. Many schools replied to these notes and I updated my records. However, many schools, although keen for me to visit and who had organised visit schedules and even had many members of the school community give me extensive time during the visit, did not reply to my follow up email. In these situations, I inferred consent from the school for my physical visit as a School Tourist and from that took assent to use notes from the visit in my research.

However, I kept my own personal journalling, my own storying of my experience to myself until I began to weave the text for the autoethnographic-we. This follows Ellis's (2007) advice to her students that they do not always need to show their autoethnographic writing to those involved but, you should be able to defend your reasons for not seeking their responses" (Ellis, 2007, p. 25) as well as being aware that you must always assume that everyone in your story will read it. Warmstead (2012) argues that when writing autoethnographically about an interaction with another person then their experience is only relevant in how it makes the autoethnographer think and feel and want to retell the story, "My colleague is... merely a character in the novel I am telling about my own life – a character far beyond my ability to theorize as an independent being" (Warmstead, 2012, p. 186). My reasons not to share these personal reflections to each school follow the advice of Ellis (2007) and Warmstead (2012), with an awareness that the stories from performing School Tourism are all connected to the complex web of my thoughts and understandings of education and I did not want each school to feel that I was unduly criticizing them. There were also times when adults during the visit shared particularly sensitive or evocative memories or strong opinions that I did not feel were appropriate to share in a document that is emailed and shared to the school and in my records. These stories were stored in my head, where I could decide to disseminate the new information internally as it may help me in my thinking and understanding of my research in the future.

Therefore, by being aware of this complexity around writing about others I ensured that I was constantly reflexive throughout. When I chose to include excerpts of my journalling in this book, I aimed to be storying from "an ethic of care" (Ellis, 2007; Noddings, 1984). Ellis's (2013) words give further guidance for ethical practice that autoethnography 'requires that we observe ourselves observing, that we interrogate what we think and believe' (2013, p. 10). I have done this by using journalling, but also by turning my journalling into ethnodramas and poems to show my developing arguments and my continued reflexivity. As well, I am hoping that this iteration of my storying supports Phillips and Bunda's (2018) argument that, "Storying is an ethically value-driven way of being and knowing the world... driven by motivations of inclusivity – to welcome and broaden audiences" (p. 105).

5   Alys the Guide

Offering this theoretical insight into the complexities around performing School Tourism hopes to engage the reader with all aspects of the approach so they are prepared to start becoming performing School Tourism themselves.

This poem attempts to show the intricacies of defining performing School Tourism:

Performing School Tourism...

Stems from curiosity
Spans rhizomatic iterative journeying

Is a relationship between people, places, feelings and objects creating an integrated assemblage,
Spins an ever-becoming performance
Encompassing the embodied encounter allowing the emotional body of the Performer to speak
In an ever-changing temporal practice
That has potentiality
And possibility to affect change
So that the agency of new experiences can be influencing new visions
Reminding others that it is the 'literal act of travelling' that makes this difference
Dancing on the patchwork quilt
Storying
Weaving-with.

6 Summary

– Issues that have arisen from troubling performing School Tourism include the role of hierarchy, patriarchy, the dangers of volun-tourism and a critique of the term 'tourist' and 'school.'
– School Tourist continues to be the term used, although this book has discredited the word 'school' and is cautious about the word 'tourist.' However, because it is the tourist *"gaze"* (Urry & Larsen, 2011) that observes these places 'educating differently,' not the inspector with a set rubric of what makes a school 'ideal' as that is not the agenda, the word 'tourist' continues to make sense. It is the ripple-effect that sharing stories from School Tourism creates, rather than top-down enforced changes from a School Inspector. The term 'tourism' is used with care and with an awareness of its level of privilege and the colonialist history that accompanies it.
– This chapter takes a feminist stance to explore the concept of OWMS (old white men with assumed privilege) and their continued role in education, including in schools and places of learning that are educating differently.
– The ethics of performing School Tourism remind the reader about the power of storying (Phillips & Bunda, 2018), that once someone has visited a school they take with them in their body and in their story an experience that they can share with others which is beyond the initial teller or school itself. This chapter reminds those performing School Tourism to share stories with an ethic of care (Ellis, 2007; Noddings, 1984). School names are only included in this book if consent was given or the author paid to visit that school on an official visit.

CHAPTER 11

Becoming a School Tourist

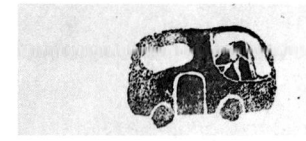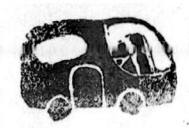

"So, what school do you advise us to send our kids to then?" is a question I get regularly asked. And for anyone who has read my whole book they will know that there is no 'Ideal School' as school is not the answer! But I can't say that to an expectant friend keen for some advice. I'm meant to be the expert after all... I can offer some of my own thoughts for my future children that I still, like Steiner Kindergarten and collective home education/ unschooling, but for many people asking me for advice that isn't what they are looking for. So I have sat with this, followed my own recommendations of inner work, and realised that performing School Tourism hasn't just been for me to learn about what schools/places of learning are out there or for pre-service teachers/current teachers to gain stories to share about 'educating differently,' it is also for parents and children.

"Perform School Tourism," I answer.

Anyone can be a School Tourist.

"Performing School Tourism is the answer... It does not even need to be about 'educating differently,' it is about your own inner journey, the embodied feelings you get from visiting schools" I explain.

"How do I go about performing School Tourism?" they ask.

"Find out what is on offer in your area, what is your budget, beliefs and then visit places and see what feels right for your children and family" I reply.

Of course, this still assumes a level of privilege and social capital (see Bourdieu, 1986), to not send your children by default to the local state-school. But for those asking, I am beginning to have some answers and for those not aware then this is where this book can help – dip in and out, read the stories and choose your own adventure around innovative education. (Mendus, From journalling on being asked for school recommendations [Cornwall, UK, September 2017/ Moreton Bay, AU, November 2020])

1   Alys the Guide

I invite you to become a school tourist yourself. I know many people I speak to want to send their child to the local state school, hoping that by choosing their local school they can be a part of their immediate community and make grass roots changes. However, I am arguing that even when a state funded school is your decision to work at, attend or for your children to attend, I suggest that you go and visit other places of learning/schools to embody which school culture, climate and environment suits you. In the UK most people are in the catchment for several schools, so I recommend that you visit these schools on open days or go to school fairs or shows. I argue that although schools are often following a national curriculum, they are all managed by different people and in different neighbourhoods, creating very different school cultures. I hope that from reading this book you will have become more informed of aspects of education that are important to you and that you can, through visiting several schools, find somewhere that is a best-fit. I am aware that I write this call for people to become School Tourists themselves from a place of privilege and that for many the closest school is where their children will attend. However, I am arguing that for whoever is able, by going out and visiting as many different innovative schools as possible, your experiences and understanding of what is possible within education broadens. These experiences of new ways of educating have the potential to become part of your future classroom, school experiences or home life, as well as your own identity and awareness of possibilities for a paradigm shift.

Expanding this further, this chapter hopes to position performing School Tourism as a mediation between creativity, arts, learning and teaching by understanding that physically performing School Tourism is a social approach to learning. It is the spontaneous learning that comes through the communication with those at the school, the journey and embodied more-than-human experience that helps shape the identity of the School Tourist. Wenger's (2010) Community of Practice, which views learning as becoming, is a helpful framing of this becoming-identity (see also Deleuze and Guattari, 1980/1987). Becoming identity from performing School Tourism is explored within this chapter, building upon important details such as what is included in a school visit, examples from working with Middle School students designing their Ideal School and from performing School Tourism with Pre-service teachers in New York. This chapter hopes to give the reader the skills to perform School Tourism themselves, as well as a deeper understanding of how visiting innovative schools can help shift understandings of education and the future of learning.

2 Alys the School Tourist: Other School Tourists...

My work sits amongst a few others who also visit schools around the world, sharing stories for change (Dintersmith, 2018; Grauer, 2016; Gravata et al., 2017; Gribble, 1998; Kamen & Shepherd, 2013; Little & Ellison, 2015; Mendus et al., 2020, Reddy, 2017). I was inspired by the late David Gribble, retired teacher and author of many books on 'educating differently,' particularly Democratic Education. His book, 'Real Education' (1998), shares his stories from 18 schools (16 of which he visited) from around the world that "decline to train children to become cogs, and indeed help children who have been so trained to lose their coggishness" (1998, p. 2). Gribble does not give his journeys to visit schools a specific term (like School Tourist), but Grauer (2016) suggests the term of 'Edu-tourism' for students and teachers travelling to visit other schools and their students around the world. Following this theme, Philippe Grier led an online-based organisation called 'Edu on Tour'[1] which aimed to mobilise change makers and educators around the world to make a difference in education. They held several six week long events for people to visit schools in a particular country and network them together so that they could skill share and host an in-country conference.

3 Alys the Theorist: What Counts as a School Visit?

> Do I need to spend a week in a school or a full year to understand how it works?
> Or is one day enough?
> And within that day must I observe lessons to really know what is going on?
> Or is a chat with teachers and being shown around enough?
> And do the students need to be there? (Mendus, Journalling about School Tourism [Cumbria, June 2017])

When creating a list of schools that I have visited around the world, all or some of the above counted as a visit and sometimes I was not a 'visitor' per se, but the teacher or visiting mentor (and yet, due to rhizomatic nature of School Tourism, as it was a new place of learning for me, I also saw myself as a School Tourist...). This is definitely not a quasi-quantitative study with each school allowed a set time for a visit with the same structure so that direct comparisons can be made. Therefore, the stories shared in Part 2 occur from a wide range of experiences and time frames. However, I am aware of the potential dangers of using my experience from a short visit to extrapolate assertions about the whole school, as this is exactly what school examiners such as OFSTED in the UK do when they turn up for two days, pass judgement and leave. How do I justify School Tourism to be different from this? My approach was critiqued by David Gribble (2017). Gribble replied to my email where I mentioned how at that point I had been to over 170 schools in 19 countries:

> I am a little startled that you have visited quite so many of them. When I was visiting schools I felt it was necessary, if possible, to spend about a week in each one, because over and over again my first impressions were neutral or negative, and it was only on the third or fourth day that I seemed to begin to understand what was happening. (Gribble, personal communication by email, 13 April 2017)

Following Urry and Larsen's (2011) definition of tourism as, "a limited breaking with established routines and practices of everyday life" (p. 3), I wonder if a week in a school, as Gribble suggests, could affect the School Tourist's position, leading to a moving beyond touristing to becoming part of the school and to be potentially intertwined with internal politics? What I am clear about is that School Tourism is an embodied intra-active practice, each visit is more than a geographical study of educational spaces, so each visit needs to include those who occupy these spaces.

Therefore, I argue that although visiting an empty school site (for example at holidays/evenings/weekends) is still an element of School Tourism, to be able to *perform* School Tourism the visit needs to be on the place of learning/ school site and include interaction with people who work and/or attend there.

4   What Do I Do as a School Tourist?

Most schools that I contacted replied to my emails, were interested in my research and helped to coordinate a visit. I realise my privilege as a Steiner Waldorf teacher, as this qualification allowed me almost instant access to all Steiner Waldorf schools around the world that I contacted. The only place that I really wanted to visit that I did not gain access to was the original Sudbury democratic school in Massachusetts, USA.

When I visit each school, whether as a teacher or as an observer, I chat with and informally 'interview' every person that I meet, the conversation usually includes me asking about their journey to be working at/attending that place of learning/school and how they run day-to-day. I argue that I see these informal

FIGURE 62
Alys performing School Tourism, New York, May 2017
(photo by Michael Kamen)

'interviews,' following Kvale (1996), as conversations with purpose, hoping to be able to create 'thick description' (Geertz, 1973) in my storying. When I speak to colleagues in education or to teachers and parents at places of learning/ schools that I visit, as well as classroom and teacher observations I need to be aware, as Peterson and Langellier (in Ellis, 2004) argue, of the power relationships in these conversations whilst being aware of the "emotional dynamics within the interview itself" (Ellis, 2004, p. 61).

I recognize that these conversations also are a performance. For example; do the people I chat to, even though informally, share what they think I want to hear, or what they truly feel? Following Spry (2011), that we make meaning about ourselves and our lives through our interactions with others, I am particularly aware of hierarchies if students are allowed to talk to the visitors alone or if these conversations are chaperoned. However, it is these performances, these conversations, that are essential to performing School Tourism as they have the potentiality of "adding alternatives to a single story" (Spry, 2011, p. 124), as well as creating a space to "radically rethink the relation between bodies, movement and space" (Sheller, 2011, p. 2), recognizing an inner feeling journey. One way to radically rethink this relationship is by becoming aware of our 'inner life' (Romero, 2015). Romero's writing on inner work helps explain how the emotional experience of performing School Tourism can lead to a shift in personal understandings and perceptions of the world (and of education) as, "what creates this inner changing, streaming within, is not our reaction of liking or not liking what is observed; rather, it is the activity unseen by the eye that lives in the thing itself" (Romero, 2015, p. 14). Therefore, as I invite you to perform School Tourism, I hope that you will enter each place of learning/ school with an open heart, ready to observe and interact with the space, ask questions and reflect on how this place is making you feel, working with where it unsettles you, brings you joy and more questions. I suggest taking heed from Blackie (2016), whose words resonate with my experiences visiting places of learning/schools:

> As I walk, my own stories begin to take shape and merge with stories past. So it is that we give birth to new stories each morning, the land and I, along these old bog roads. I set out as one creature and may return home another. (Blackie, 2016, p. 184)

5   Alys the School Tourist: Group and Solo School Tourism

Most of the School Tourism that has occurred within this book was carried out alone, which was mostly down to the solo journey of the PhD, but not the definition of School Tourism. Meeting Michael Kamen in March 2017 and being invited to join him and three students from Southwestern University, Texas to visit schools in New York in May 2017 gave me an opportunity to share my School Tourism performances with others. It was an exciting and formative experience.

FIGURE 63   Group School Tourism, New York, May 2017. L–R: Abigail Earle, Sarah Buchanan, Alys Mendus, Kelli McLaughlin, Michael Kamen, Adaire Kamen

This poem shares my initial reactions to group School Tourism.

Watching the students wonder (like me) at the examples we are seeing

Worried I am talking too much, asking too much...
I am not so self conscious when I am on my own.

The camaraderie of the group
The recap coffee with Michael
Helps me see the bigger picture
Refocusses me on the gems when I get lost by my annoyances.

With the group I need to justify myself or be gently reminded
To stop bitching and finding fault in every place I visit
My writing changes, my memories shift
I am no longer sitting recalling every moment of a visit in great detail as if paint-
ing a picture of my shadow following me around the schools
I'm now focussing on the key points
The possible gems, the things I will take away.
(Mendus, First thoughts on group School Tourism [New York, May 9th 2017])

With hindsight, I see that through writing the poem above I was able to realise that, through performing School Tourism as part of an intentional group, I had become more accountable for my opinions, feelings and thoughts. In contrast, the week after visiting schools in New York, I carried out some solo School Tourism where I felt a little lost and lonely without having colleagues to discuss and reflect on the experience. However, thinking with Braidotti (2012) helps remove the concept of the solo, separate School Tourist and looks at the act of performing School Tourism as a nomadic vision of the body, going in and out of places of learning/schools, "as multifunctional and complex, as a transformer of flows and energies, affects, desires, and imaginings" (p. 24). Therefore, even when I was carrying out these later place of learning/school visits alone, I was not alone, but part of a wider network.

Reflecting back on Goffman's (1959) idea of front and back stage conversations, I realise that group School Tourism does provide a level of hierarchies. Michael worked very hard to make sure that I was introduced not as one of his students but as a peer, but I was aware that, unfortunately, often cultural norms defer to the older man as the 'expert' and I realised that I was not always allowed the more personal and deep and open conversations that often happen when I visit places alone.

It is interesting to reflect on the role the 'tourist' can play in the size of a group performing School Tourism, as the School Tourist is a guest into a busy organisation of a school or place of learning. Urry and Larsen also argue that tourism is "about the body-as-seen, displaying, performing and seducing visitors with skill, charm, strength, sexuality and so on..." (Urry & Larsen, 2011, p. 22). So, although I may argue that the School Tourist brings stories from other places and shares reflections and insights with the teachers who are often too busy to visit schools elsewhere, they are also taking up time, resources and energy from children and adults involved in the school. I am aware, however, that the same time is required to show a School Tourist around, answer questions and observe lessons for one or for six people. Maybe it is easier for a school to have a larger group than several solo School Tourists?

Nevertheless, I know that I can ask more questions when I go alone. However, other people think differently and I learn from their questions and from having the opportunity to debrief afterwards. Therefore, I think there is a strength to my stories in Part 2, as they weave these differing experiences of solo and group School Tourism and share my developing understandings and reflection.

6 Alys Educating-Differently: Working with School Students to Find the Ideal School

6.1 *Leysin American School, Switzerland, March 2017*

Dr Paul Magnuson runs the Leysin American School research faculty (LASER) where I have worked twice during my PhD journey as a visiting scholar. Leysin American School is an international boarding school which focuses on International Baccalaureate for its 9–12 Grade students. The younger students (7/8 Grade) are part of an innovative Middle School programme. Knowing about my research, Magnuson devised a project on the 'Ideal School' where groups of middle schoolers, using the eduScrum approach (explained in Chapter 9) were given the challenge of:

> Presenting their ideal schools in a poster session at a conference... to which all of our seventh through tenth graders would come, as well as some students and faculty members from other schools. We also told them that an expert in ideal schools, Alys, would arrive in the last weeks of the project to give feedback on the students' ideal schools based on her many school visits across the world. (Magnuson & Mendus, 2017, p. 51)

I have given talks about my journey 'Searching for the Ideal School' around the world to undergraduate students at Plymouth university and post-graduates at the University of Hull and it often leads to fascinating discussions, especially when I ask them to design their 'Ideal School.' Running a similar concept with young people currently in school was a fascinating experience and I hoped it would reveal authentic opinions from children in 2017.

However, following Hughes's work on 'imagining otherwise' which argues "how could young people possibly imagine a school with no classrooms or even walls if they have no knowledge or experience of it?" (2015, p. 239), I worked with the middle schoolers for two weeks and tried very hard to offer them lots of radical stories of 'educating differently' to hopefully allow them the opportunity to be brave with their ideas. With hindsight, I recognised that it was still a school project and that the system is hierarchical, with students predisposed to please the teacher. So, it was not surprising that:

> On the surface it appeared that four out of the six schools seemed very similar to LAS [Leysin American School], which on the one hand was a credit to the current system, but on the other hand raised questions of how seriously the students had taken up the challenge to design their own 'Ideal School.' However, once Alys began to get to know the students she was able to dig further and extrapolate what made each school unique. (Magnuson & Mendus, 2017, p. 51)

I used my approach of looking for 'gems' from performing School Tourism with the poster presentations from each of the schools that the students designed and in my talk about 'Searching for the Ideal School' I found examples internationally that had similarities to the group's ideal. Reflecting on the project in class, the students gave their own suggestions of changes that could occur

FIGURE 64   Ideal School poster 1, Switzerland, March 2017

in their current school that would make it more 'ideal' for them, see Figures 64 and 65 for examples of the students work. One student gave an interesting opinion on what is 'school':

> There was unanimous support for their Ideal School having classes, although Alys had repeatedly emphasised that the Ideal School does not need to be in a building nor even have a time-table, sharing with students notions about "Democratic Education." One sceptical student responded: "Our ideal school would have classes because without classes the school isn't a school." (Magnuson & Mendus, 2017, p. 52)

This was a fascinating project to be involved with and I recognised that, although the students came from 14 different countries, the costs of attending Leysin American School added another level of privilege and background to the opinions of these students on what is 'school.' However, I think it opens up many possibilities of entering into 'Ideal School' projects with other students around the world whereby children are encouraged to question the status quo from a young age, hopefully resulting in a higher likelihood for future change. By visiting and experiencing other schools I argue that young people could have more examples and understandings of what is school and begin to demand something different for their future. The sudden, overnight, international transformation to at-home learning around the world in 2020 means that the current generation of school children know that physical school is not the only answer to education. Even though Sahlberg argued that 'at home' learning during the pandemic was not necessarily innovative as "learning from home has been mostly based on the old logic of consuming information and knowledge rather than creating or co-creating new ideas and solutions to real-life problems" (2020, p. 359). Many of this same generation have also

FIGURE 65
Ideal School poster 2, Switzerland,
March 2017

been involved in grass-roots activism with the monthly climate strikes, realizing that their voice counts and can be part of the change (Martiskainen, Axon, Sovacool, Sareen, Del Rio, & Axon, 2020).

7   Alys the School Tourist: Visiting Innovative Schools with Preservice Teachers

7.1   *The Innovative School Class, New York, May 2017*

In contrast to working with school students, I was very lucky to join Professor Michael Kamen, his daughter Adaire and three of his students from Southwestern University, Texas on a week's school tourism visiting innovative schools in New York city in May 2017. Michael Kamen and I met at the Beyond Words conference at the University of Plymouth, March 2017. The week in New York was part of an elective course on the pre-service teacher training. In 5 days, we visited a range of state-funded and private schools using a variety of pedagogical approaches, including Progressive and Democratic, as well as targeting issues of social justice and rebelling against high stakes testing. Some stories from these school visits are included in Part 2. The students had to write reflective journals on the school visits and had to design their own Ideal Schools. In comparison to the middle schoolers, these students had a wider range of experiences to draw from although, quite surprising to me, they were not much more radical. However, Michael and I realised that the experience of visiting schools had a longer-term affect on these teachers becoming-teacher identity. As a group, we all wrote into the experience of visiting schools and its continuing legacy and created a collaborative ethnodrama which was performed at the Performing the World conference in NYC in September 2018. This play script has been crafted into a chapter for a book on Affect and Performance in Education which is being published in December 2020 (Mendus et al., 2020). The following two excerpts from the collaborative ethnodrama are shared here: the section from Scene 4, as an example of our collective voices discussing visiting innovative schools, and the section from Scene 8, to share the continuing dialogue between Michael and I about the importance of visiting innovative schools and our responsibilities to pre-service teachers and to education.

> *Scene 4: "They call teachers by their first names..."*
> STAGE NOTES: Location: Group walking out of a school gate of a Progressive school in NYC, May 2017.
> Alys: One of the things I loved about that school was how the students called the teachers by their first names. I'm very interested

in unpacking hierarchies and societal norms in the classroom. I think by using first names there is an opportunity to connect as people. An opportunity for mutual respect, instead of superficiality or arbitrary customs.

Kelli: It was so interesting to observe it in action! I think I actually like the idea of having the students call teachers and administrators by their first names. I think it really does eliminate some of the weird authoritative-like stigma that comes from calling someone Mr. or Mrs. As the students put it, it really does make you feel like you're talking on the same level as someone. This could be something to take with me into my future teaching career. I've always said that I would like to be Ms. Kelli, since I don't really like the way my last name sounds, but now I'm thinking of throwing out the Ms. as well.

Abby: Uhh... I'm not sure if I agree with that idea – with students and teachers being on the same level. A teacher is still an adult. I think if a student still used Mrs. or Mr. in front of the first name, that might work for the teacher and student relationship. But... I still like last names used, especially with secondary students.

Sarah: I think I'm with you. I'm not sure how I feel about letting students call teachers by their first name. I agree that simply putting a Mr. or Mrs. in front of a person's name doesn't automatically make you respect them, but I do think that it is one step towards respecting them. I think I need to learn more about that before deciding about my own classroom.

(Mendus et al., 2020, pp. 225–226)

Scene 8: Michael and Alys Video Call Following the NYC School Visits
STAGE NOTES: Recorded video chat.

Alys: When we visit schools, we need to be aware of our privilege. We are white, able-bodied, and able to afford to study/work at university and to spend a week in New York. When we walk into these schools each day we need to hold an awareness of this. We, too, are part of the performance. We wear our privileges as we visit schools, and in turn the schools perform to us and share what they want us to see. There are many unspoken themes, topics and judgements left hanging in the air. We had one challenge with the patriarchy and what I know we discussed later as 'white saviour' concept. What responsibility do we have in not only visiting schools but in sharing the stories from these places we visit? How do we tell these stories? What language do we use?

Michael: Yes, and in turn you and I have the responsibility of choosing which schools we visit and which schools we choose for the students to experience.

Alys: Exactly. New York is unique in that way. We managed to choose several places that tackle diversity, social justice, and inclusion in numerous ways. I was impressed by one school we visited that had created a sliding scale of tuition fees in an attempt to include more students, but I was frustrated when I realised that this still is not an option for families from the poorest areas. It was unsettling in some ways to visit some exciting and innovative schools and know that many were only accessible to affluent families.

Michael: That's why we're visiting public schools as well as private schools. We even visited a public school that doesn't participate in high-stakes testing at all. We toured a few others that have made social justice a key part of their curriculum.

Alys: It's been such a treat to visit so many schools and to have a group of people to talk about each experience with. I have felt that these discussions have really helped my thinking and ability to reflect on different places and to unpick my own privileges, assumptions, and biases. Although I do wonder about our responsibility.

Michael: Oh, interesting. What do you mean?

Alys: Well, by being upfront about my dislike of hierarchy and the use of titles like Mr, Miss it may have unfairly influenced the students...

Michael: I can see that. Although by explaining why you dislike hierarchy, it means that the students are beginning to question thoughts and beliefs they might have had about education. I think that some of them are now less bothered by the use of first-names for teachers, for example, which provides the opportunity to look further at what that school has to offer.

Alys: So although we need to be aware of our privileges and position in these school visits, we may also be able to help the students extend their thinking and understanding about educational possibilities.

(Mendus et al., 2020, pp. 229–231)

8   Alys the Theorist: Becoming-Identity

By performing School Tourism, I argue that these students I am talking about in
Scene 8, and anyone else who chooses to visit schools, is part of a wider entanglement for change, where these relational encounters can affect identity, ideas
and understandings about education, self and the wider world. Seeing this
becoming-identity (influenced by Deleuze and Guattari's 1980/1987 work on
becoming) through affect theory, which Massumi (2015) defines as, "When you
affect something, you are at the same time opening yourself up to be affected
[influenced] in turn, and in a slightly different way" (p. 4), helps develop a
framework for understanding the role that performing School Tourism could
have in beginning to understand what is the future for education/learning. As
Mendus et al. (2020) argued, developing the idea of becoming-teacher through
performing School Tourism, "The embodied nature of these experiences [visit-
ing schools] empowers reflection and growth" (p. 220) as it acknowledges the
importance of an 'experience-in-the-making' (Massumi, 2015) and an embodied encounter (Massumi, 2017).

    This embodied encounter can include non-human elements that in turn
can influence our identity as well as our understanding of the future of education. Examples of this have been covered in the autoethnographic-we stories
of Part 2 where I describe the place of learning/school environment: including
weather, smells, colour, objects and physical layout. Viewing these places of
learning/school visits as affective-encounters or a "relational matrix" (Massumi, 2017, p. 49) helps frame the experience further by recognising that each
person performing School Tourism is having different and equally important
experiences which they will in turn share in differing ways. I argue that not
only is the physical experience different for each person, so is the internal
experience. This follows Romero (2015), who argues that what is shared is also
influenced by 'inner work.' Therefore, it can also be hard to put an experience
into words, to tell other people exactly what a School Tourist feels when they
visit a school, but this "inner changing" (Romero, 2015, p. 14) can influence a
person's outlook and connectivity to a school, people or educational approach.

    Wenger's (2010) concept of Communities of Practice can be used to sup-
port the relationship between performing School Tourism as a pre-service
teacher/current teacher and the 'becoming teacher' identity by recognising
the importance of spontaneous learning that happens through and with each
place of learning/school visit. Wenger argues that when "learning is becoming, when knowledge and knower are not separated, then the practice is also
about enabling such becoming" (Wenger, 2010, p. 3). So, by physically visiting
places educating differently, these different experiences are part of enabling

the becoming-teacher identity, which is dynamic and iterative as different, "[school/learning] communities emerge, merge, split, compete, complement each other, and disappear. And the boundaries between the practices [pedagogies/ideals/curriculums] involved are not necessarily peaceful or collaborative" (Wenger, 2010, p. 4). The key issue here is that, through performing School Tourism, change could happen in education on a grass-roots level that begins to create momentum for new understandings and could speed up the affect of the ripple-effect to change the current system. This would be a political mission, knowing that most people's experience and understanding of what is a 'school' is from their own childhood experiences. For many, if they attended a traditional school, this is a narrow place to project education for the future, which makes the call for all people to begin performing School Tourism even more timely.

9 Alys the Guide

This chapter concludes by arguing that as more people perform School Tourism then the spontaneous learning experiences of what is school/education/learning in the relational matrix of our society increases, so "the impact of school tourism and visiting those innovative schools continues to permeate our understanding and beliefs" (Mendus et al., 2020, p. 232) and has the potentiality that even more people can begin to think differently.

10 Summary

– You can be a School Tourist!
– I encourage you to go and visit all types of places of learning/schools at open days and school fairs so you can experience the many current possibilities of education and learning.
– I visited most places for a morning or a full day. Whilst at a place of learning/school I would observe lessons, have a tour of the site, talk to staff, students and, if possible, to senior management. At some places I also gave a talk about my work and at some schools I worked as a teacher.
– Each school visit is a performance, a relational experience with those who attend or work at that place. The performance is also with yourself and it is not always possible to give words to the affect of each visit on your inner being, except for its potential influence on your growing understanding of the possibilities for education and learning.

– Performing School Tourism can be carried out alone or with a group of others. Each approach leads to different possible experiences and conversations.
– Young people can be encouraged to think differently about education through running Ideal School projects and by actually visiting other schools or learning about their approaches online.
– Using performing School Tourism with Pre-service teachers is invaluable to diversify their experiences of what is possible as they are developing their becoming-teacher identity.
– Physically performing School Tourism is a mediation between creativity, arts, learning and teaching. The spontaneous learning leads to change as it helps shape the identity of the School Tourist and allows them to add these new experiences and understandings of the possibilities for education to the collective consciousness of the world. This is the Earth-we, explored further in Chapter 12.

Note

1   https://eduontour.tumblr.com/

Composting the Rhizome: The Earth-We

1   Alys the Guide

This chapter aims to take a tentative step into the unthought. The Earth-we, so far defined to be similar to 'Gaia,' the collective consciousness of the planet Earth both human and non-human. Therefore reminding Alys-we that it is not all about Alys, by acknowledging that Alys-we is rhizomatically part of the Earth-we: the multiplicity of voices on this Earth, human and non human that is calling out for a 'New Story' (see Berry, 1978).

This chapter explores first steps into this 'New Story,' coming back to the idea of the 'edge-ucation' explored in Part 1. Therefore, this chapter can be seen as a starting point, a wading in the ecotone of edge-ucation where, by exploring the Earth-we, it can begin to be used to problematise possibilities for the future. Come with me! Jump into the entanglement so we can be making these changes together!

FIGURE 66
Large tree on our local walk, Australia, July 2020

© KONINKLIJKE BRILL NV, LEIDEN, 2022 | DOI: 10.1163/9789004506039_013

This chapter shares two vignettes, 29 and 30, nodal points; a wet and wild weekend van-camping in Devon, UK in 2016 and the other two films created from the assemblages of my Come Dance my PhD workshops in Cumbria, UK in 2018. My theoretical responses to these experiences help develop and define the Earth-we further, moving beyond the more simplified cry for a 'New Story' and becoming a rich compost (Haraway, 2016) of possibilities.

2   Alys the Theorist: Discussing the Big Picture

Vignette 29 is important as it shares how attending the Dark Mountain Weekend at Embercombe community in Devon, UK in September 2016 influenced the dialogue of my research. This experience reminded me to connect to non-human influences and to step away from being too focussed on the detail of 'types' of school/schooling and to question not just 'education' but the relationship of humanity and the natural world. Through positioning this book within the 'New Story' (Berry, 1978), the argument moves the role of School Tourism to a meta-level beyond the Alys-we to the consciousness and collective-awareness of the Earth-we. The Earth-we builds upon the performative autoethnographic-we (Spry, 2016), creating a complex web of the multiplicities of the Alys-we, the voices of other School Tourists and those lives they interact with within the schools that are visited, as well as multiplicities of the stories themselves. At the same time being aware that the Earth-we doesn't forget the dirt, the sticky, claggy earth of the land, the places in which schools are built, where learning happens, as well as the physical objects, that create the assemblage of lives on the planet. Vignette 29 is very much from that squelchy, damp earth.

3   Vignette 29: Alys the Edge-Dweller – Learning from the Dark Mountain Weekend

The stars shone brightly. The shooting stars dropped out the sky leaving luminescent traces of their stories in the sky. In the half light of the stars, my friends, Dan, Annie and I stood mesmerised by the twinkling lights, surrounded by the heaving boughs of the orchard. I wandered off to scrump some apples, soon the tangy juice of harvest was wetting my lips and dripping onto my chin. We all wondered and wandered at our very existence in this universe. The conversation ebbed and flowed along the lines of the stories we had heard, the assumptions and critiques of the event, our own budding research and dreams for society and our life as three friends.

Here I was at the 'Dark Mountain Gathering Basecamp,' a weekend for people interested in the Dark Mountain Project:

> A network of writers, artists and thinkers who have stopped believing the stories our civilisation tells itself. We see that the world is entering an age of ecological collapse, material contraction and social and political unravelling, and we want our cultural responses to reflect this reality rather than denying it. (The Dark Mountain Project, 2017)

The people at the Dark Mountain weekend felt like a mix of lives lived in different cities and rural places across the land, except that the room was white, ghostly white. The hues of the bodies, covered in oil, sliding around in workshops at other alternative gatherings that I attended this summer of alabaster white, through pale browns to deep chocolate hues to almost black were not represented here. They are in other alternative events I attend, so where were their voices this weekend?

> *It made me feel uneasy, like a strange gathering of 'otherness' in our gathering of inclusivity. The white privilege, patriarchy and status of people at this event was unsettling. The power of who can speak and who is not just invisible at the gathering but not even there at all, means that although this event allowed some people to begin to think differently, it is too small to be representative in any capacity of the Earth-we. This issue needs to be addressed further through encouraging more diverse groups of people to have access to performing School Tourism and knowing about the possibilities of educating differently to the traditional neoliberal approaches.*

One keynote speaker was David Abram (1996, 2011) who spoke of our connection with all living beings and the interconnectedness of all life on this planet, yet we were an under-represented example of the human species. Were we stuck in that bubble that Dan worried about, "not really making any change?"

However, I believe, as the main storytellers Martin Shaw and David Abram and others suggested, that the power of the story is not just in the telling but in the ripple effect that happens next as the words, the archetypes, permeate down into my soul, unearthing and processing ideas and hidden 'gems' buried deep down under the rocks.

> *This mention of rocks makes me think of my partner, Bozz, who at the same time that Martin Shaw was sharing his story at the event, was cave-digging in Somerset with Annie's parents, Alice and Tony, unearthing rocks and*

> *debris trapped in the mouth of the cave. They liberate the pieces that were*
> *blocking access to the underworld and carefully and manually as a team, a*
> *community, lift, carry and winch them back to the surface.*

Part of me felt belittled in the awe of the great storyteller, I wanted him to be my teacher. How can I tell stories as well as him? Or is that really what I am aspiring to be, to be like Martin Shaw?

> Then I am back looking up at Martin Shaw (for I am on a cushion on the floor) and my brain is trying to question the concept of hero worshipping and hierarchy and, yes, it is another OWM up there. (Mendus, 2017b)

Chatting to Dan and Annie, we enjoyed the "alchemy that can happen when you honour the spaces that open in-between" (Strang, 2016, para. 6) all the talks, workshops and performances of the weekend. At one stage we found ourselves talking disgruntledly about 'Brexit' and I share stories about the Democratic schools that I have visited, telling them that I find the consensus approach really scary and it reminds me about how I feel that a step beyond the current version of democracy is needed.

On Sunday morning another OWM steps up onto the most awaited stage, the audience squeezed into the hall, all waiting expectantly. This time it was a wild looking man with big glasses perched on his nose and his body moving theatrically like a puppet on a string. I have known about David Abram's work since 2007. Abram's first book (1996) comes from his PhD and it weaves a chapter of creative, eloquent story illustrating his arguments with a more theoretical chapter throughout. His second book (2011) strongly argues the importance of oral language as a contact between oneself and others:

> Oral language gusts through us – our sounded phrases borne by the same air that nourishes the cedars and swells the cumulus clouds. Laid out and immobilised on the flat surface, our words tend to forget that they are sustained by this windswept earth; they begin to imagine that their primary task is to provide a *representation* of the world (as though they were outside of, and not really *a part of,* this world). (Abram, 2011, p. 11)

I put my hand up and asked, "If we are looking at the future of education then do we need to look at the relationship between the current focus on the written word and literacy, and oral cultures?"

Abram replied in detail, explaining in his organisation AWE (Association of Wild Ethics) that it was of *"ECOLOGICAL IMPERATIVE TO RESTORE ORAL*

CULTURE." He argued that instead of reading bedtime stories parents should be telling stories with gestures and these stories should be told to children in the correct seasons, in the place on the land that the story is from and with an accompanying dance and music. He reiterated that not all stories should be written down as he had argued earlier that it changes the connection to a place once the 'spell of spelling' has taken over. He finished by reminding the audience, *"DO NOT WRITE ALL STORIES DOWN!"*

4   Alys the Guide

I sat there wondering if by writing down a story or experience then it becomes positioned temporally and spatially. In terms of performing School Tourism, maybe I need to recognise the importance of the oral sharing of stories (or even the unspoken embodied stories that come from the feeling journey of actually being in each 'school' environment) as being as important or even more important than my written observations? Positioning this idea within the Earth-we makes sense, as the oral/aural/embodied stories that occur when performing School Tourism can never be written down verbatim. Even if an experience was filmed or recorded, only one dimension of the experience would have been captured including only a short period of time, it would not include the after affect. As I have argued earlier, in performative autoethnography the role of performance is the unknown and potentially ongoing aspect of its impact on the audience. Therefore, through performing School Tourism, new experiences are added to the collective-consciousness of the world, allowing the Earth-we to begin to gain momentum towards a paradigm shift.

5   Alys-We Performing School-Tourism for the 'New Story'

The Anthropocene (see Bonneuil & Fressoz, 2017) is the name for the new geological epoch described by Grusin (2015) as a time "that humans must now be understood as climatological or geological forces on the planet" (Grusin, 2015, p. vii). Therefore, placing performing School Tourism temporally and spatially within the Anthropocene gives it agency, a role to intra-act (Barad, 2007) with the multiplicities of the Earth-we. This then follows Abram (2011) who argued for the importance of sharing oral stories on the collective consciousness (linked here to those from performing School Tourism) and St. Pierre (2014) who argues that the language that matters is spoken and heard. As Abram explained:

> The journey from one ecosystem into another is precisely a journey from
> one state of mind into another, different, state. From one mode of aware-
> ness, flavoured by salt and the glint of sunlight on waves, to an altered,
> inland awareness wherein the cries of those gulls become only a vague,
> half-remembered dream. (Abram, 2011, p. 139)

Other understandings of the Anthropocene have concentrated on the effects
of climate change (Klein, 2014) and the ongoing possibility of the 'sixth-extinc-
tion' (Kolbert, 2014). However, Kingsnorth (2017) (one of the founders of the
Dark Mountain Project) is concerned that the over focus on sustainability has
disconnected the focus on wild places for their own sake, which he is calling
'dark ecology.' Kingsnorth, like others (Macy & Johnstone, 2012; Ploktin, 2008)
are searching (like this book) for new ways forward towards what some are
calling the 'New Story' (Berry, 1978; New Story Hub, 2017).

Macy and Johnstone (2012) argue that we need to engage in what they call
the 'Great Turning' (2012, p. 26). Their work suggests that by engaging with
'Active Hope' and an inner journey, a mutually reinforcing self and world connection can happen (what I am understanding as the Earth-we) but this needs
"compassion and insight into radical interconnectivity" (Macy & Johnstone,
2012, p. 102). My connection to inner work has iteratively moved throughout
this thesis from its central tenet in Steiner Waldorf education and Anthroposophy and its growing role as an aspect of performing School Tourism. Here
again in my understandings towards the 'New Story,' conscious inner work
(Macy & Johnstone, 2012) is also connected to the more-than-human psyche
of the collective awareness (Abram, 2011), again seen here as the Earth-we. I
see resonance in performing School Tourism with Abram's (2011) idea that as
we travel we connect to the psyche of the land/place (or school) which impacts
our own self-awareness and even if we stay in one place then the collective
shifts of awareness impact everyone through "delicate changes unfolding in
the local mind-scape, changes that imperceptibly – but inevitably – affect our
emotions, our thoughts, and our actions" (Abram, 2011, p. 139).

So, through sharing stories from the edge-ucation, those 'gems' can have a
ripple-effect of changing the world's imagination or psyche (Abram, 2011), the
Earth-we. Abram (2011) also argues for educators (or, I argue, for all people) to
share stories from the land so to be "renewing the sensory craft of listening,
and the sensuous art of storytelling" (Abram, 2011, p. 288) and to be becoming
part of "a fresh perception [which] is slowly shaping itself – a clarified encounter between the human animal and its elemental habitat" (Abram, 2011, p. 299).
I want to acknowledge here that these ideas of Abram, of knowing and listening to the land have a long history and I pay heed to the work of Indigenous

scholars and those working with Indigenous knowledges (Country et al., 2019; Phillips & Bunda, 2018; Wooltorton et al., 2020). As Wooltorton, Collard and Horwitz (2017) explain, "Stories are embedded across landscapes" (p. 63), positioning this within Noongar Country, Western Australia reminding us all to listen:

> The Noongar word for alive is the same word as to speak. The land is alive, and the land speaks. In Noongar language, there can be no argument. The land still speaks, but these days it seems comparatively few people hear it. (Wooltorton, Collard, & Horwitz, 2017, p. 63)

Ploktin (2008) also argues for an education that supports each individual becoming part of the greater earth community (becoming part of the world's psyche, or Earth-we). He still argues for the need of learning the basics (literacy, numeracy) but questions the need of formal compulsory secondary education beyond that which is self-designed. By returning here to the questions raised by Peim (2016), to unthink education as the solution, reminds me that education as we know it will change in the 'New Story' as the greater collective consciousness of the Earth-we rhizomatically interacts with the post-human Anthropocene. You, my reader, have the power to be part of this change. By performing School Tourism, extending your embodied knowledge of what is available, particularly in terms of innovative education, society becomes closer to the critical mass of people needed to make changes to the current mainstream paradigm of what is education.

6 The Queering of Bad-Alys: Moving beyond the 'New Story'

With hindsight, when I think with the Earth-we I realise that deciding we need a 'New Story' does not reiterate the complexity of the "past, present, and to come" (Haraway, 2015, p. 160) and that I do not want to end the book with only a call for a 'New Story.' So, I have found Donna Haraway's book, 'Staying with the Trouble' (2016), helpful in developing the Earth-we. Haraway uses the term 'Chthulucene' to help understand the entanglement between the human and the non-human world, defining the Chthulucene as "a kind of timeplace for learning to stay with the trouble of living and dying in response-ability on a damaged earth" (Haraway, 2016, p. 2). The Chthulucene is unlike the Anthropocene as it is "made up of ongoing multispecies stories and practices of becoming-with in times that remain at stake, in precarious times" (Haraway, 2016, p. 55). Therefore, I hear Haraway's (2016) call for 'making-kin' with the more-than-human world. Perhaps the Earth-we could be part of this making-kin, in particular by making "oddkin"; where through our stories "we require each other in unexpected collaborations and combinations, in hot compost piles" (p. 4). The idea of hot compost piles excites me as Haraway explains further that 'we are compost' (2016, p. 97):

> We relate, know, think, world, and tell stories through and with other stories, worlds, knowledges, thinkings, yearnings. So do all the other critters of Terra, in all our bumptious diversity and category-breaking speciations and knottings. (Haraway, 2016, p. 97)

Nevertheless, following Haraway's 'compost,' humans are not separate, nor superior to other species or the non-human for "We are humus, not Homo, not anthropos; we are compost" (2016, p. 55) as "we make with, and we become with each other" (Haraway in Franklin, 2017, p. 50). In the interview with Franklin (2017), Haraway is referring to the term "sympoiesis," meaning "making-with" (2016, p. 58), which could be extrapolated to view the Earth-we as something that is never alone. Therefore, the compost of the Earth-we is vast, in between the stories from the school visits, the people involved, the places, the non-human elements; the van, that cup of coffee or even the smell of linseed rubbed on the wooden floors. Haraway sees this as, "material-semiotic composting, as theory in the mud, as muddle" (2016, p. 31). Using the idea of compost adds depth to the Earth-we, there is a muddle of stories that are beginning to increase awareness that life, education and society could be different to the current paradigm. This is because the 'doings' and lives of humans performing School Tourism 'matter' (Haraway, 2016) as each one has an integral role within the Earth-we. However, this needs to be approached with an awareness that "It matters what stories tell stories" (Haraway, 2016, p. 35), as each story shared has the power for change and at the same time a deep knowledge that "human beings are not the only important actors in the Chthulucene... and the biotic and abiotic powers of this earth are the main story" (Haraway, 2016, p. 55).

Therefore, the Earth-we which I have defined earlier is in many ways similar to Lovelock and Margulis's (1974) concept of 'Gaia,' a greater human consciousness. It is also more than this, it is also the dirt, the mud under your fingernails, as "human beings are with and of the earth" (Haraway, 2016, p. 55). There is a connection here between compost to the flowering rhizome of a water lily that dies and replenishes the plant as compost, it is also about "living and dying... those who will return our flesh to the Earth are in the making of compost" (Haraway in Franklin, 2017, p. 51). Figure 67, a nature ring, shows this rhizomatic compost of flowers, fire and needle-felted pumpkins!

FIGURE 67
Autumn nature ring

Vignette 30, 'Come Dance my PhD' shares where Alys-we created a composting of the assemblage of the nomadology of 'Searching for the Ideal School around the world,' through creating two films, 'A cup of instant coffee: A van-dwellers' assemblage' (Mendus, 2018a) and 'Come Dance My PhD' (Mendus, 2018b).

> I made art. Art in this project was collaborative improvised dance, movement, play based workshops, assemblages, maps and in-situ installations in nature and old buildings alongside photographs and lino-cuts. (Mendus, 2019, p. 52)

7 Vignette 30: Come Dance My PhD

> Inspired by Shane Waltener's (2010) woven stairwell at Dovecot Gallery, Edinburgh, I wove a stairwell in an old working Corn Mill in Cumbria [UK] with ribbons, creating an interactive dream-catcher, a helix of my rhizomatic PhD. I then worked with exploring movement, dance and trans-materiality. Following the call from the annual Dance your PhD competition I led two nomadic workshops in different locations inspired by my interactive stairwell installation to connect to my van and nature with the same ribbons that had threaded the stairwell. (Mendus, 2019, p. 53)

Collecting my compost was a fascinating aspect of this arts-based project. I collated photos and objects from my journeys as a van-dweller, from performing

FIGURE 68
Stairwell weave looking down, Cumbria,
April 2018

School Tourism and my life and travels during my PhD studies. I created montages for the participants to dance through, with and in, things that connected to the van and nature which can be seen as the backdrop of both films. The first film shows the deliberate weaving of the stairwell, "the growing assemblage of ribbons, objects, maps and textures of the life of an itinerant van-dwelling PhD student" (Mendus, 2019, p. 54).

Realising that through making these films as "an arts-based response to living itinerantly" that my life itself was unusual as I was "constantly travelling and in relation with so many different things – both human and non-human" (Mendus, 2019, p. 54), I began to see the power of things, both physical and tangible. I argued that:

> I began with a "thing," an object from the assemblage, a *"cup of cold, instant coffee."* I was using the work of Jane Bennett (2004) on "Thing Power" to give agency to the objects that directed my study and influenced my life on a diffracted sphere. (Mendus, 2019, p. 54)

I argue that my thinking has moved on since 2019, that the objects (back to that special enamel cup again!) did have agency and an important role, but it was also the non-human environment, the rain, the rivers, the buzzing bees that had an impact on my journeys. I am also reminded that emotion is important here, as for Ahmed, "Emotions are not 'after-thoughts' but shape how bodies are moved by the worlds they inhabit" (Ahmed, 2010, p. 237). My

FIGURE 69
Alys presenting the Come Dance my PhD films
at the British Autoethnography conference,
Bristol, UK, July 2018 (photo by Tessa Wyatt)

emotions influenced my nomadology and how I intra-acted with the objects along my path. For example, I realised I may not have found the 'Ideal School,' but I had fallen in love. Love, an emotion with an essential role in influencing response-ability with objects [and people], became a key theme within the research. I met Bozz whilst spending a week in Melbourne visiting schools in February 2016 and he moved to the UK in May 2016. We spent the next 18 months living in our van, travelling the UK, visiting schools, having fun and exploring. As I write now, that love and support continues as we live currently as fixed-home-dwellers in Australia with our energetic and delightful toddler. Outside our home sits our third van, ready for us to escape at any moment! The move from solo journeys to one with a partner transformed the assemblage; the places I went, but also the emotional wellbeing of the author as I now had a confidante, lover, copy editor, fellow adventurer and traveller. The photos from this time were hung from threads attached to the same ribbons that threaded the stairwell.

I recognise the 'thing-thought' (Harris & Holman Jones, 2019) of these photos and the montages I created, interwoven by the ribbons, that they are objects "in relation to one another, carrying on with each other without regard to what the human animals might be thinking or doing or feeling in relation to those worldings" (Harris & Holman Jones, 2019, p. 12). For example, the "The thought-thing interaction" (Harris & Holman Jones, 2019, p. 91) can be seen:

> In the middle of the film the visual cuts from the stairwell to the newest van (not the one we lived in during the PhD). The van is parked and via

FIGURE 70
Bozz and Alys surrounded by a heart
of roses, Netherlands, June 2017
(photo by Margo Bruins)

> the same ribbons in the stairwell is woven into the Spring landscape of
> the Lake District. Here I aimed to highlight the place-based, if ever itin-
> erant, aspect of van-dwelling. The objects: the photos, the ribbons, the
> van all set up and welcoming gives the viewer a glimpse of van-life and
> a more open installation of the assemblage than being closed within a
> multi-layered helix in the stairwell. (Mendus, 2019, p. 54)

By inviting others into these performance spaces with the assemblage of the
Alys-we, it could be viewed as a way of 'making kin' (Haraway, 2016) with our
bodies, the objects and nature, "the wind, the sheep bleating, the cries of the
dancers" (Mendus, 2019, p. 58). As,

> These films and the workshops are about movement and dance, about
> the way that different groups of people relate to each other, the environ-
> ment, the assemblage and my words through dance and play. Through
> "voicing the body" (Erb, 2018) this work values the unspoken voice of the
> body. (Mendus, 2019, p. 53)

I am reminded that this is also a performance as a political act, connecting
Vignette 30 back to the Introduction chapter where the Guided Meditation

that I shared with the workshop participants is written in full. There was a magical moment on top of a hill under a Spring oak tree festooned in my ribbons where I "introduced a game: people were invited to pick a word from a basket and then to speak that word as they moved around the space" (Mendus, 2019, p. 58). Watching the clip in the film brings me joy as the participants run in and out from the tree shouting at the top of their voices, "reiterating not only the key themes of "centre and periphery" but also that of being "Fed up with the System" [as]... This is a film, a PhD and a life fundamentally about subverting the current paradigm" (Mendus, 2019, p. 58).

Watch these films again to see this composting in action, A cup of instant coffee: A van-dwellers' assemblage and Come Dance My PhD (Mendus, 2018a, 2018b), the intra-actions and storying happening within the assemblage.

> The twisting, growing and receding of the ribbons in the stairwell,
> the moment when the group intuitively placed their hands together and
> spiral upwards,
> the sticky mud on the parade up the windy hillside,
> the wind blowing the ribbons in the trees,
> the handmade dolls on the bed in the van
> Making-with each other
> Becoming the Earth-we.

FIGURE 71
Stairwell weave looking up, Cumbria,
April 2018

8   The Multiplicities of the Alys-We and the Earth-We

Using Phillips and Bunda's (2018) five principles of storying can be helpful here to share how the Earth-we is entangled within the storying of places and experiences. Thinking-with these principles is helpful when re-reading this book, seeing examples where "(1) storying nourishes thought, body and soul" (p. 43) for example where performing School Tourism is growing exponentially with the possibility of each becoming identity. Or with "(2) storying claims voice in the silenced margins" (p. 43) allows more people to know about ways of educating differently. Or with "(3) storying is embodied relational meaning making" (p. 43) connects to the interconnected consciousness of the Earth-we. Where "(4) storying intersects the past and present as living oral archives" (p. 43) connects to Haraway's work on the Chthulucene and "(5) storying enacts collective ownership and authorship"(p. 43) supports the multiplicities of the Earth-we, Alys-we and more-than-human world.

The more that I understand about the storying of the Earth-we, the more I realise that the voices of the Alys-we have an impact on who listens and how loud the call for change from the Earth-we can be. Therefore, as this book heads to a close I also realise that other voices of Alys-we are emerging and need to be heard, others may need to be let go of so that the stories can change. For example, I am no longer Alys the PhD Student/Theorist, but Dr. Alys. I am no longer Alys the future parent, but Alys the parent of a delightful toddler. Hopefully I will not need to be Alys the traditional, mainstream teacher again (but I doubt I can be now as I bring so many stories with me even if I step foot into a traditional mainstream classroom). This means that I realise that the performance piece I presented in multiple voices of the Alys-we Searching for the Ideal School at the International Congress of Qualitative Inquiry in May 2017 (Mendus, 2017a, 2017b) only included certain voices and that now I would add in other voices of the Alys-we. Therefore, I have included here the voice of 'Ecological-Alys' from the term 'ecological self' introduced by Arne Naess (2008) and described as the "wider sense of identity that arises when our self-interest includes the natural world" (Macy & Johnstone, 2012, p. 94). Macy and Johnstone explain further that when we recognise "ourselves as part of the living body of Earth [it] opens us to a great source of strength" (2012, p. 94) and importantly pays respects to First Nations people's understanding of the world that, "we are an intrinsic part of the living Earth" (Macy & Johnstone, 2012, p. 94).

Addendum: The rhizome is global 'Ecological-Alys' speaks...

Alys-we imagines themselves now perched up on the ridge of a Cumbrian
fell side

Their home-land
Feeling the hard stone and springy moss beneath their body
Breathing deep and
Sending a golden-thread into a deeper consciousness
Whilst glancing down the valley
Looking at the light skimming across the lake and pulling their attention to
the horizon
As the sun is beginning to rise
For this morning is midsummer – the longest day...
Looking up, Alys-we realises they are surrounded, collectively marvelling in
the sunrise.
Remembering that the School Tourist is not alone.

Let us position then performing School Tourism temporally and spatially
beyond the epoch of the Anthropocene
maybe within Haraway's (2016) definition of Chthulucene
Becoming-with others in precarious times
Learning from Indigenous knowledges (Country et al., 2019)
That the wild-places and the nonhuman speak
What may have started as the embodied rhizome of the Alys-we
Has 'motion and emotion' (see Sheller, 2004a)
The stories from the edge-ucation that are shared have agency – they move
beyond the teller
They intra-act with others and others and others
Moving on a global scale
The Earth-we
A compassionate, collective inner journey of radical interconnectivity follow-
ing Macy & Johnstone (2012)
A more-than-human psyche of the collective awareness (Abram, 2011)
Where local then global mind-scapes can change through the storying of
The Earth-we.
Daring to unthink education as the solution (Peim, 2016)
As the greater collective consciousness of the Earth-we rhizomatically intra-
acts with the possibilities of the Chthulucene
Stepping beyond the 'New Story' (Berry, 1978)
by
Making odd-kin
In hot compost piles
(Haraway, 2016)

As the dazzling rays of the sun-light bring hope for a new day.

FIGURE 72   The view of Skiddaw from my childhood home, Lake District, UK

9   Alys the Guide

This chapter moved the dialogue of the potentiality of performing School Tourism for a paradigm shift in education onto a new level with the exploration of the Earth-we. The Earth-we argues that we are all part of a collective-consciousness and, through becoming aware of ways of educating (and living) differently through performing School Tourism, we add these experiences to a collective understanding, realising that the current established neoliberal systems can be changed.

This reminds me that education as we now know will change through the lens of the Earth-we as the greater collective consciousness and assemblage rhizomatically intra-acts. The Earth-we in relation to education is everything. For example, it could be the physical human bodies within the 'school' buildings and institutions, the intra-actions between the humans, the emotions, the objects that identify with 'school,' the journey including nature, the sounds, the smells, the dog you walk when you get home, even the dirt you stand on in the school yard. The chance here is that we can be more than a New Story, we can be compost. So there is scope to unthink education as the solution, giving space for the unthought to shine.

I invite you to be part of this change by performing School Tourism.

10   Summary

- The Earth-we is the collective consciousness of the planet Earth, both human and non-human, calling out for a new story about education and learning.
- The edge-ucation thinks beyond the types of school or approaches to learning pedagogy, to question current relationships of humanity and the natural world.
- Vignette 29 of the experience at the Dark Mountain Project aims to trouble that even when people collectively come together wishing for change, it is not easy to shake off issues of privilege and power. This is where the Earth-we can help as it includes the role of sharing stories of not just places educating differently but also different ways of living, therefore expanding the collective-consciousness towards a paradigm shift.
- Placing performing School Tourism temporally and spatially within the Anthropocene, aware that it is a human construct, gives it agency, a role to intra-act (Barad, 2007) with the multiplicities of the Earth-we.
- Using Haraway's (2016) definition of the Chthulucene is helpful to give space for multi-species stories and a making-kin with the unexpected including human, non-human and the more-than-human, seen as 'making compost.'
- The Come Dance my PhD assemblage and workshops are an example of an arts-based response to living itinerantly and studying for a PhD showing the 'thing-power' (Bennett, 2004) of the objects, places and journeys.
- A reminder that this book was written in particular voices of Alys-we, but that it is continually changing and new voices such as Alys the parent and Ecological-Alys are added into the mix. This book also gives space for the ever-changing voices of the reader as their identity changes as they envision education, and life, in new ways.

Concluding Thoughts

1   **Alys the Nomad: New Van, New Possibilities, New Hope**

Gubbi Gubbi Country, Queensland, Australia, Wednesday 27th January 2021. It's a hot sunny January day and I sit typing in our new van, parked up under the shade of a large eucalyptus tree in our yard. It feels strange as someone from the North West of England to write 'hot and sunny' about January and to use words like 'yard' and not mean a small, hard-covered, outdoor space. I suppose that I am finding my feet and becoming on this land on which I now live. In Australia, I have learnt that a yard is your garden and the place where we have ended up has a yard that is almost an acre. We have veg gardens growing with a sprawling pumpkin and watermelon patch, a bright row of sunflowers and a sandpit that is currently being played in. My partner, Bozz, has endless sheds (and space for all his motorcycles!) and he is currently strumming on the ukulele whilst our toddler makes sandcastles and I type. I am taken back to the drawing room at Hawkwood College in Stroud, UK where with friends and colleagues from ANI-net (now CANI-net) we wrote into our lived experience, made art and shared our words aloud (see Kirkpatrick, Porter, Spry & Wyatt, 2021). I feel in this moment a corporeality, an embodied lived moment of my words, clasping at an experience going on around me, within me and through me. Ginny is now splashing in a bucket of water washing off the sand and I am sipping on a lukewarm cup of espresso coffee in my little enamel cup. Some 'things' that lived in our old vans will live in this van too, even if spectre-like. Traces of the old journeys and experiences, whispers of our nomadology overlay our new van with the promise of travel, journeys into the unknown, remindings of stepping into the unthought.

The thing-thought (Harris & Holman Jones, 2019) layers my experience. Our old van was a collage of our experiences: postcards, photos, decorations, old receipts, candles and drawings. We had a cork board stapled to the walls for us to adorn and if you look back at photos of the van in this book (see Figures 5, 7 & 15) you will get glimpses of that changing collage. Today I have a new sketch, drawn this morning, very early when the dew was still heavy on the grass, of

FIGURE 73 Sketch of the new van, 'Valerie,' Australia, 27 January 2021

the new van under the eucalyptus, and I currently have it resting on the seat in front of me. We have named the new van Valerie, in memory of my wonderful Grandma who died at 95 in March 2020 and who holds such an important place in my life and identity.

Looking out of the window I see our compost pile. I like to think with Haraway that "we are compost" (2016, p. 97) as that compost pile hides stories and memories of our lives over the last 7 months that we have lived here on Gubbi Gubbi Country in Moreton Bay, Queensland, Australia. I am drawn by other life experiences and voices of Alys now to Alys the Archaeologist, who hasn't spoken in this book but was prominent 19 years ago when I worked for the New Zealand Historic Places Trust in Wellington, New Zealand. I am thinking of 'middens,' the place where people bury their waste, and the stories and the storying that archaeologists create from those excavations. I think-with middens, compost heaps and old vans, following Ingold's concept of tracings (2007), whilst sitting here with the light breeze softly tickling my face, full of hope.

Most children go back to school today in Australia and now, almost a year later from writing my preface, the children in the UK are back to learning at-home. I realise that it is a strange time to be writing a book calling out for embodied change in education, to be asking people to be visiting places of learning/schools that are educating differently when very few people (in the UK) are even allowed into school buildings due to the risk of COVID-19. However, the stories I share in this book of gems from places educating differently, and my wish that I will engage my readers to begin performing School Tourism themselves, sits in a place of hope. A place of hope and potentiality for moving into a new paradigm beyond our current understandings of what is education, learning and society.

By sharing my storying of my nomadology performing School Tourism through multiple arts-based approaches from places educating differently around the world, I hope that this book can be a rigorous addition to the scholarship and global perspectives for societal and educational change.

I remind my reader that performing School Tourism is a mediation between creativity, arts, learning and teaching. This spontaneous learning leads to change as it helps shape the identity of those performing School Tourism and allows them to add these new experiences and understandings of the possibilities for education to the Earth-we, the collective consciousness of the world.

I finish with a reminder of our own response-ability, we can all be part of the change in perspectives about what is possible for the future.

I invite you all to perform School Tourism!

References

Abram, D. (1996). *The spell of the sensuous: Perception and language in a more-than-human world.* Pantheon Books.

Abram, D. (2011). *Becoming animal: An earthly cosmology.* Vintage Books.

Adams, T. E., Ellis, C., & Holman Jones, S. (2015). *Handbook of autoethnography.* Left Coast Press.

Adler, A. (1930). *The education of the child.* Greenburg.

Adler, J. (1989). Travel as performed art. *American Journal of Sociology, 94*, 1366–1391.

Ahmed, S. (2006). *Queer phenomenology: Orientations, objects, others.* Duke University Press.

Ahmed, S. (2010). *The promise of happiness.* Duke University Press.

Alexander, B. K. (2013). Teaching autoethnography and autoethnographic pedagogy. In S. Holman Jones, T. Adams, & C. Ellis (Eds.), *Handbook of autoethnography* (pp. 538–556). Left Coast Press.

Alliance for Public Waldorf Education. (2015). *About.* http://publicwaldorf.org/

Amsler, S. (2015). *The education of radical democracy.* Routledge.

Ashley, M. (2009). Education for freedom: The goal of Steiner/Waldorf Schools. In W. A. Woods & G. J. Woods (Eds.), *Alternative education for the 21st century philosophies, approaches, visions* (pp. 209–226). Palgrave Macmillan.

Attwood, M. (1986). *The handmaid's tale.* Houghton Mifflin.

Au, W. (2016). Social justice and resisting neoliberal education reform. *FORUM, 58*(3), 315–325.

Avison, K. (2015). *Grow prosper flourish brochure.* http://www.steinerwaldorf.org/education/wp-content/uploads/2015/09/grow-prosper-flourish-brochure-201509.pdf

Back, L., & Puwar, N. (2012). A manifesto for live methods: Provocations and capacities. *The Sociological Review, 60*(1), 6–17. https://doi.org/10.1111/j.1467-954X.2012.02114.x

Baldwin, N. R. (2009). *You are your child's first teacher: What parents can do with and for their children from birth to age six* (4th ed.). Hawthorn Press.

Barad, K. (2007). *Meeting the universe halfway: Quantum physics and the entanglement of matter and meaning.* Duke University Press.

Bauman, Z. (2011). Tourists and vagabonds: Or, living in postmodern times. In J. E. Davis (Ed.), *Identity and social change* (pp. 13–26). Transaction Publishers.

Benbenishty, R., Zeira, A., Astor, R. A., & Khoury-Kassabri, M. (2002). Maltreatment of primary school students by educational staff in Israel. *Child Abuse and Neglect, 26*, 763–782.

Bennett, J. (2004). The force of things. Steps toward an ecology of matter. *Political Theory, 32*(3), 347–372. http://www.jstor.org/stable/4148158

Bennett, J. (2015). Systems and things on vital materialism and object-oriented philosophy. In R. Grusin (Ed.), *The nonhuman turn* (pp. 223–235). University of Minnesota Press.

Berger, R. (2003). *An ethic of excellence building a culture of craftsmanship with students*. Heinemann.

Berger, R. (2012). *Austin's butterfly: Building excellence in student work* [Video]. https://vimeo.com/38247060

Berry, T. (1978). *The new story*. ANIMA Books.

Bettinger, E. P. (2011). Paying to learn: The effect of financial incentives on elementary school test scores. *Review of Economics and Statistics, 94*(3), 686–698. https://doi.org/10.1162/REST_a_00217

Biesta, G. J. J. (2006). *Beyond learning: Democratic education for a human future*. Paradigm Publishers.

Biesta, G. J. J. (2010). *Good education in an age of measurement: Ethics, politics, democracy*. Paradigm Publishers.

Biesta, G. J. J. (2013). Receiving the gift of teaching: From "learning from" to "being taught by." *Studies in Philosophy and Education, 32*(5), 449–461. https://doi.org/10.1007/s11217-012-9312-9

Blackie, S. (2016). *If women rose rooted: A journey to authenticity and belonging*. September Publishing.

Bloch, E. (1986). *The principle of hope* (N. Plaice, S. Place, & P. Knight, Trans.). MIT Press. (Original work published 1954)

Boland, N. (2014). Sticking wings on a caterpillar? *Journal of Waldorf/Rudolf Steiner Education, 16*(2), 8–9.

Boland, N. (2015). The globalisation of Steiner education: Some considerations. *Research on Steiner Education Journal, 6*, 192–202.

Boland, N. (2016). Sticking wings on a caterpillar? *Pacifica Journal, 49*(1), 4–6.

Boland, N. (2017). Travels in education: Towards Waldorf 2.0. *Educational Journal of Living Theories, 10*(2), 51–81. https://ejolts.net/node/310

Boland, N., & Demirbag, J. (2017). (Re)inhabiting Waldorf education: Honolulu teachers explore the notion of place. *Educational Journal of Living Theories, 10*(2), 20–50. http://ejolts.net/node/308

Bonk, C. J., & Graham, C. R. (Eds.). (2006). *The handbook of blended learning: Global perspectives*. Local Designs.

Bonneuil, C., & Fressoz, J.-B. (2017). *The shock of the Anthropocene: The Earth, history and us*. Verso.

Bourdieu, P. (1986). The forms of capital. In J. Richardson (Ed.), *Handbook of theory and research for the sociology of education* (pp. 241–258). Greenwood.

Bradbury-Jones, C., & Isham, L. (2020). The pandemic paradox: The consequences of COVID-19 on domestic violence. *Journal of Clinical Nursing, 29*, 2047–2049. https://doi.org/10.1111/jocn.15296

Braidotti, R. (2012). *Nomadic theory: The portable Rosi Braidotti.* Columbia University Press.

Bransby, K., & Mendus, A. (2012). *A case study of active storytelling in Derbyshire.* Derbyshire County Council.

Bruce, B. C. (2013). Editorial for the series of three issues: Progressive education: Past, present and future. *International Journal of Progressive Education, 9*(1), 7–9. https://ir.uwf.edu/islandora/object/uwf%3A22764/datastream/PDF/view

Bunda, T. (2017, June 26). *Research through, with and as storying.* The Australian Association for Research in Education Theory Workshop. Southern Cross University Gold Coast Campus.

Burbules, N. C. (2013). Learning is not education. In P. Smeyers & M. Depaepe (Eds.), *Educational research: The attraction of psychology* (pp. 159–166). Springer.

Butler, J. (2005). *Giving an account of oneself.* Forham University Press.

Chaltain, S. (2010). *Using rewards in the classroom: Short-term crutch or long term strategy?* http://www.samchaltain.com/?s=rewards

Chemi, T. (2020). It is impossible: The teacher's creative response to the Covid-19 emergency and digitalized teaching strategies. *Qualitative Inquiry.* https://doi.org/10.1177/1077800420960141

Chilton, G., & Leavy, P. (2014). Arts-based research practice: Merging social research and the creative arts. In P. Leavy (Ed.), *The Oxford handbook of qualitative research* (pp. 403–422). Oxford University Press.

Cisneros, S. (2002). *Caramelo.* Vintage Contemporaries.

Clandinin, D. J., Huber, J., Huber, M., Murphy, M. S., Murray Orr, A., Pearce, M., & Steeves, P. (2006). *Composing diverse identities. Narrative inquiries into the interwoven lives of children and teachers.* Routledge.

Clouder, C., & Rawson, M. (2003). *Waldorf education.* Floris Books.

Code, J. M. (2020). Considering Waldorf education's contributions to global citizenship education. *Steiner Studies. Internationale Zeitschrift für Kritische Steiner-forschung, 1,* 33. http://doi.org/10.12857/STS.951000140-2

Collins, S. (2008). *The hunger games.* Scholastic Press.

Country, B., Suchet-Pearson, S., Wright, S., Lloyd, K., Tofa, M., Sweeney, J., Burarrwanga, L., Ganambarr, R., Ganambarr-Stubbs, M., Ganambarr, B., & Maymuru, D. (2019). Goŋ Gurtha: Enacting response-abilities as situated co-becoming. *Environment and Planning D: Society and Space, 37*(4), 682–702. https://doi.org/10.1177/0263775818799749

Crouch, C. (2004). *Post-democracy.* Polity Press.

Crouch, D. (2005). Flirting with space: Tourism geographies as sensuous/expressive practice. In C. Cartier & A. Lew (Eds.), *Seductions of places: Geographical perspectives on globalization and touristed landscapes* (pp. 23–25). Routledge.

Csikszentmihalyi, M. (1990). *Flow: The psychology of optimal experience.* Harper and Row.

Dahlin, B. (2014). Review of: Transforming criticisms of Anthroposophy and Waldorf education – Evolution, race and the quest for a global ethics. *RoSE – Research on Steiner Education, 5*(1), 156–159. https://www.rosejourn.com/index.php/rose/article/view/195

Dahlin, B. (2017). *Rudolf Steiner: The relevance of Waldorf Education*. Springer.

Deci, E. L., Koestner, R., & Ryan, R. M. (2001). Extrinsic rewards and intrinsic motivation in education: Reconsidered once again. *Review of Educational Research, 17*, 1–27.

De Jesus, P. (2018). Thinking through enactive agency: Sense-making, bio-semiosis and the ontologies of organismic worlds. *Phenomenology and the Cognitive Sciences, 17*, 861–887. https://doi.org/10.1007/s11097-018-9562-2

Deleuze, G., & Guattari, F. (1980). *A thousand plateaus: Capitalism and schizophrenia* (Translated from French by B. Massumi, 1987). University of Minnesota Press.

De Meyer, K. (2016). The mind of the educator. In H. E. Lees & N. Noddings (Eds.), *The Palgrave international handbook of alternative education* (pp. 17–30). Macmillan.

Denjean, A. (2014). Curricula in Kiswahili, Arab, French. *Journal of the Pedagogical Section at the Goetheanum, 51*, 19–22.

Denzin, N. (2003). *Performance ethnography: Critical pedagogy and the politics of culture*. Sage.

Denzin, N. (2006). Analytic autoethnography or deja vu all over again? *Journal of Contemporary Ethnography, 35*(4), 419–428.

Department for Education. (2016). *Behaviour and discipline in schools: Advice for headteachers and school staff*. Crown copyright. https://www.gov.uk/government/uploads/system/uploads/attachment_data/file/488034/Behaviour_and_Discipline_in_Schools_-_A_guide_for_headteachers_and_School_Staff.pdf

Department for Education. (2018). *Mental health and behaviour in schools: Departmental advice for school staff*. Crown copyright. https://assets.publishing.service.gov.uk/government/uploads/system/uploads/attachment_data/file/755135/Mental_health_and_behaviour_in_schools__.pdf

Dewey, J. (1900). *The school and society being three lectures* (2017 ed.). http://www.gutenberg.org/files/53910/53910-h/53910-h.htm

Dewey, J. (1938). *Experience and education*. Macmillan.

Dewey, J. (1966). *Democracy and education: An introduction to the philosophy of education*. The Free Press.

Dintersmith, T. (2018). *What school could be*. Princeton University Press.

Dreikurs, R. (1972). *Discipline without tears*. Penguin.

Duckworth, E. (1987). *"The having of wonderful ideas" and other essays on teaching and learning*. Teachers College Press.

Edensor, T. (2010). Introduction: Thinking about rhythm and space. In T. Edensor (Ed.), *A geography of rhythms* (pp. 1–20). Ashgate.

Edmonds, F. (2005). *An introduction to Anthroposophy*. Sophia Books.

Edu on Tour. (2014). About. https://eduontour.tumblr.com/

eduScrum. (2021). About. https://www.eduscrum.nl/about/eduscrum

Edwards, C., Gandini, L., & Forman, G. (Eds.). (2011). *The hundred languages of children The Reggio Emilia experience in transformation* (3rd ed.). Praeger.

Ellis, C. (2004). *The ethnographic I: A methodological novel about autoethnography.* Alta Mira Press.

Ellis, C. (2007). Telling secrets, revealing lives: Relational ethics in research with intimate others. *Qualitative Inquiry, 13,* 3–29.

Ellis, C., Adams, T. E., & Bochner, A. P. (2010). Autoethnography: An overview. *Forum Qualitative Sozialforschung/Forum: Qualitative Social Research, 12*(1), Art. 10. https://doi.org/10.17169/fqs-12.1.1589

Erb, J. (2018). *Stumbling through the contours of bodily experience: Nomadic Embodiment of the female counsellor* [Doctoral dissertation]. University of Edinburgh, UK.

Etherington, K. (2002). Narrative ideas and stories of disability. In K. Etherington (Ed.), *Rehabilitation counselling in physical and mental health* (pp. 219–239). Jessica Kingsley Publishers.

Etherington, K. (2004). *Becoming a reflexive researcher – Using our selves in research.* Jessica Kingsley.

Epstein, R. (2007). *The case against adolescence: Rediscovering the adult in every teen.* Quill Driver Books/Word Dancer Press.

Facer, K. (2016). Using the future in education: Creating space for openness, Hope and novelty. In H. E. Lees & N. Noddings (Eds.), *The Palgrave international handbook of alternative education* (pp. 63–78). Macmillan.

Fielding, M., & Moss, P. (2010). *Radical education for the common school: A democratic alternative.* Routledge.

Franklin, S. (2017). Staying with the Manifesto: An interview with Donna Haraway. *Theory, Culture & Society, 34*(4), 49–63. doi:10.1177/0263276417693290 journals.sagepub.com/home/tcs

Freire, P. (1970). *Pedagogy of the oppressed.* Continuum.

Frielingsdorf, V. (Ed.). (2012). *Waldorfpädagogik in der Erziehungswissenschaft: Ein Überblick* [Steiner education and educational science: An overview]. Beltz Juventa.

Fryer, L. (2016). *Concentrating your turmoil. Experiences in alternative adolescent education.* Author.

Gale, K. (2014). Moods, tones, flavors: Living with intensities as inquiry. *Qualitative Inquiry, 20*(8), 1–7. https://doi.org/10.1177/1077800413513725

Gale, K. (2017, April). *Now you see me, now you don't: Using Whitehead's process philosophy to animate inquiry in contemporary education research* [Paper presentation]. Beyond Words conference, University of Plymouth, UK.

Gardner, H. (1983). *Frames of mind: The theory of multiple intelligences.* Basic Books.

Gatto, J. T. (2009). *Weapons of mass instruction: A schoolteacher's journey through the dark world of compulsory schooling*. New Society Publishers.

Geertz, C. (1973). *The interpretations of cultures*. Basic Books.

German Association of Waldorf Schools (Bund Der FreienWaldorfschulen). (2007, October). *Stuttgart declaration [Adopted policy]*. Stuttgart, Germany.

Gibbon, P. (2019). John Dewey: Portrait of a progressive thinker. *Humanities, 40*(2). https://www.neh.gov/article/john-dewey-portrait-progressive-thinker

Gidley, J. (2008). Beyond homogenisation of global education: Do alternative pedagogies such as Steiner education have anything to offer an emergent globalising world? In M. Bussey, S. Inayatullah, & I. Milojević (Eds.), *Alternative educational futures: Pedagogies for an emergent world* (pp. 242–258). Sense.

Gingrich-Philbrook, C. (2014). A knock at the door: Speculations on theatres and thresholds. *Departures in Critical Qualitative Research, 3*(1), 24–36. doi:10.1525/dcqr.2014.3.1.24

Giroux, H. A. (2005). *Border crossings cultural workers and the politics of education* (2nd ed.). Routledge.

Goertz, D. B. (2001). *Children who are not yet peaceful preventing exclusion in the early elementary classroom*. Frog, Ltd.

Goffman, E. (1959). *The presentation of self in everyday life*. Random House.

Golden, J. (1997). *Narrative – The use of story in Waldorf education*. Annual Meeting of American Educational Research Association.

Goleman, D. (1995). *Emotional intelligence*. Bantam.

Grauer, S. (2016). *Fearless teaching: Collected stories*. Alternative Education Resource Organization.

Gravata, A., Piza, C., Mayumi, C., & Shimahara, E. (2017). *Around the world in 14 schools: Glimpses of the future in the present*. Coletivo Educ-acao.

Gray, P. (2009). Play as a foundation for hunter-gatherer social existence. *American Journal of Play, 1*, 476–522.

Gray, P. (2015). *Free to learn why unleashing the instinct to play will make our children happier, more self-reliant, and better students for life*. Basic Books.

Gray, P. (2016). Mother nature's pedagogy: How children educate themselves. In H. E. Lees & N. Noddings (Eds.), *The Palgrave international handbook of alternative education* (pp. 49–62). Macmillan.

Gray, P., & Feldman, J. (2004). Playing in the zone of proximal development: Qualities of self-directed age mixing between adolescents and young children at a democratic school. *American Journal of Education, 110*, 108–145.

Gray, P., & Riley, G. (2013). The challenges and benefits of unschooling according to 232 families who have chosen that route. *Journal of Unschooling and Alternative Learning, 7*, 1–27. https://jual.nipissingu.ca/wp-content/uploads/sites/25/2014/06/v72141.pdf

Greenberg, D. (1987). *The Sudbury Valley School experience.* Sudbury Valley School Press.

Greenberg, D. (1995). *Free at last: The Sudbury Valley School.* Boynton/Cook.

Greenberg, D. (2014). *Do children need guidance?* Sudbury Valley School Press.

Greenberg, D., & Sadofsky, M. (2008). *Starting a Sudbury School: A summary of the experiences of fifteen start-up groups.* Sudbury Valley School Press.

Greene, M. (1995). *Releasing the imagination: Essays on education, the arts, and social change.* Jossey-Bass.

Green School. (2017). *Green School Bali.* https://www.greenschool.org/

Gribble, D. (1998). *Real education varieties of freedom.* Libertarian Education.

Gribble, D. (2012). *Progressive education.* https://www.davidgribble.co.uk/progressive-education.htm

Grusin, R. (2017). Introduction. Anthropocene feminism: An experiment in collaborative theorizing. In R. Grusin (Ed.), *Anthropocene feminism* (pp. vii–xviii). University of Minnesota Press.

Hamera, J. (2011). Performance ethnography. In N. K. Denzin & Y. Lincoln (Eds.), *Handbook of qualitative research* (4th ed., pp. 317–330). Sage.

Haralambous, B. (2016). *Surfing the wave of emergent renewal: Re-imagining Steiner's vision for teachers' research and professional learning* [Doctoral dissertation]. University of Canberra, Canberra, Australia. https://researchsystem.canberra.edu.au/ws/portalfiles/portal/33656956/file

Haraway, D. (2015). Anthropocene, capitalocene, plantationocene, chthulucene: Making kin. *Environmental Humanities, 6,* 159–165. https://doi.org/10.1215/22011919-3615934

Haraway, D. J. (2016). *Staying with the trouble: Making kin in the Chthulucene.* Duke University Press. http://ebookcentral.proquest.com/lib/unimelb/detail.action?docID=4649739

Harold, V. L., & Corcoran, T. (2013). On behaviour: A role for restorative justice? *International Journal of School Disaffection, 10*(2), 45–61.

Harris, A. (2014). *The creative turn toward a new aesthetic imaginary.* Sense Publishers.

Harris, A., & Holman Jones, S. (2016). *Writing for performance.* Sense Publishers.

Harris, A., & Holman Jones, S. (2019). *The queer life of things: Performance, affect, and the more-than-human.* Lexington Books.

Hart, R. (2010). Classroom behaviour management: Educational psychologists' views on effective practice. *Emotional and Behavioural Difficulties, 15,* 353–371. doi:10.1080/13632752.2010.523257

Hartkamp, P. (2016). *Beyond coercive education: A plea for the realisation of the rights of the child in education.* The Quantum Company.

Hauskeller, M. (2014). Utopia in trans- and posthumanism. In R. Ranisch & S. L. Sorgner (Eds.), *Post- and transhumanism: An introduction* (pp. 101–108). Peter Lang.

Hayden, C., & Pike, S. (2004). *Challenging behaviour in schools: An evaluation of Team-Teach: A whole setting holistic approach to behaviour management* [eBook]. ICJS University of Portsmouth.

Hecht, Y. (2010). *Democratic education: A beginning of a story.* Innovation Culture.

Hellawell, D. (2006). Inside–out: Analysis of the insider–outsider concept as a heuristic device to develop reflexivity in students doing qualitative research. *Teaching in Higher Education, 11*(4), 483–494.

Heller, A. (1995). Where are we at home? *Thesis Eleven N, 41.*

Hoffman, V. (2016). Creating place-based Waldorf festivals: An ethnographic study of festivals in two non-European Waldorf schools. *RoSE – Research on Steiner Education, 7*(2), 88–104. https://www.rosejourn.com/index.php/rose/article/view/353/334

Holman Jones, S. (2016). Living bodies of thought: The "critical" in critical autoethnography. *Qualitative Inquiry, 22*(4), 228–237. https://doi.org/10.1177/1077800415622509

Holman Jones, S., & Harris, A. (2018). *Queering autoethnography.* Routledge.

Holmgren, D. (2006). *Permaculture principles & pathways beyond sustainability.* Holmgren Design Services.

Holt, J. (1967). *How children learn.* Penguin.

Holzman, L. (1997). *Schools for growth radical alternatives to current educational models.* Lawrence Erlbaum Associates.

hooks, b. (1984). *Feminist theory: From margin to center.* South End Press.

Horton, J., & Kraftl, P. (2014). *Cultural geographies: An introduction.* Routledge.

Hougham, P. (2012). *Dialogues of destiny: A postmodern appreciation of Waldorf education.* Sylvan Associates.

Hughes, G. (2015). 'Imagining otherwise' or tinkering with the system? In C. Cooper, S. Gormally, & G. Hughes (Eds.), *Socially just, radical alternatives for education and youth work practice. Re-imaging ways of working with young people* (pp. 220–244). Palgrave Macmillan.

Huxley, A. (1932). *Brave new world.* Harper Brothers.

Ilgunas, K. (2013). *Walden on wheels: On the open road from debt to freedom.* Houghton Mifflin Harcourt.

Illich, I. (1971). *Deschooling society.* Harper and Row.

Ingold, T. (2007). *Lines: A brief history.* Routledge.

Jackson, A. Y., & Mazzei, L. A. (2008). Experience and "I" in autoethnography: A deconstruction. *International Review of Qualitative Research, 1*(3), 299–317.

Jiron, P. (2010). Repetition and difference: Rhythms and mobile place-making in Santiago de Chile. In T. Edensor (Ed.), *Geographies of rhythm: Nature, place, mobilities and bodies* (pp. 129–143). Ashgate.

Johnston, R., Wilson, D., & Burgess, S. (2007). Ethnic segregation and educational performance at secondary school in Bradford and Leicester. *Environment and Planning, 39*(3), 609–629.

Joldersma, C. W. (2016). Promise and peril of neuroscience for alternative education. In H. E. Lees & N. Noddings (Eds.), *The Palgrave international handbook of alternative education* (pp. 79–96). Macmillan.

Kamen, M., & Erickson Shepherd, D. (2013). Exploring innovative schools with pre-service teachers. In L. V. Shavinina (Ed.), *The Routledge international handbook of innovation education* (pp. 288–300). Routledge.

Kaufmann, V., & Montulet, B. (2008). Between social and spatial mobilities: The issue of social fluidity. In W. Canzler, V. Kaufmann, & S. Kesselring (Eds.), *Tracing mobilities: Towards a cosmopolitan perspective* (pp. 288–300). Ashgate.

Kennedy, J. H., & Kennedy, C. E. (2004). Attachment theory: Implications for school psychology. *Psychology in the Schools, 41,* 247–259.

Khasnabish, A., & Haiven, M. (2012). Convoking the radical imagination: Social movement research, dialogic methodologies, and scholarly vocations. *Cultural Studies ↔ Critical Methodologies, 12*(5), 408–421. https://doi.org/10.1177/1532708612453126

Kilteni, K., Groten, R., & Slater, M. (2012). The sense of embodiment in virtual reality. *Presence: Teleoperators and Virtual Environments, 21*(4), 373–387. http://diposit.ub.edu/dspace/bitstream/2445/53294/1/634024.pdf

Kirkpatrick, D., Porter, S., Speedy, J., & Wyatt, J. (Eds.). (2021). *Collaborative artful inquiry: Writing and making qualitative research.* Routledge.

Kirschner, D. H. (2008). *Producing unschoolers: Learning through living in a U.S. education movement* [Doctoral dissertation]. University of Pennsylvania, USA. http://repository.upenn.edu/dis sertations/AAI3309459

Kingsnorth, P. (2017). *Confessions of a recovering environmentalist.* Faber & Faber.

Klaus, P. (2016). An ordinary day. In H. E. Lees & N. Noddings (Eds.), *The Palgrave international handbook of alternative education* (pp. 31–48). Macmillan.

Klein, N. (2014). *This changes everything: Capitalism vs. the climate.* Simon and Schuster.

Knight, S. (2016). Forests school: A model for learning holistically and outdoors. In H. E. Lees & N. Noddings (Eds.), *The Palgrave international handbook of alternative education* (pp. 289–304). Macmillan.

Kohn, A. (1999). *Punished by rewards: The trouble with gold stars, incentive plans, A's, praise, and other bribes* (2nd ed.). Houghton Mifflin.

Kolb, D. A. (1984). *Experimental learning: Experience as the source of learning and development.* Prentice-Hall.

Kolbert, E. (2014). *The sixth extinction: An unnatural history.* Bloomsbury.

Kozol, J. (2006). *The shame of the nation: The restoration of apartheid schooling in America.* Three Rivers Press.

Kraftl, P. (2013). *Geographies of alternative education. Diverse learning spaces for children and young people.* Policy Press.

Krishnamurti, J. (1953). *Education and the significance of life.* Krishnamurti Writings Inc.

Kvale, S. (1996). *Interviews: An introduction to qualitative research interviewing.* Sage Publications.

Labonté, R. (2011). Reflections on stories and a story/dialogue method in health research. *International Journal of Social Research Methodology, 14*(2), 153–163.

Laurier, E., Lorimer, H., Brown, B., Jones, O., Juhlin, O., Noble, A., Perry, M., Pica, D., Sormani, P., Strebel, I., Swan, L., Taylor, A. S., Watts, L., & Weilenmann, A. (2008). Driving and passengering: Notes on the ordinary organisation of car travel. *Mobilities, 3*(1), 1–23.

Leavy, P. (2010). A/r/t: A poetic montage. *Qualitative Inquiry, 16*(4), 240–243. https://doi.org/10.1177/1077800409354067

Leavy, P. (2015). *Method meets art: Arts-based research practice.* The Guildford Press.

Lees, H. E., & Noddings, N. (Eds.). (2016). *The Palgrave international handbook of alternative education.* Macmillan.

Levitas, R. (2013). *Utopia as method: The imaginary reconstitution of society.* Palgrave MacMillan.

Lewis, A. (2012, November 2). *What every parent should know about Steiner-Waldorf schools.* The Quackometer Blog. http://www.quackometer.net/blog/2012/11/what-every-parent-should-know-about-steiner-waldorf-schools.html

Lillard, A. S. (2007). *Montessori: The science behind the genius.* Oxford University Press.

Lillard, A. S., Heise, M. J., Richey, E. M., Tong, X., Hart, A., & Bray, P. M. (2017). Montessori preschool elevates and equalizes child outcomes: A longitudinal study. *Frontiers in Psychology, 8*, 1783. https://doi.org/10.3389/fpsyg.2017.01783

Lillard, A. S. (2019). Shunned and admired: Montessori, self-determination, and a case for radical school reform. *Educational Psychology Review, 31*, 939–965. https://doi.org/10.1007/s10648-019-09483-3

Lissau, R. (2005). *Rudolf Steiner: His life, work, inner path and social initiatives* (2nd ed.). Hawthorn Press.

Little, T. (2013). 21st century learning and progressive education: An intersection. *International Journal of Progressive Education, 9*(1), 84–96.

Little, T., & Ellison, K. (2015). *Loving learning: How progressive education can save America's schools.* W.W. Norton & Company.

Lovelock, J. E., & Margulis, L. (1974). Atmospheric homeostasis by and for the biosphere: The Gaia hypothesis. *Tellus, Series A, 26*(1–2), 2–10. http://tellusa.net/index.php/tellusa/article/view/9731

Lupinacci, J. (2019). Teaching to end human supremacy <=> Learning to recognize equity in all species. In C. Drew et al. (Eds.), *Education for total liberation: Critical animal pedagogy and teaching against speciesism.* Peter Lang.

Lupinacci, J. (2020, September) *Scholar activism: Radical praxis in support of democracy in dangerous times.* Seminar for Sustainability, Environment and the Arts in Education' (SEAE) Research Cluster, Southern Cross University, Australia.

MacLure, M. (2010). The offence of theory. *Journal of Education Policy, 25*, 277–286. https://doi.org/10.1080/02680930903462316

MacLure, M. (2013a). Classification or wonder: Coding as an analytic practice in qualitative research. In R. Coleman & J. Ringrose (Eds.), *Deleuze and research methodologies*. Edinburgh University Press.

MacLure, M. (2013b). The wonder of data. *Cultural Studies ↔ Critical Methodologies, 13*(4), 228–232. https://doi.org/10.1177/1532708613487863

Macy, J., & Johnstone, C. (2012). *Active hope: How to face the mess we're in without going crazy*. New World Library.

Madison, S. D. (2008). Narrative poetics and performative interventions. In N. K. Denzin, Y. S. Lincoln, & L. T. Smith (Eds.), *Handbook of critical and Indigenous methodologies* (pp. 391–405). Sage.

Magnuson, P., & Mendus, A. (2017). The search for the ideal school. *The International School Parent Magazine,* Summer, 50–53. https://alysmendus.files.wordpress.com/2017/03/the-ideal-school-article-2017-dragged.pdf

Manning, E. (2015). Artfulness. In R. Grusin (Ed.), *The nonhuman turn* (pp. 45–75). University of Minnesota Press.

Marshall, C. (2017). Montessori education: A review of the evidence base. *NPJ Science of Learning, 2*, 11. https://doi.org/10.1038/s41539-017-0012-7

Martin, R. A. (2002, April). *Alternatives in education: An exploration of learner-centered, progressive, and holistic education*. Paper presented at AERA, New Orleans.

Martiskainen, M., Axon, S., Sovacool, B. K., Sareen, S., Del Rio, D. F., & Axon, K. (2020). Contextualizing climate justice activism: Knowledge, emotions, motivations, and actions among climate strikers in six cities, *Global Environmental Change, 65*. https://doi.org/10.1016/j.gloenvcha.2020.102180

Maslow, A. H. (1943). A theory of human motivation. *Psychological Review, 50*(4), 430–437.

Massumi, B. (2015). *Politics of affect*. Polity Books.

Massumi, B. (2017). *The principle of unrest: Activist philosophy in the expanded field*. Open Humanities Press.

Mason, K. (2009). *Empowering citizen green: Prefigurative politics, autonomous geographies and hoping against hope* [Doctoral dissertation]. University of Aberystwyth, Wales. http://www.academia.edu/14121405/Empowering_Citizen_Green_thesis

Mason, P. (2015). *Postcapitalism: A guide to our future*. Allen Lane.

Masters, B. (2005). *Adventures in Steiner education: An introduction to the Waldorf approach*. Sopia Books.

McEachern, A. G., Aluede, O., & Kenny, M. C. (2008). Emotional abuse in the classroom: Implications and interventions for counselors. *Journal of Counselling and Development, 86*, 3–10.

Meier, D. (2002). *In schools we trust creating communities of learning in an era of testing and standardization*. Beacon Press.

Mendus, A. (2007). *Using Waldorf methods to teach light to Year 8* [Unpublished Master's research assignment]. Sheffield Hallam University, Sheffield, UK.

Mendus, A. (2012). *'A gold star for good sitting,' moving from rewards and punishments to effective communication* [Masters thesis]. Sheffield Hallam University, Sheffield, UK. https://alysmendus.files.wordpress.com/2013/09/august-final-ma.pdf

Mendus, A. (2013a). "You are the coyote": Notes from my visit to alternative schools on the East Coast of the U.S. January–March 2013. *Other Education, 2*(2). http://www.othereducation.org/index.php/OE/article/view/66/66

Mendus, A. (2013b). Education: How schools can be different. *JUNO, 33*, 14–15.

Mendus, A. (2016a). Letters from Lesbos: A recounting of emergency pedagogy in action. *Other Education, 5*(1). http://www.othereducation.org/index.php/OE/article/view/161/147

Mendus, A. (2016b). Transforming pedagogy in primary schools: A case study from Australia. *FORUM, 58*(3), 389–394.

Mendus, A. (2017a, May). *'Searching for the ideal school' through performing School Tourism*. Paper presented at the International Congress of Qualitative Inquiry, University of Illinois, Champaign-Urbana, USA.

Mendus, A. (2017b, May). *Alys Mendus 'Searching for the ideal school' through performing School Tourism* [Video]. YouTube. https://youtu.be/Z8owyJfMS_A

Mendus, A. (2017c). *A rhizomatic edge-ucation: Searching for the ideal school through School Tourism and performative autoethnographic-we* [Doctoral dissertation]. University of Hull, UK. https://hydra.hull.ac.uk/assets/hull:16594a/content

Mendus, A. (2018a). *A cup of instant coffee: A van-dwellers' assemblage* [Video]. YouTube. https://youtu.be/gEfexXuvz28

Mendus, A. (2018b). *Alys Mendus: Come dance My PhD* [Video]. YouTube. https://youtu.be/GllsJd89ioY

Mendus, A. (2019). An epilogue to two films: A cup of instant coffee – A van-dwellers's assemblage and come dance my PhD. *Murmurations: Journal of Transformative Systemic Practice, 2*(1), 51–60. https://doi.org/10.28963/2.1.6

Mendus, A. (2020, July). *Round table: Collaborative artful narrative inquiry*. Seminar for Sustainability, Environment and the Arts in Education' (SEAE) Research Cluster, Southern Cross University, Australia. https://youtu.be/ZwVQoxgBkr4

Mendus, A. (2021). Bad-alys and the Bad-Folx: Edge-dwelling, Hope and how to get your voice heard. *International Review of Qualitative Research, 14*(1), 55–66. https://doi.org/10.1177/1940844720968193

Mendus, A., Kamen, M., Kamen, A., Buchanan, S., Earle, A., Luna, A., & McLaughlin, K. (2020). They call teachers by their first names! An ethnodrama of pre-service teachers visiting innovative schools. In A. Harris & S. Holman Jones (Eds.), *Affective movements, Methods and pedagogies* (pp. 219–233). Routledge.

Moller, V. (2020). *Leading practices of Steiner school principals: A reflective practice perspective* [Doctoral dissertation]. University of Sydney, Australia. https://hdl.handle.net/2123/22139

Montessori, M. (1948). *To educate the human potential.* Kalakshetra Publications.

Montessori, M. (1989). *To educate the human potential.* Clio Press.

Montessori, M. (1994a). *Creative development in the child I* (R. Ramachandran, Trans.). Kalakshetra Press.

Montessori, M. (1994b). *From childhood to adolescence.* Clio Press.

Montessori, M. (1995). *The absorbent mind.* Henry Holt. (Original work published 1949)

Montgomery, C., & Hope, M. A. (2016). Thinking the yet to be thought: Envisioning autonomous and alternative pedagogies for socially just education. *FORUM, 58*(3), 307–314.

Munoz, J. E. (2009). *Cruising utopia: The then and there of queer futurity.* NYU Press.

Naaeke, A., Kurylo, A., Grabowski, M., Linton, D., & Radford, M. L. (2011). Insider and outsider perspective in ethnographic research. *Proceedings of the New York State Communication Association, 2010*(9).

Naess, A. (2008). *Ecology, community and lifestyle: Outline of an ecosophy.* Cambridge University Press.

Neill, A. S. (1960). *Summerhill: A radical approach to child rearing.* Hart Publishing Company.

Nesbit, W. C., & Philpott, D. F. (2002). Confronting subtle emotional abuse in classrooms. *Guidance and Counselling, 17*, 32–38.

New Story Hub. (2017). About. http://newstoryhub.com/about/

Nichol, J. (2016). *Bringing the Steiner Waldorf approach to your early years practice* (3rd ed.). Routledge.

Noaparast, K. B. (2016). Islamic education as asymmetrical democratic interaction. In H. E. Lees & N. Noddings (Eds.), *The Palgrave international handbook of alternative education* (pp. 339–353). Macmillan.

Noddings, N. (1984). *Caring, a feminine approach to ethics & moral education.* University of California Press.

NOVA Institute. (2021). *Mission & vision of Nova Institute.* https://www.novainstitute.org/mission.htm

Olsen, N. (2020). *What is radical unschooling?* https://unschoolers.org/radical-unschooling/what-is-radical-unschooling/

Orwell, G. (1949). *1984.* Secker and Warburg.

Osswald, F. (2017). Löst der pädagogische Impuls Rudolf Steiners bei Ihnen Begeisterung aus? [Does Steiner's pedagogical impulse make you enthusiastic?]. *Rundbrief der Pädagogischen Sektion am Goetheanum, 60*, 8–9.

Oxford University Press. (2021). Oxymoron. In *Lexico.* https://en.oxforddictionaries.com/definition/oxymoron

Palmer, P. J. (1998). *The courage to teach.* Jossey-Bass.

Parker, R., Rose, J., & Gilbert, L. (2016). Attachment aware schools: An alternative to behaviourism in supporting children's behaviour? In H. E. Lees & N. Noddings (Eds.), *The Palgrave international handbook of alternative education* (pp. 463–484). Macmillan.

Pascoe, B. (2014). *Dark emu: Black seeds: Agriculture or accident?* Magabala Books.

Patel, F., & Lynch, H. (2013). Glocalization as an alternative to internationalization in higher education: Embedding positive glocal learning perspectives. *International Journal of Teaching and Learning in Higher Education, 25*(2), 223–230. http://www.isetl.org/ijtlhe/

Pattison, H., & Thomas, A. (2016). Great expectations: Agenda and authority in technological, hidden and cultural curriculums. In H. E. Lees & N. Noddings (Eds.), *The Palgrave international handbook of alternative education* (pp. 129–144). Macmillan.

Patton, A. (2012). *Work the matters: The teacher's guide to project-based learning.* Paul Hamlyn Foundation. http://www.innovationunit.org/wp-content/uploads/2017/04/Work-That-Matters-Teachers-Guide-to-Project-based-Learning.pdf

Pavlov, I. P. (1927). *Conditional reflexes.* Dover Publications.

Peim, N. (2016). Alternatives to education? Impotentiality and the accident: New bearings in the ontology of the present. In H. E. Lees & N. Noddings (Eds.), *The Palgrave international handbook of alternative education* (pp. 145–158). Macmillan.

Pelias, R. (2004). *A methodology of the heart: Evoking academic and daily life.* AltaMira Press.

Pelias, R. (2013). Writing autoethnography: The personal, poetic, and performative as compositional strategies. In S. Holman Jones, T. Adams, & C. Ellis (Eds.), *Handbook of autoethnography* (pp. 384–405). Left Coast Press.

Perrow, S. (2012). *Therapeutic storytelling: 101 healing stories for children.* Hawthorn Press.

Phillips, L. G., & Bunda, T. (2018). *Research through, with and as storying.* Routledge.

Piaget, J., & Inhelder, B. (1972). *Psychology of the child.* Basic Books.

Ploktin, B. (2008). *Nature and the human soul cultivating wholeness and community in a fragmented world.* New World Library.

Pollock, D. (2006). Memory, remembering, and histories of change. In D. S. Madison & J. Hamera (Eds.), *The Sage handbook of performance studies* (pp. 87–105). Sage.

Poulos, C. N. (Ed.). (2008). Special issue: Autoethnography. *Iowa Journal of Communication, 40*(1).

Randoll, D., & Peters, J. (2015). Empirical research on Waldorf education. *Educar em Revista, 56,* 33–47. http://www.scielo.br/pdf/er/n56/0101-4358-er-56-00033.pdf

Rawson, M., Richter, T., & Avison, K. (2014). *Tasks and content of the Steiner-Waldorf curriculum* (2nd ed.). Floris Books.

Reay, D. (2012). What would a socially just education system look like? Saving the minnows from the pike. *Journal of Education Policy, 27*(5), 587–599. https://doi.org/10.1080/02680939.2012.710015

Reay, D. (2016). How possible is socially just education under neo-liberal capitalism? Struggling against the tide? *FORUM, 58*(3), 325–332.

Reddy, R. (2017, January 26). Around the world in 18 schools. *Education Revolution Podcast* [Podcast]. https://player.fm/series/education-revolution-podcast/episode-5-roopa-reddy-around-the-world-in-18-schools

Reed-Danahay, D. (2017). Bourdieu and critical autoethnography: Implications for research, writing, and teaching. *International Journal of Multicultural Education, 19*(1), 144–154. http://dx.doi.org/10.18251/ijme.v19i1.1368

Reiach, S., Averbeck, C., & Cassidy, V. (2012). The evolution of distance education in Australia: Past, present, future. *Quarterly Review of Distance Education, 13*(4), 247–252, 269–270. https://search.proquest.com/scholarly-journals/evolution-distance-education-australia-past/docview/1356976073/se-2?accountid=12372

Riley, G. (2020). *Unschooling exploring learning beyond the classroom.* Palgrave Macmillan. https://doi.org/10.1007/978-3-030-49292-2

Romero, L. (2015). *Developing the self through the inner work path in the light of Anthroposophy.* Steiner Books.

Rose, R. (2013). *Transforming criticisms of Anthroposophy and Waldorf education – Evolution, race and the quest for a global ethics.* Centre for Philosophy and Anthroposophy, UK.

Rowe, A. C., & Tuck, E. (2017). Settler colonialism and cultural studies: Ongoing settlement, cultural production, and resistance. *Cultural Studies ↔ Critical Methodologies, 17*(1), 3–13. https://doi.org/10.1177/1532708616653693

Roth, V. (2012). *Divergent.* Harper Collins.

Sahlberg, P. (2020). Will the pandemic change schools? *Journal of Professional Capital and Community, 5*(3/4), 359–365. https://doi.org/10.1108/JPCC-05-2020-0026

Saldaña, J. (2005). *Ethnodrama: An anthology of reality theatre.* AltaMira Press.

Schaub, M. (2010). Parenting for cognitive development from 1950 to 2000: The institutionalization of mass education and the social construction of parenting in the United States. *Sociology of Education, 83*(1), 46–66. https://doi.org/10.1177/0038040709356566

Schultz, K., & Ravitch, S. M. (2013). Narratives of learning to teach: Taking on professional identities. *Journal of Teacher Education, 64*(1), 35–46. https://doi.org/10.1177/0022487112458801

Seo, D. (2009). The profitable adventure of threatened middle-class families: An ethnographic study on homeschooling in South Korea. *Asia Pacific Education Review, 10*, 40–22.

Shaw, G. B. (2009). *Man and superman.* SMK Books. (Original work published 1903).

Sheller, M. (2004). Automotive emotions: Feeling the car. *Theory, Culture & Society*, *21*(4–5), 221–242. https://doi.org/10.1177/0263276404046068

Sheller, M. (2011). *Mobility*. Sociopedia.isa. www.sagepub.net/isa/resources/pdf/mobility.pdf

Sheller, M. (2014). The new mobilities paradigm for a live sociology. *Current Sociology*, *62*(6), 789–811. https://doi.org/10.1177/0011392114533211

Sheller, M., & Urry, J. (2006). The new mobilities paradigm. *Environment and Planning*, *38*, 207–226.

Shread, C., & Osorio, M. (2019). *School circles: Every voice matters* [Video file]. https://schoolcirclesfilm.com/

Singer, H. (2016). Innovative experiences in holistic education inspiring a new movement in Brazil. In H. E. Lees & N. Noddings (Eds.), *The Palgrave international handbook of alternative education* (pp. 211–226). Macmillan.

Skeggs, B. (2004). *Class, self, culture*. Routledge.

Smyth, J. (2016). Geographies of trust: A politics of resistance for an alternative education. In H. E. Lees & N. Noddings (Eds.), *The Palgrave international handbook of alternative education* (pp. 385–400). Macmillan.

Snell, D. (n.d). *Welcome from PLANS*. http://www.waldorfcritics.org/

Speedy, J. (2000). The storied helper: Narrative ideas and practices in counselling and psychotherapy. *European Journal of Psychotherapy, Counselling and Health*, *3*, 361–374.

Springgay, S., & Truman, S. E. (2018). *Walking methodologies in a more-than-human world*. Routledge.

Spry, T. (2001). Performing autoethnography: An embodied methodological praxis. *Qualitative Inquiry*, *7*(6), 706–732. http://www.nyu.edu/classes/bkg/methods/spry.pdf

Spry, T. (2005). Performative autoethnography: Critical embodiments and possibilities. In N. K. Denzin & Y. S. Lincoln (Eds.), *The Sage handbook of qualitative research* (3rd ed., pp. 497–511). Sage.

Spry, T. (2011). *Body, paper, stage writing and performing autoethnography*. Left Coast Press.

Spry, T. (2016). *Autoethnography and the other*. Routledge.

Stanley, P. (2013). *A critical ethnography of 'Westerners' teaching English in China: Shanghaied in Shanghai*. Routledge.

Stanley, P. (2017). *A critical auto/ethnography of learning Spanish: Intercultural competence on the gringo trail?* Routledge.

Staudenmaier, P. (2008). Race and redemption: Racial and ethnic evolution in Rudolf Steiner's Anthroposophy. *Nova Religio*, *11*(3), 4–36.

Steer, A. (2005). *Learning behaviour: The report of the Practitioners Group on School Behaviour and Discipline*. Department for Education and Skills.

http://www.educationengland.org.uk/documents/pdfs/2005-steer-report-learning-behaviour.pdf

Steiner, R. (1910). *Mission of the Folk Souls, 76.* https://wn.rsarchive.org/Lectures/GA121/English/APC1929/19100610p01.html

Steiner, R. (1965). *The education of the child in the light of Anthroposophy* (G. M. Adams, Trans.). Rudolf Steiner Press. (Original work published 1909)

Steiner, R. (1966). *The study of man: General education course* (D. Harwood & H. Fox, Trans.). Rudolf Steiner Press. (Original work published 1932) https://wn.rsarchive.org/Lectures/GA293/English/RSP1966/StuMan_index.html

Steiner, R. (1984). *The mission of Michael: The revelation of the intrinsic secret of the human being elemental beings and human destinies.* http://wn.rsarchive.org/Lectures/19191206p01.html (Original work published 1919)

Steiner, R. (1989). *Anthroposophical leading thoughts: The path of knowledge of Anthroposophy: The Michael mystery.* Rudolf Steiner Verlag. (Original work published 1924)

Steiner, R. (1993). *Vom Leben des Menschen und der Erde* [On the life of man and of the earth]. Rudolf Steiner Verlag. (Original work published 1923)

Steiner, R. (1996a). *The foundations of human experience* (R. F. Lathe, Trans.). Anthroposophic Press. (Original work published 1919)

Steiner, R. (1996b). *Rudolf Steiner in the Waldorf School: Lectures and addresses to children, parents, and teachers 1919–1924* (C. E. Creeger, Trans.). Anthroposophic Press.

Steiner, R. (1997). *Discussions with teachers* (H. Fox, Trans.). Anthroposophic Press. https://wn.rsarchive.org/Lectures/GA293/English/RSP1966/19190905a01.html (Original work published 1919)

Steiner, R. (1998). *Faculty meetings with Rudolf Steiner 1922–1924, Vol. 2* (R. F. Lathe & N. Parsons Whittaker, Trans.). Anthroposophic Press.

Steiner Education Australia. (2019). *Reconciliation action plan.* https://www.steinereducation.edu.au/wp-content/uploads/Final-SEA-RAP-7.pdf

Steiner Education Development Trust. (2017). *The New Zealand certificate of Steiner education.* https://sedt.co.nz/

St. Pierre, E. A. (2011). Refusing human being in humanist qualitative inquiry. In N. K. Denzin & M. A. Giardina (Eds.), *Qualitative Inquiry and globe crises.* Left Coast Press.

St. Pierre, E. A. (2014). An always already absent collaboration. *Cultural Studies ↔ Critical Methodologies, 14*(4), 374–379. https://doi.org/10.1177/1532708614530309

St. Pierre, E. A. (2016). The empirical and the new empiricisms. *Cultural Studies ↔ Critical Methodologies, 16*(2), 111–124. https://doi.org/10.1177/1532708616636147

Strang, D. (2016, February 10). The Dark Mountain gathering base camp: Embercombe September 2nd–4th 2016. *Dark Mountain Blog.* http://dark-mountain.net/blog/the-dark-mountain-gathering-base-camp-embercombe-september-2nd-4th-2016/

Stronach, I., & Piper, H. (2009). The touching example of Summerhill School. In W. A. Woods & G. J. Woods (Eds.), *Alternative education for the 21st century philosophies, approaches, visions* (pp. 49–64). Palgrave Macmillan.

Tedlock, B. (2011). Braiding narrative ethnography with memoir and creative nonfiction. In N. Denzin & Y. Lincoln (Eds.), *The Sage handbook of qualitative research* (4th ed., pp. 331–340). Sage.

Te Ra Waldorf School and Kapiti Waldorf Trust. (2012, November). *Equity statement.* https://tera.school.nz/about-us/equity-statement/

The Dark Mountain Project. (2017). About. http://dark-mountain.net/about/the-dark-mountain-project/

Tickell, C. (2011). *The early years: Foundations for life, health and learning. An independent review on the early years foundation stage.* Department for Education. http://www.educationengland.org.uk/documents/pdfs/2011-tickell-report-eyfs.pdf

Ullrich, H. (2008). *Rudolf Steiner* (J. Duke & D. Balestrini, Trans.). Bloomsbury.

Urry, J. (2000). *Sociology beyond societies.* Routledge.

Urry, J. (2002). Mobility and proximity. *Sociology, 36*(2), 255–274.

Urry, J. (2007). *Mobilities.* Polity Press.

Urry, J., & Larsen, J. (2011). *The tourist gaze (3.0).* Sage.

Waks, L. J. (2013). John Dewey and the challenge of progressive education. *International Journal of Progressive Education, 9*(1), 73–83.

Waltener, S. (2010). *Stairwell weave-in* [Video]. YouTube. https://www.youtube.com/watch?v=gil1nCBUOrM

Wamsted, J. (2012). Borges & bike rides: Toward an understanding of autoethnography. *Qualitative Research in Education, 1*(2), 179–201. http://dx.doi.org/10.4471/qre.2012.09

Weale, S. (2016, October). Almost a third of teachers quit state sector within five years of qualifying. *The Guardian.* https://www.theguardian.com/education/2016/oct/24/almost-third-of-teachers-quit-within-five-years-of-qualifying-figures

Wenger, E. (2010). Communities of practice and social learning systems: The career of a concept. In C. Blackmore (Ed.), *Social learning systems and communities of practice* (pp. 179–198). Springer. https://doi.org/10.1007/978-1-84996-133-2_11

Williams, M. K. (2017). John Dewey in the 21st century. *Journal of Inquiry and Action in Education, 9*(1), 91–102. https://digitalcommons.buffalostate.edu/jiae/vol9/iss1/7

Winter, R., Buck, A., & Sobiechowska, P. (1999). *Professional experience and the investigative imagination: The art of reflective writing.* Routledge.

Wolf, A. D. (1995). *A parents' guide to the Montessori classroom.* Parent Child Press.

Wooltorton, S., Collard, L., & Horwitz, P. (2017). The land still speaks: Ni, Katitj! *PAN: Philosophy, Activism, Nature, 13,* 57–67. https://doi.org/10.4225/03/5ab86d416356c

Wooltorton, S., White, P., Palmer, M., & Collard, L. (2020). Learning cycles: Enriching ways of knowing place. *Australian Journal of Environmental Education,* 1–18. doi:10.1017/aee.2020.15

Wrigley, T. (2016). Opening up pedagogies: Making a space for children. *FORUM, 58*(3), 333–340.

Wunderlich, F. M. (2010). The aesthetics of place-temporality in everyday urban space: The case of Fitzroy Square. In T. Edensor (Ed.), *A geography of rhythms* (pp. 45–56). Ashgate.

Wyatt, J., & Gale, K. (2013). Getting out of selves: An assemblage ethnography? In S. A. Holman Jones, T. E. Adams, & C. Ellis (Eds.), *The handbook of autoethnography* (pp. 300–312). Left Coast Press.

Zembylas, M. (2003). Emotions and teacher identity: A poststructural perspective. *Teachers and Teaching, 9*(3), 213–238.

Index

Printed in the United States
by Baker & Taylor Publisher Services